DOUBLESPEAK

DOUBLESPEAK

From "Revenue Enhancement" to "Terminal Living"

How Government, Business, Advertisers, and
Others Use Language to Deceive You

WILLIAM LUTZ

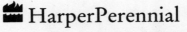
HarperPerennial
A Division of HarperCollins*Publishers*

A hardcover edition of this book was published in 1989 by Harper & Row, Publishers.

First HarperPerennial edition published 1990.

The Library of Congress has catalogued the hardcover edition as follows:

Lutz, William.
  Doublespeak/William Lutz.
    p. cm.
  Includes index.
  ISBN 0-06-016134-5
  1. Jargon (Terminology) 2. English language—Jargon. I. Title.
P409.L88   1989
427'.973—dc20   89-45051

ISBN 0-06-091993-0 (pbk.)
90 91 92 93 94 FG 10 9 8 7 6 5 4 3 2 1

For my wife, Denise

CONTENTS

ACKNOWLEDGMENTS

I gratefully acknowledge the support of the Rutgers University Research Council for grants that assisted in constructing a data base of examples of doublespeak, thus making the writing of this book a manageable task. I also gratefully acknowledge the National Council of Teachers of English for allowing me to use material from the *Quarterly Review of Doublespeak*.

I would like to thank the gracious women of the Four Arts Club of Elkhart, Indiana, who listened to an early version of Chapter II and laughed at all the right places. My thanks, too, to Harry Brent and Murl Barker, colleagues and good friends, who read earlier versions of parts of this book and were generous with their helpful comments. My thanks also to Jean Nagger and Hugh Van Dusen for their faith in this project and their support. And special thanks to all the readers of the *Quarterly Review of Doublespeak* who sent me examples of doublespeak, many of which I have used in the *Review* and in this book. But, most of all, I want to give very special thanks to my wife, Denise, who, in addition to providing me with the perfect writing environment, convinced me that I could write this book and then served as my best, most helpful critic and reader, even while writing her second novel. I owe her more than I can say, or ever repay.

PREFACE

*Most people who bother with the matter at
all would admit that the English language is
in a bad way.*
—GEORGE ORWELL
"Politics and the English Language," 1946

There are many people who agree with Orwell. Indeed, there
are quite a few who believe that the situation has deteriorated to the point where there is little hope left for the
English language. I am not among either of these groups.
The English language is doing quite well, thank you; it is we who
use the English language who are not doing well, not doing well
at all.

Nor will America be the death of English. For all the supposed
misfortunes the English language has suffered in recent years, it
gives every sign of continuing as a living, prosperous, effective
language for quite a while. If anything, English is growing. Each
year more and more people learn and use the language as an
integral part of their lives. Some estimates place the number of
people who use English as their first or second language as high
as one billion. Rather than causing the death of English, America
has been one of its greatest supporters, spreading the language
throughout the world.

The issue is not what we are doing *to* the language, but what
we are doing *with* the language. The issue is not just whether

subjects and verbs agree, but whether statements and facts agree. As Orwell also observed in his 1946 essay, the "defense of the English language . . . has nothing to do with correct grammar and syntax, which are of no importance so long as one makes one's meaning clear . . . or with having what is called a 'good prose style.' What is above all needed is to let the meaning choose the word, and not the other way about."

Language is a tool, just like any of the tools human beings have invented. Like any tool—a knife, a screwdriver, a computer, a space satellite—language is used to do something, to achieve a goal. A knife can be used to carve a roast or carve a relative; a computer can be used to keep lists of people who donate money to charity or to keep lists of people marked for summary execution by the government; a satellite can provide information on the weather or navigational directions for nuclear missiles to hit their targets. Language can be used to write the Constitution of the United States or to write the laws of apartheid; to write *King Lear* or pornography; to write the lyrics of John Keats or plans for a winnable nuclear war. The fault lies not in the language but in us, the creators and users of language.

I have in this book brought together some of the examples of doublespeak that I have collected since I became a member of the Committee on Public Doublespeak of the National Council of Teachers of English, and since I became editor of the *Quarterly Review of Doublespeak*. In an attempt to make the text as readable as possible, I have not used footnotes to document my source for each example of doublespeak I have cited. However, I can document every example of doublespeak I have used, as I do in every issue of the *Review*.

My goal has been to make this book more than a simple collection of the most egregious examples of doublespeak. I have tried to show that doublespeak is not a slip of the tongue, or language used out of ignorance, but is instead a very conscious use of language as a weapon or tool by those in power to achieve their ends at our expense. While some doublespeak is funny, much of it is frightening. We laugh and dismiss doublespeak as empty or meaningless words at our own peril, for, as George Orwell saw so clearly, the great weapon of power, exploitation, manipulation, and oppression is language. It is only by being aware of the pervasiveness of doublespeak and its function as a tool of social, economic, and political control that we can begin to fight those who would use language against us.

CHAPTER 1

Involuntary Conversions, Preemptive Counterattacks, and Incomplete Successes: The World of Doublespeak

There are no potholes in the streets of Tucson, Arizona, just "pavement deficiencies." The Reagan Administration didn't propose any new taxes, just "revenue enhancement" through new "user's fees." Those aren't bums on the street, just "non-goal oriented members of society." There are no more poor people, just "fiscal underachievers." There was no robbery of an automatic teller machine, just an "unauthorized withdrawal." The patient didn't die because of medical malpractice, it was just a "diagnostic misadventure of a high magnitude." The U.S. Army doesn't kill the enemy anymore, it just "services the target." And the doublespeak goes on.

Doublespeak is language that pretends to communicate but really doesn't. It is language that makes the bad seem good, the negative appear positive, the unpleasant appear attractive or at least tolerable. Doublespeak is language that avoids or shifts responsibility, language that is at variance with its real or purported meaning. It is language that conceals or prevents thought; rather than extending thought, doublespeak limits it.

Doublespeak is not a matter of subjects and verbs agreeing; it is a matter of words and facts agreeing. Basic to doublespeak is incongruity, the incongruity between what is said or left unsaid,

1

and what really is. It is the incongruity between the word and the referent, between seem and be, between the essential function of language—communication—and what doublespeak does—mislead, distort, deceive, inflate, circumvent, obfuscate.

How to Spot Doublespeak

How can you spot doublespeak? Most of the time you will recognize doublespeak when you see or hear it. But, if you have any doubts, you can identify doublespeak just by answering these questions: Who is saying what to whom, under what conditions and circumstances, with what intent, and with what results? Answering these questions will usually help you identify as doublespeak language that appears to be legitimate or that at first glance doesn't even appear to be doublespeak.

First Kind of Doublespeak

There are at least four kinds of doublespeak. The first is the euphemism, an inoffensive or positive word or phrase used to avoid a harsh, unpleasant, or distasteful reality. But a euphemism can also be a tactful word or phrase which avoids directly mentioning a painful reality, or it can be an expression used out of concern for the feelings of someone else, or to avoid directly discussing a topic subject to a social or cultural taboo.

When you use a euphemism because of your sensitivity for someone's feelings or out of concern for a recognized social or cultural taboo, it is not doublespeak. For example, you express your condolences that someone has "passed away" because you do not want to say to a grieving person, "I'm sorry your father is dead." When you use the euphemism "passed away," no one is misled. Moreover, the euphemism functions here not just to protect the feelings of another person, but to communicate also your concern for that person's feelings during a period of mourning. When you excuse yourself to go to the "rest room," or you mention that someone is "sleeping with" or "involved with" someone else, you do not mislead anyone about your meaning, but you do respect the social taboos about discussing bodily functions and sex in direct terms. You also indicate your sensitivity to the feelings of your audience, which is usually considered a mark of courtesy and good manners.

However, when a euphemism is used to mislead or deceive, it becomes doublespeak. For example, in 1984 the U.S. State Department announced that it would no longer use the word "killing" in its annual report on the status of human rights in countries around the world. Instead, it would use the phrase "unlawful or arbitrary deprivation of life," which the department claimed was more accurate. Its real purpose for using this phrase was simply to avoid discussing the embarrassing situation of government-sanctioned killings in countries that are supported by the United States and have been certified by the United States as respecting the human rights of their citizens. This use of a euphemism constitutes doublespeak, since it is designed to mislead, to cover up the unpleasant. Its real intent is at variance with its apparent intent. It is language designed to alter our perception of reality.

The Pentagon, too, avoids discussing unpleasant realities when it refers to bombs and artillery shells that fall on civilian targets as "incontinent ordnance." And in 1977 the Pentagon tried to slip funding for the neutron bomb unnoticed into an appropriations bill by calling it a "radiation enhancement device."

Second Kind of Doublespeak

A second kind of doublespeak is jargon, the specialized language of a trade, profession, or similar group, such as that used by doctors, lawyers, engineers, educators, or car mechanics. Jargon can serve an important and useful function. Within a group, jargon functions as a kind of verbal shorthand that allows members of the group to communicate with each other clearly, efficiently, and quickly. Indeed, it is a mark of membership in the group to be able to use and understand the group's jargon.

But jargon, like the euphemism, can also be doublespeak. It

can be—and often is—pretentious, obscure, and esoteric terminology used to give an air of profundity, authority, and prestige to speakers and their subject matter. Jargon as doublespeak often makes the simple appear complex, the ordinary profound, the obvious insightful. In this sense it is used not to express but impress. With such doublespeak, the act of smelling something becomes "organoleptic analysis," glass becomes "fused silicate," a crack in a metal support beam becomes a "discontinuity," conservative economic policies become "distributionally conservative notions."

Lawyers, for example, speak of an "involuntary conversion" of property when discussing the loss or destruction of property through theft, accident, or condemnation. If your house burns down or if your car is stolen, you have suffered an involuntary conversion of your property. When used by lawyers in a legal situation, such jargon is a legitimate use of language, since lawyers can be expected to understand the term.

However, when a member of a specialized group uses its jargon to communicate with a person outside the group, and uses it knowing that the nonmember does not understand such language, then there is doublespeak. For example, on May 9, 1978, a National Airlines 727 airplane crashed while attempting to land at the Pensacola, Florida airport. Three of the fifty-two passengers aboard the airplane were killed. As a result of the crash, National made an after-tax insurance benefit of $1.7 million, or an extra 18¢ a share dividend for its stockholders. Now National Airlines had two problems: It did not want to talk about one of its airplanes crashing, and it had to account for the $1.7 million when it issued its annual report to its stockholders. National solved the problem by inserting a footnote in its annual report which explained that the $1.7 million income was due to "the involuntary conversion of a 727." National thus acknowledged the crash of its airplane and the subsequent profit it made from the crash, without once mentioning the accident or the deaths. However, because airline officials knew that most stockholders in the company, and indeed most of the general public, were not familiar with legal jargon, the use of such jargon constituted doublespeak.

Third Kind of Doublespeak

A third kind of doublespeak is gobbledygook or bureaucratese. Basically, such doublespeak is simply a matter of piling on words, of overwhelming the audience with words, the bigger the words and the longer the sentences the better. Alan Greenspan, then chair of President Nixon's Council of Economic Advisors, was quoted in *The Philadelphia Inquirer* in 1974 as having testified before a Senate committee that "It is a tricky problem to find the particular calibration in timing that would be appropriate to stem the acceleration in risk premiums created by falling incomes without prematurely aborting the decline in the inflation-generated risk premiums."

Nor has Mr. Greenspan's language changed since then. Speaking to the meeting of the Economic Club of New York in 1988, Mr. Greenspan, now Federal Reserve chair, said, "I guess I should warn you, if I turn out to be particularly clear, you've probably misunderstood what I've said." Mr. Greenspan's doublespeak doesn't seem to have held back his career.

Sometimes gobbledygook may sound impressive, but when the quote is later examined in print it doesn't even make sense. During the 1988 presidential campaign, vice-presidential candidate Senator Dan Quayle explained the need for a strategic-defense initiative by saying, "Why wouldn't an enhanced deterrent, a more stable peace, a better prospect to denying the ones who enter conflict in the first place to have a reduction of offensive systems and an introduction to defensive capability? I believe this is the route the country will eventually go."

The investigation into the Challenger disaster in 1986 revealed the doublespeak of gobbledygook and bureaucratese used by too many involved in the shuttle program. When Jesse Moore, NASA's associate administrator, was asked if the performance of the shuttle program had improved with each launch or if it had remained the same, he answered, "I think our performance in terms of the liftoff performance and in terms of the orbital performance, we knew more about the envelope we were operating under, and we have been pretty accurately staying in that. And so I would say the performance has not by design drastically improved. I think we have been able to characterize the performance more as a function of our launch experience as opposed to it improving as a function of time." While this language may appear to be jargon, a close look will reveal that it is really just gobbledygook laced with jargon. But you really have to wonder if Mr. Moore had any idea what he was saying.

Fourth Kind of Doublespeak

The fourth kind of doublespeak is inflated language that is designed to make the ordinary seem extraordinary; to make everyday things seem impressive; to give an air of importance to people, situations, or things that would not normally be considered important; to make the simple seem complex. Often this kind of doublespeak isn't hard to spot, and it is usually pretty funny. While car mechanics may be called "automotive internists," elevator operators members of the "vertical transportation corps," used cars "pre-owned" or "experienced cars," and black-and-white television sets described as having "non-multicolor capability," you really aren't misled all that much by such language.

However, you may have trouble figuring out that, when Chrysler "initiates a career alternative enhancement program," it is really laying off five thousand workers; or that "negative patient care outcome" means the patient died; or that "rapid oxidation" means a fire in a nuclear power plant.

The doublespeak of inflated language can have serious consequences. In Pentagon doublespeak, "pre-emptive counterattack" means that American forces attacked first; "engaged the enemy on all sides" means American troops were ambushed; "backloading of augmentation personnel" means a retreat by American troops. In the doublespeak of the military, the 1983 invasion of Grenada was conducted not by the U.S. Army, Navy, Air Force, and Marines, but by the "Caribbean Peace Keeping Forces." But then, according to the Pentagon, it wasn't an invasion, it was a "predawn vertical insertion."

Doublespeak Throughout History

Doublespeak is not a new use of language peculiar to the politics or economics of the twentieth century. In the fifth century B.C., the Greek historian Thucydides wrote in *The Peloponnesian War* that

> revolution thus ran its course from city to city. . . .
> Words had to change their ordinary meanings and to
> take those which were now given them. Reckless
> audacity came to be considered the courage of a loyal
> ally; prudent hesitation, specious cowardice; moderation
> was held to be a cloak for unmanliness; ability to see all
> sides of a question, inaptness to act on any. Frantic
> violence became the attribute of manliness; cautious
> plotting, a justifiable means of self-defense. The advocate
> of extreme measures was always trustworthy; his
> opponent, a man to be suspected.

Julius Caesar, in his account of the Gallic Wars, described his brutal and bloody conquest and subjugation of Gaul as "pacifying" Gaul. "Where they make a desert, they call it peace," said an English nobleman quoted by the Roman historian Tacitus. When traitors were put to death in Rome, the announcement of their execution was made in the form of saying "they have lived." "Taking notice of a man in the ancestral manner" meant capital punishment; "the prisoner was then lead away" meant he was executed.

In his memoirs, *V-2*, Walter Dornberger, commanding officer of the Peenemünde Rocket Research Institute in Germany during World War II, describes how he and his staff used language to get what they needed from the Bureau of Budget for their rocket experiments. A pencil sharpener was an "Appliance for milling wooden dowels up to 10 millimeters in diameter," and a typewriter was an "Instrument for recording test data with rotating roller." But it was the Nazis who were the masters of doublespeak, and they used it not just to achieve and maintain power but to perpetrate some of the most heinous crimes in the history of the human race.

In the world of Nazi Germany, nonprofessional prostitutes were called "persons with varied sexual relationships"; "protective custody" was the very opposite of protective; "Winter Relief" was a compulsory tax presented as a voluntary charity; and a "straightening of the front" was a retreat, while serious difficulties became "bottlenecks." Minister of Information (the very title is doublespeak) Josef Goebbels spoke in all seriousness of "simple pomp" and "the liberalization of the freedom of the press."

Nazi doublespeak reached its peak when dealing with the "Final Solution," a phrase that is itself the ultimate in doublespeak. The notice, "The Jew X.Y. lived here," posted on a door, meant the occupant had been "deported," that is, killed. When mail was returned stamped "Addressee has moved away," it meant the person had been "deported." "Resettlement" also meant deportation, while "work camp" meant concentration camp or incinerator, "action" meant massacre, "Special Action Groups" were army units that conducted mass murder, "selection" meant gassing, and "shot while trying to escape" meant deliberately killed in a concentration camp.

George Orwell and Language

In his famous and now-classic essay, "Politics and the English Language," which was published in 1946, George Orwell wrote that the "great enemy of clear language is insincerity. When there is a gap between one's real and one's declared aims, one turns as it were instinctively to long words and exhausted idioms, like a cuttlefish squirting out ink." For Orwell, language was an instrument for "expressing and not for concealing or preventing thought." In his most biting comment, he observed that, "in our time, political speech and writing are largely the defense of the indefensible. . . . [P]olitical language has to consist largely of euphemism, question-begging and sheer cloudy vagueness. . . . Political language . . . is designed to make lies sound truthful and murder respectable, and to give an appearance of solidity to pure wind."

Orwell understood well the power of language as both a tool and a weapon. In the nightmare world of his novel, *1984*, Orwell depicted a society where language was one of the most important tools of the totalitarian state. Newspeak, the official state language in the world of *1984*, was designed not to extend but to *diminish* the range of human thought, to make only "correct" thought possible and all other modes of thought impossible. It was, in short, a language designed to create a reality that the state wanted.

Newspeak had another important function in Orwell's world of *1984*. It provided the means of expression for doublethink, the mental process that allows you to hold two opposing ideas in your mind at the same time and believe in both of them. The classic example in Orwell's novel is the slogan, "War Is Peace." Lest you think doublethink is confined only to Orwell's novel, you need only recall the words of Secretary of State Alexander Haig when he testified before a congressional committee in 1982 that a continued weapons build-up by the United States is "absolutely essential to our hopes for meaningful arms reduction." Or remember what Senator Orin Hatch said in 1988: "Capital punishment is our society's recognition of the sanctity of human life."

At its worst, doublespeak, like newspeak, is language designed to limit, if not eliminate, thought. Like doublethink, doublespeak enables speaker and listener, writer and reader, to hold two opposing ideas in their minds at the same time and believe in both of them. At its least offensive, doublespeak is inflated language that tries to give importance to the insignificant.

The Doublespeak All Around Us

Orwell was concerned primarily with political language because it is the language of power, but it is not just political language that is so misleading these days. Everywhere you turn you encounter the language with which Orwell was so concerned. It's not an economic recession but, according to the Reagan Administration, a "period of accelerated negative growth" or simply "negative economic growth." There's no such thing as acid rain; according to the Environmental Protection Agency, it's just "poorly buffered precipitation" or, more impressively, "atmospheric deposition of anthropogenetically-derived acidic substances." And those aren't gangsters, mobsters, the Mafia, or La Cosa Nostra in Atlantic City; according to the "New Jersey Division of Gaming Enforcement" (a doublespeak title that avoids the use of that dreaded word, "gambling") they're just "members of a career-offender cartel."

Military Doublespeak

Military doublespeak seems to have always been around. In 1947 the name of the Department of War was changed to the more pleasing if misleading Department of Defense. How much easier it is to spend hundreds of billions of dollars for defense instead of war. During the Vietnam War the American public learned that it was an "incursion" into Cambodia, not an invasion; a "protective reaction strike" or "a limited duration protective reaction strike" or "air support," not bombing.

When asked why U.S. forces lacked intelligence information on Grenada before they invaded the island in 1983, Admiral Wesley L. McDonald told reporters that "We were not micromanaging Grenada intelligence-wise until about that time frame." In today's armed forces it's not a shovel but a "combat emplacement evacuator," not a bullet hole but a "ballistically induced aperture in the subcutaneous environment."

Business Doublespeak

The world of business has produced large amounts of doublespeak. If an airplane crash is one of the worst things that can happen to an airline company, a recall of automobiles because of a safety defect is one of the worst things that can happen to an automobile company. In April of 1972, when the Ford Motor Company had to recall 423,000 1972 Torino and Mercury Montego models to correct "mechanical deficiencies," the company sent a letter to all those who had bought the defective cars. In its letter, Ford said that the rear axle bearings of the cars "can deteriorate" and went on to say "Continued driving with a failed bearing could result in disengagement of the axle shaft and adversely affect vehicle control." This is the language of nonresponsibility. What are "mechanical deficiencies"—poor design, bad workmanship? The rear axle bearings "can deteriorate," but will they deteriorate? If they do deteriorate, what causes the deterioration? Note that "continued driving" is the subject of the sentence, which suggests that it is not Ford's poor manufacturing that is at fault but the driver who insists on driving the defective car. Note, too, the expression "failed bearing," which implies that the bearing failed, not Ford. Finally, the phrase "adversely affect vehicle control" means simply that, because of the mechanical defect, the driver could lose control of the car and get killed.

If you ask the questions for examining language to see if it's doublespeak (who is saying what to whom, under what conditions and circumstances, with what intent, and with what results), you can quickly discover the doublespeak here. What Ford should be saying to its customers is that the car Ford sold them has a serious defect that should be corrected immediately, otherwise the customer runs the risk of being seriously injured or killed. But you have to find this message beneath the doublespeak that Ford has used to disguise its embarrassing and unpleasant message. We will never know how many customers didn't bring their cars in for repairs because they didn't understand from that letter just how serious the problem was and that they'd better get their car to the service department fast.

When it comes time to fire or lay off employees, business has produced more than enough doublespeak to deal with the unpleasant situation. Employees are, of course, never fired or laid off. They are "selected out," "placed out," "non-retained," "released," "dehired," or "non-renewed." A corporation will "eliminate the redundancies in the human resources area," assign "candidates for derecruitment" to a "mobility pool," "revitalize the department" by placing executives on "special assignment," "enhance the efficiency of operations," "streamline the field sales organization," or "further rationalize marketing efforts." The reality behind all this doublespeak is that companies are firing or laying off employees, but no one wants to acknowledge to the stockholders, public, or competition that times are tough, business is bad, and people have to go.

When the oil industry was hit hard by declining sales and a surplus of oil, after years of great prosperity and a shortage of oil, the doublespeak flowed thicker than crude oil. Because of "reduced demand for product," which results in "space refining capacity" and problems in "down-stream operations," oil companies have been forced to "re-evaluate and consolidate their operations" and take "appropriate cost-reduction actions," in order to "enhance the efficiency of operations," which has meant the "elimination of marginal outlets," "accelerating our divestment program," and the "disposition of low throughput marketing units." This doublespeak really means that oil companies have fired employees, cut back on expenses, and closed gas stations and oil refineries because there's a surplus of oil and people are not buying as much gas and oil as in the past.

One oil company faced with declining business sent a memorandum to its employees advising them that the company's "business plans are under revision and now reflect a more moderate approach toward our operating and capital programs." The result of this "more moderate approach" is a "surplus of professional/technical employees." To "assist in alleviating the surplus, selected professional and technical employees" have been "selected to participate" in a "Voluntary Program" providing "incentives" for employees who "resign voluntarily." What this memorandum means, of course, is that expenses must be

cut because of declining business, so some employees will have
to go.

Wall Street produces doublespeak right along with the junk
bonds. It is rare to read in a trade publication that the stock
market "fell." Others might say the stock market fell, but those
who work on Wall Street prefer to say that the stock market
"retreated," "eased," made a "technical adjustment" or a "technical correction," or perhaps that "prices were off due to profit
taking," or "off in light trading," or "lost ground." In October
1987, when the stock market collapsed, losing billions of dollars,
one brokerage house called the collapse a "fourth quarter equity
retreat." As a side note, it is interesting to observe that the stock
market never rises because of a "technical adjustment" or "correction," nor does it ever "ease" upward. Stock prices always
"climb," "advance," "move forward," "edge up," or "surge."

Business magazines, corporate reports, executive speeches,
and the business sections of newspapers are filled with words
and phrases such as "marginal rates of substitution," "equilib-
rium price," "getting off margin," "distributional coalition,"
"non-performing assets," and "encompassing organizations."
Much of this is jargon or inflated language designed to make the
simple seem complex, but there are other examples of business
doublespeak that misleads or is designed to avoid a harsh reality.
What should you make of such expressions as "negative deficit"
or "revenue excesses" (i.e., profit), "invest in" (spend money or
buy something), "price enhancement" or "price adjustment"
(price increase), "shortfall" (mistake in planning), or "period of
accelerated negative growth" or "negative economic growth" (recession)?

Business doublespeak often attempts to give substance to pure
wind (to use Orwell's term), to make ordinary actions seem complex. Executives "operate" in "timeframes" within the "context"
of which a "task force" will serve as the proper "conduit" for all
the necessary "input" to "program a scenario" that, within acceptable "parameters," and with the proper "throughput," will
"generate" the "maximum output" for a "print out" of "zero defect terminal objectives" which will "enhance the bottom line."

Education Doublespeak

Politicians, members of the military, and businesspeople are not the only ones who use doublespeak. People in all parts of society use it. Education has more than its share of doublespeak. On some college campuses, what was once the Department of Physical Education is now the "Department of Human Kinetics" or the "College of Applied Life Studies." You may have called it Home Economics, but now it's the "School of Human Resources and Family Studies." These days, you don't go to the library to study; you go to the "Learning Resources Center."

Those aren't desks in the elementary school classroom, they're "pupil stations." Teachers, who are "classroom managers" applying an "action plan" to a "knowledge base," are concerned with the "basic fundamentals," which are "inexorably linked" to the "education user's" "time-on-task." Students don't take simple tests; now it's "criterion-referenced testing" that measures whether a student has achieved the "operational curricular objectives." A school system in Pennsylvania, making absolutely no mention of whether the student learned anything, uses the following grading system on its report cards: "no effort, less than minimal effort, minimal effort, more than minimal effort, less than full effort, full effort, better than full effort, effort increasing, effort decreasing."

B. W. Harlston, president of City College in New York, said in 1982 that some college students in New York come from "economically nonaffluent" families, while a spokesperson at Duke University said in 1982 that coach Red Wilson wasn't being fired, "He just won't be asked to continue in that job." An article in a scholarly journal suggests teaching students three approaches to writing to help them become better writers: "concretization of goals, procedural facilitation, and modeling planning."

In its August 3, 1981 issue, *Newsweek* magazine reported that the prestigious National Bureau of Economic Research published a working paper by Brown University economist Herschel I. Grossman entitled "Familial Love and Intertemporal Optimality." Professor Grossman reached this conclusion about family love: "An altruistic utility function promotes intertemporal efficiency. However, altruism creates an externality that implies that satisfying the conditions for efficiency does not insure intertemporal optimality."

A research report issued by the U.S. Office of Education in 1966 contains this sentence: "In other words, feediness is the shared information between toputness, where toputness is at a time just prior to the inputness." At times, doublespeak seems to be the primary product of educators.

Deadly Doublespeak

There are instances, however, where doublespeak becomes more than amusing, more than a cause for a laugh. At St. Mary's Hospital in Minneapolis in 1982, an anesthetist turned the wrong knob during a Cesarean delivery, giving a fatal dose of nitrous oxide which killed the mother and unborn child. The hospital called it a "therapeutic misadventure." In its budget request to Congress in 1977, the Pentagon called the neutron bomb "an efficient nuclear weapon that eliminates an enemy with a minimum degree of damage to friendly territory." The Pentagon also calls the expected tens of millions of civilian dead in a nuclear war "collateral damage," a term the Pentagon also applies to the civilians killed in any war. And in 1977 people watching the Dick Cavett show on television learned from former Green Beret Captain Bob Marasco that during the Vietnam war the Central Intelligence Agency created the phrase "eliminate with extreme prejudice" to replace the more direct verb "kill."

President Reagan and the Doublespeak of Politics

Identifying doublespeak can at times be difficult. For example, on July 27, 1981, President Ronald Reagan said in a speech televised to the American public that "I will not stand by and see those of you who are dependent on Social Security deprived of the benefits you've worked so hard to earn. You will continue to receive your checks in the full amount due you." This speech had been billed as President Reagan's position on Social Security, a subject of much debate at the time. After the speech, public opinion polls revealed that the great majority of the public believed that the president had affirmed his support for Social Security and that he would not support cuts in benefits. However, only days after the speech, on July 31, 1981, an article in the *Philadelphia Inquirer* quoted White House spokesperson David Gergen as saying that President Reagan's words had been "carefully chosen." What President Reagan had meant, according to Gergen, was that he was reserving the right to decide who was "dependent" on those benefits, who had "earned" them, and who, therefore, was "due" them.

The subsequent remarks of David Gergen reveal the real intent of President Reagan as opposed to his apparent intent. Thus, the criteria for analyzing language to determine whether it is doublespeak (who is saying what to whom, under what conditions and circumstances, with what intent, and with what results), when applied in light of David Gergen's remarks, reveal the doublespeak of President Reagan. Here, indeed, is the insincerity of which Orwell wrote. Here, too, is the gap between the speaker's real and declared aim.

Doublespeak and Political Advertisements

During the 1982 congressional election campaign, the Republican National Committee sponsored a television advertisement that pictured an elderly, folksy postman delivering Social Security checks "with the 7.4% cost-of-living raise that President Reagan promised." The postman then adds that "he promised that raise and he kept his promise, in spite of those sticks-in-the-mud who tried to keep him from doing what we elected him to do." The commercial was, in fact, deliberately misleading. The cost-of-living increases had been provided automatically by law since 1975, and President Reagan had tried three times to roll them back or delay them but was overruled by congressional opposition. When these discrepancies were pointed out to an official of the Republican National Committee, he called the commercial "inoffensive" and added, "Since when is a commercial supposed to be accurate? Do women really smile when they clean their ovens?"

Again, applying the criteria for identifying doublespeak to this advertisement reveals the doublespeak in it, once you know the facts of past actions by President Reagan. Moreover, the official for the Republican National Committee assumes that all advertisements, whether for political candidates or commercial products, do not tell the truth; in his doublespeak, they do not have to be "accurate." Thus, the real intent of the advertisement was to mislead, while the apparent purpose of the commercial was to inform the public of President Reagan's position on possible cuts in Social Security benefits. Again there is insincerity, and again there is a gap between the speaker's real and declared aims.

Alexander Haig and Doublespeak

One of the most chilling and terrifying uses of doublespeak in recent memory occurred in 1981 when then Secretary of State Alexander Haig was testifying before congressional committees about the murder of three American nuns and a Catholic lay worker in El Salvador. The four women had been raped and then shot at close range, and there was clear evidence that the crime had been committed by soldiers of the Salvadoran government. Before the House Foreign Affairs Committee, Secretary Haig said:

> I'd like to suggest to you that some of the investigations
> would lead one to believe that perhaps the vehicle the
> nuns were riding in may have tried to run a roadblock,
> or may accidentally have been perceived to have been
> doing so, and there'd been an exchange of fire and then
> perhaps those who inflicted the casualties sought to
> cover it up. And this could have been at a very low level
> of both competence and motivation in the context of the

issue itself. But the facts on this are not clear enough for anyone to draw a definitive conclusion.

The next day, before the Senate Foreign Relations Committee, Secretary Haig claimed that press reports on his previous testimony were "inaccurate." When Senator Claiborne Pell asked whether the secretary was suggesting the possibility that "the nuns may have run through a roadblock," he replied, "You mean that they tried to violate . . . ? Not at all, no, not at all. My heavens! The dear nuns who raised me in my parochial schooling would forever isolate me from their affections and respect." Then Senator Pell asked Secretary Haig, "Did you mean that the nuns were firing at the people, or what did 'an exchange of fire' mean?" The secretary replied, "I haven't met any pistol-packing nuns in my day, Senator. What I meant was that if one fellow starts shooting, then the next thing you know they all panic." Thus did the secretary of state of the United States explain official government policy on the murder of four American citizens in a foreign land.

Secretary Haig's testimony implies that the women were in some way responsible for their own fate. By using such vague wording as "would lead one to believe" and "may accidentally have been perceived to have been doing so," he avoids any direct assertion. The use of the phrase "inflicted the casualties" not only avoids using the word "kill" but also implies that at the worst the killings were accidental or justifiable. The result of this testimony is that the secretary of state has become an apologist for rape and murder. This is indeed language in defense of the indefensible; language designed to make lies sound truthful and murder respectable; language designed to give an appearance of solidity to pure wind.

The Dangers of Doublespeak

These previous three examples of doublespeak should make it clear that doublespeak is not the product of carelessness or sloppy thinking. Indeed, most doublespeak is the product of clear thinking and is carefully designed and constructed to appear to communicate when in fact it doesn't. It is language designed not to lead but mislead. It is language designed to distort reality and corrupt thought. In the world created by doublespeak, if it's not a tax increase, but rather "revenue enhancement" or "tax base broadening," how can you complain about higher taxes? If it's not acid rain, but rather "poorly buffered precipitation," how can you worry about all those dead trees? If that isn't the Mafia in Atlantic City, but just "members of a career-offender cartel," why worry about the influence of organized crime in the city? If Supreme Court Justice William Rehnquist wasn't addicted to the pain-killing drug his doctor prescribed, but instead it was just that the drug had "established an interrelationship with the body, such that if the drug is removed precipitously, there is a reaction," you needn't question that his decisions might have been influenced by his drug addiction. If it's not a Titan II nuclear-armed intercontinental ballistic missile with a warhead 630 times more powerful than the atomic bomb dropped on Hiroshima, but instead, according to Air Force Colonel Frank Horton, it's just a "very large, potentially disruptive reentry system," why be concerned about the threat of nuclear destruction? Why worry about the neutron bomb escalating the arms race if it's just a "radiation enhancement weapon"? If it's not an invasion, but a "rescue mission" or a "predawn vertical insertion," you won't need to think about any violations of U.S. or international law.

Doublespeak has become so common in everyday living that many people fail to notice it. Even worse, when they do notice doublespeak being used on them, they don't react, they don't protest. Do you protest when you are asked to check your packages at the desk "for your convenience," when it's not for your convenience at all but for someone else's? You see advertisements for "genuine imitation leather," "virgin vinyl," or "real counterfeit diamonds," but do you question the language or the supposed quality of the product? Do you question politicians who don't speak of slums or ghettos but of the "inner city" or "substandard housing" where the "disadvantaged" live and thus avoid talking about the poor who have to live in filthy, poorly heated, ramshackle apartments or houses? Aren't you amazed that patients don't die in the hospital anymore, it's just "negative patient-care outcome"?

Doublespeak such as that noted earlier that defines cab drivers as "urban transportation specialists," elevator operators as members of the "vertical transportation corps," and automobile mechanics as "automotive internists" can be considered humorous and relatively harmless. However, when a fire in a nuclear reactor building is called "rapid oxidation," an explosion in a nuclear power plant is called an "energetic disassembly," the illegal overthrow of a legitimate government is termed "destabilizing a government," and lies are seen as "inoperative statements," we are hearing doublespeak that attempts to avoid responsibility and make the bad seem good, the negative appear positive, something unpleasant appear attractive; and which seems to communicate but doesn't. It is language designed to alter our perception of reality and corrupt our thinking. Such language does not provide us with the tools we need to develop, advance, and preserve our culture and our civilization. Such language breeds suspicion, cynicism, distrust, and, ultimately, hostility.

Doublespeak is insidious because it can infect and eventually destroy the function of language, which is communication between people and social groups. This corruption of the function of language can have serious and far-reaching consequences. We live in a country that depends upon an informed electorate to make decisions in selecting candidates for office and deciding issues of public policy. The use of doublespeak can become so pervasive that it becomes the coin of the political realm, with speakers and listeners convinced that they really understand such language. After awhile we may really believe that politicians don't lie but only "misspeak," that illegal acts are merely "inappropriate actions," that fraud and criminal conspiracy are just "miscertification." President Jimmy Carter in April of 1980 could call the aborted raid to free the American hostages in Teheran an "incomplete success" and really believe that he had made a statement that clearly communicated with the American public. So, too, could President Ronald Reagan say in 1985 that "ultimately our security and our hopes for success at the arms reduction talks hinge on the determination that we show here to continue our program to rebuild and refortify our defenses" and really believe that greatly increasing the amount of money spent building new weapons would lead to a reduction in the number of weapons in the world. If we really believe that we understand such language and that such language communicates and promotes clear thought, then the world of *1984,* with its control of reality through language, is upon us.

CHAPTER II

Therapeutic Misadventures, the Economically Nonaffluent, and Deep-Chilled Chickens: The Doublespeak of Everyday Living

Airline Doublespeak

After fighting the traffic all the way to the airport, parking your car in the expensive and overcrowded parking garage, standing in long lines waiting to check in, and then boarding your flight, you can at last settle back in your uncomfortable seat for your direct flight to Denver. Or so you thought. As the plane begins its descent into the Kansas City airport, you innocently ask the flight attendant why the plane is landing. After all, you specifically asked for a direct flight to Denver. Without batting an eye, the flight attendant replies, "It is indeed a direct flight; it just isn't nonstop."

Welcome to the world of everyday doublespeak. Through such unpleasant and sometimes even painful experiences, you learn how doublespeak affects your life. Someplace along the line, the airlines invented a distinction between the terms "direct" and "nonstop," but the airlines forgot to tell you. When a lawyer who specializes in aviation law petitioned to put an end to what he called the "deception of airline passengers," Mike Clark, a spokesperson for Pan American World Airways, denied that passengers were being misled: "It's just a question of semantics," he said.

If you travel by airplane at all, you quickly become aware of the doublespeak used by airlines. Only airlines can get away with calling four crackers and some artificial cheese spread or a package of twelve peanuts a "snack." Trans Florida Airlines provides its passengers with a set of instructions to be followed "in case of a non-routine operation." Other airlines give you instructions to follow in the event of a "water landing." The little paper sack is "for motion discomfort." At one airport, American Airlines transports its passengers from the departure gate to the airplane on a "customer conveyance mobile lounge," which certainly sounds a lot more impressive than a bus. After all, you didn't pay all that money to ride a bus, did you?

If you have ever arrived at the airport only to find that your plane is full, don't charge the airline with overbooking the flight. Airlines prefer to call the practice of selling more tickets than there are seats on the airplane "space planning," "capacity management," or "revenue control," which is part of their "inventory-management system" handled by "space controllers" who seek to avoid "spoilage," or empty seats.

The next really important doublespeak you learn (after the distinction between direct and nonstop flights) is that you do not fly in an airplane or a jet plane or even an airliner. Sometimes you might fly in an aircraft, but far more often you fly in "equipment," as in, "The equipment has arrived and is now being serviced prior to our beginning the preboarding process." Or as in, "Ladies and gentlemen, because of a technical difficulty there will be a change of equipment. Will you please deplane at this time." Of course, this last statement means the airplane is broken and won't fly, so they have to get you off that plane and on another—if there's some other "equipment" that works. If you want to know what kind of airplane you'll be flying on this trip, just ask the ticket agent, "What's the 'equipment' on this flight?" Without hesitation you'll be told 727, L-1011, or something similar.

The airlines, I am sure, think that the word "equipment" sounds much more solid, reliable, and far less frightening than the simple, common, ordinary word "airplane." But to me, flying is scary enough without feeling that I'm not even going to be flying in an airplane but in a piece of equipment, which sounds like I'm going to be thirty-six thousand feet from the solid earth surrounded by old washing machine parts, pieces of a 1948 Hudson, and a few leftover manual typewriters. I don't want to strap myself into a seat on the "equipment"; I want to sit in an airplane.

Before you ever make it to the equipment, however, you must go through the "preboarding process," as in, "Ladies and gentlemen, in a few minutes we will begin the preboarding process." It's not just preboarding; it's a "preboarding *process.*" I live for the day when I will see someone actually "preboard the equipment." I want to see someone board the airplane before boarding it, and I want to see the process someone has to go through in order to preboard.

Airlines like to talk about "carry-on items," not baggage, as in, "All carry-on items must fit conveniently beneath the seat in front of you or in the overhead compartments." Airlines never speak of first-class passengers, but always of "passengers in the first-class section." And did you ever notice that, while there may be a first-class section, there's never a second-class section? You probably ride in the "coach" section, as I do. American Airlines has even eliminated the first-class section. On their planes it's the "main cabin." I wonder, where does that leaves the rest of us?

The Doublespeak of Food

Even if you don't fly very often, you can still find plenty of doublespeak close to home. On your next trip to the grocery store—or supermarket, as they like to call them these days—pay attention to the language of food and the food business. Little things in this business try to mean a lot.

Wegmans Food Markets in Rochester, New York advertised for "part-time career associate scanning professionals," or what used to be called check-out clerks when I worked stocking shelves in a grocery store. Some of the clerks at the Pathmark supermarkets in New York wear nametags that list their job as "Price Integrity Coordinator." What do they do? They check to make sure all the items in the store have the correct prices on them.

Before you rush off to the store that's open twenty-four hours a day, you'd better check its hours. The Pathmark supermarket chain in New York advertised in bold headlines that their stores were open twenty-four hours a day, but then in small print there was the note, "Check local store for exact hours." There are supermarkets in Williamstown and North Adams, Massachusetts that advertise they are "Open 24 hours a day. Hours: 9 am to Midnight. Sundays 12 to 6."

In the food business, words mean money—your money. Use the right words, and people will pay more for the product. A study conducted by a Connecticut consumer research group a few years ago revealed that people were willing to pay 10 percent more for what they thought were natural foods. Almost 50 percent of the people interviewed approved of paying more for such foods. No one has ever accused the food industry of ignoring a trend, especially when it means making lots of money just by using a few meaningless words. An article in *The New York Times Magazine* for November 29, 1987, quotes William D. Parker, vice-president of meat merchandising for Kroger food stores, who was discussing the "natural" and "lite" or "light" beef products that have recently become hot items: "It's a niche-market type item in upper-income areas where people have more money than sense," he said.

Put the magic words on the package and you can jack up the price, even if the contents aren't all that much different from those in the package without the magic words. "Lean" is a magic word, as in "lean beef." The U.S. Department of Agriculture defines "lean" red meat or poultry as having no more than 10 percent fat. Now, I know that I'm supposed to eat lean beef, as opposed to fat beef, I guess. If that's true, why do cattle ranchers spend so much time and money fattening up their cattle before selling them to the slaughterhouses, or meat processors, as they like to call themselves? Why not start a diet program for cattle, so we'll have nothing but lean beef? Why not have "fat farms" for cattle, where they can lose all their fat before they end up on our dinner tables?

But the Department of Agriculture's definition of "lean" does not apply to ground beef. In fact, the fat content of ground beef varies widely. The Center for Science in the Public Interest did a survey in 1988 and found that the fat content in "lean" ground beef ranged anywhere from 20 to 30 percent. Nor do you do any better with "extra lean" ground beef. The U.S. Department of Agriculture conducted a series of experiments in which they discovered that there was only one gram of fat difference between three and one-half ounces of cooked regular beef and the same amount of "extra lean" ground beef. And that single gram of fat (which is about one-twenty-eighth of an ounce) equals nine calories. For those nine fewer calories, you pay more for the extra-lean beef.

The National Academy of Sciences issued a report in 1988 pointing out that terms such as "lean" and "lite" are misleading. "Extra lite" doesn't guarantee reduced calories. Under Federal rules the term may simply refer to a product's color, flavor, or texture. "Lean" frozen dinners may use meat and other ingredients containing large amounts of fat.

While you may think you know what those magic words on food packages mean, you probably don't, because those words have a special meaning that seems to be known only to the food manufacturers and the four government agencies that oversee food labeling and safety. For example, the word "enriched" means that vitamins, minerals, or protein have been added to the product, usually because these nutrients were eliminated from the food during processing. In other words, "enriched" simply means that the food is back where it started, nutritionally speaking, before it was processed. However, "fortified" means that vitamins, minerals, or proteins not originally removed or reduced during processing have been added as supplements, thus increasing the nutritional value the food had before it was processed.

As you probably guessed, there's an exception to these meanings of "enriched" and "fortified," and that exception is flour. Almost all the flour sold in supermarkets today is labeled "enriched," because flour can be called "enriched" if the iron, niacin, thiamine, and riboflavin that were removed during processing are replaced. However, the zinc, fiber, copper, and other vitamins and minerals that were removed during processing don't have to be replaced. So you want to buy "fortified" flour, not "enriched" flour, but the other food you buy should be "enriched" not "fortified." Got that? Just when you thought you had their definitions straight, they still manage to confuse you, don't they?

If you buy "dietetic" foods, you'd better be careful. According to current regulations, foods with such terms as "dietetic," "diet," "low calorie," and "reduced calorie" on their labels must have either one-third fewer calories than the standard versions or fewer than 40 calories per 100-gram serving. The question, of course, is how many calories are in that standard version, whatever that may be. Moreover, some foods can be labeled "dietetic" and still have the same number of calories as the standard version, as long as they have a reduced sodium content. To top it all off, the calorie count on the label only has to be within 20 percent of the actual number of calories in the food. Thus, the frozen diet dinner that claims to contain only 200 calories can contain as few as 160 calories or as many as 240 calories; there's no way you can know for sure.

So you skip the diet dinner and go for the "sugar free" or "sugarless" food, in the innocent belief that food labels mean what they say. Wrong again. "Sugar free" and "sugarless" simply mean that the food contains no sucrose, which is nothing more than ordinary table sugar. However, the food can contain honey, dextrose (which is corn sugar), fructose (which is fruit sugar), mannose, glucose, sorbitol, or any other of a number of sweeteners that contain just as many calories as sucrose. Isn't that an interesting definition of "sugar free"? Don't you think the food industry and the government should let you in on their private definitions of words, especially since it's your health and waistline that are at stake? Remember, doublespeak is language that

pretends to communicate but really doesn't; it is language designed to mislead.

One of the most popular words in the food business these days
is "natural." Sometimes it seems as if everything sold in the
supermarket is natural, including detergent, soap, shampoo, pet
food, and candy bars. The meaning of the word "natural" is
obvious, right? (If you answered "yes" to that rhetorical question,
take a piece of paper and write a one-sentence definition of the
word "natural" before you continue reading the rest of this discussion.)

In the food business, the word "natural" doesn't mean anything. A food labeled "natural" or "all natural" can contain any
number of chemicals, including flavor enhancers, thickeners,
emulsifiers, and preservatives such as BHA and BHT. Does this
list of ingredients agree with your written or unwritten definition of "natural"? The last time I looked, the dictionary definition
of "natural" said something about "not artificial, synthetic, or
processed," but then maybe those government agencies and the
food manufacturers don't use the same dictionary you and I use.
Maybe they use their own private dictionary, the one they write
but forget to publish so you can read it.

In 1980, *Consumer Reports* magazine reported that "Langendorf Natural Lemon Flavored Creme Pie" contains no cream but
does contain sodium propionate, certified food colors, sodium
benzoate, and vegetable gum. When L. A. Cushman, Jr., who
chairs American Bakeries Company, the Chicago firm that owns
Langendorf, was asked about this label, he explained that the
word "natural" modifies "lemon flavored" and the pie contains
oil from lemon rinds. "The lemon flavor," Mr. Cushman is
quoted as saying, "comes from natural lemon flavor as opposed
to artificial lemon flavor, assuming there is such a thing as artificial lemon flavor."

Then there are "Pillsbury Natural Chocolate Flavored Chocolate Chip Cookies," which contain, among other ingredients, artificial flavor and BHA. "We're not trying to mislead anybody,"
claimed a company representative, who explained that the word
"natural" modifies only "chocolate flavored." I guess you'd better

brush up on the syntactic structure of modification if you want to be able to read food labels these days.

A great example of the doublespeak of food is the claim on the label that the product doesn't contain something it wouldn't contain anyway, a kind of negative doublespeak. For example, a jar of jelly or jam may have the words "no preservatives" on it. Since sugar is all the preservative jams and jellies need, they have never had preservatives added to them. The same is true for canned products, which are preserved by the heat of the canning process. So think twice before buying the can of corn or the jar of jelly just because it is labeled "no preservatives added." You might also notice that these magic words are usually accompanied by that other magic word, "natural."

The use of the word "natural" on products reached a certain degree of absurdity when Anheuser-Busch proudly advertised its newest line of beer, "Anheuser-Busch Natural Light Beer," which the Miller Brewing Company derided, and then attacked. Miller correctly pointed out that beers are "highly processed, complex products, made with chemical additives and other components not in their natural form." The fight between the two big brewers caused some concern in the beer industry. *The Wall Street Journal* quoted William T. Elliot, president of C. Schmidt & Sons, a Philadelphia brewery, as saying, "One thing they [other brewers] are worried about is all the fuss over ingredients. Publicity about that issue is disclosing to beer drinkers that their suds may include sulfuric acid, calcium sulfate, alginic acid, or amyloglucosidase." So much for natural beer.

After eight years of trying to regulate advertising claims involving "natural foods," the Federal Trade Commission decided in 1982 to give up. Companies are not required to make a calorie disclosure for foods that have such magic words as "energy," "natural," or "lite" on their labels. You're on your own when you try to figure out what these words on any food label mean.

Deep-Chilled Chicken

Even that all–American food, chicken, can be the victim of deceptive labeling. You may have learned at one time that, at a temperature of thirty-two degrees Fahrenheit, water and other things freeze. But chicken doesn't freeze at that temperature, at least not according to the U.S. Department of Agriculture and the chicken processors, who consider processed chickens "fresh" not "frozen" if they have been chilled to twenty-eight degrees Fahrenheit. Bill Haffert, the editor of the trade journal *Broiler Industry*, said in 1981 that the industry term is "deep-chilling" and that such chickens have not been frozen but "deep-chilled" and can therefore be sold as "fresh" chickens. Maybe the people who thought up this doublespeak should be packed in ice and have their temperature lowered to twenty-eight degrees Fahrenheit. Then we could ask them if they're "fresh," "deep-chilled," or "frozen."

But even the twenty-eight-degree standard hasn't really applied, because chickens are considered fresh and not frozen if government inspectors can depress the flesh of the chicken with their thumbs. So in 1988 the Department of Agriculture announced that it was considering a new policy. The word "fresh" could not be used on any chicken if it had been frozen or previously reduced to a temperature of twenty-six degrees Fahrenheit or below. The chicken industry immediately fought the proposed standard. It makes you wonder just how "fresh" all those "deep-chilled" chickens being sold these days are. The next time you buy "fresh" chicken, you might ask whether the chicken has been "deep-chilled."

Picowaved Food

The latest innovation in the food industry is irradiated food, or food that has been treated with ionizing or gamma radiation to extend shelf life or kill insects. While ionizing or gamma radiation isn't radioactive, it is suspected of causing chemical changes in food, changes whose safety has been questioned by some scientists and consumer groups. But the government and the food industry decided to go ahead with irradiated food. Now, nobody in the food industry wanted to put the word "radiation" on a food package. As Ellen Green, a spokesperson for the National Food Processors Association, said, "The word 'radiation' is a scary word." What, then, could the food industry and the Food and Drug Administration do? At first the FDA recommended that irradiated food carry labels referring to "gamma" and "ionized" radiation, but the Department of Health and Human Services, the agency with final say in these matters, opposed any form of labeling. However, the agency gave in to public pressure and sought a "creative" solution. It considered the labels "gamma" and "ionized" to be "too negative," so it chose the word "picowave" instead.

The word "picowave" has no real meaning. It was created by a company in California and was designed to be similar to the word "microwave," which is a completely different kind of radiation, but it's a word very familiar to the public. Thus, foods that have been irradiated will be labeled "picowaved." An industry spokesperson said that, "from a public relations standpoint, it is more pleasant to the ear than gamma radiation or electromagnetic energy." Secretary of Health and Human Services Margaret Heckler called the labeling "an important step forward for consumers." Said U.S. Senator Howard Metzenbaum, "It's the ultimate in untruth in advertising."

Picowaved food will also carry an international symbol which looks like a little flower inside a broken circle. The circle is supposed to represent the radiation facility. There is a black dot in the middle of the circle, which is supposed to represent the source of the radiation, and the petals of the flowers represent the irradiated food. Before you buy the picowaved food with the cute little flower symbol on it, you might ask yourself what it is you're really buying.

Mechanically Separated Meat

The next time you want to buy some hot dogs, sausage, luncheon meat, scrapple, or canned spaghetti with meat sauce, you might want to read the list of ingredients on the label very carefully. Does the list of ingredients include "Mechanically Separated Meat"? Do you know what MSM (as it's called in the food trade) is? Here's the recipe. Take the salvaged remnants of slaughtered animals, remnants that include bones, connecting tissue, and attached scraps of meat, pass this collection of scraps through a grinder, and then press the mixture through sieves until most of the bone is filtered out. (Some pieces of ground bone are always left in the mixture, but, hey, no process is perfect.)

Until 1982 this stuff was called "salvaged meat," but for some reason it just wasn't selling, probably because manufacturers were required to label the amount of "powdered bone" the mixture contained. Then the U.S. Department of Agriculture came to the rescue. Suddenly "salvaged meat" became "Mechanically Separated Meat" and the list of ingredients on a label would no longer have to include "ground bone." All that would have to be listed was "Mechanically Separated Meat" and the amount of "calcium" in the average serving.

The meat processing industry still wasn't happy, though, so in 1988 Bob Evans Farms, Inc., the Odom Sausage Company, the Sara Lee Corporation, and Owen Country Sausage, Inc. petitioned the Department of Agriculture to allow hot dogs and other products to contain up to 10 percent MSM without listing it as an ingredient on the label. Read those food labels fast, because soon even the innocuous phrase "Mechanically Separated Meat" will no longer be there. But don't worry; the amount of "calcium" per serving will still be listed, because the ground bone will still be there.

Lite Up Your Life

Words sell food, and they sell beer, too, but you have to ask yourself what the words really mean. Diet beer was around for years, but it certainly didn't sell. After all, what real man wants to belly up to the bar and order a diet beer? Them's fighting words, partner. But along come the marketing geniuses of the Miller Brewing Company, who changed the word "diet" to "lite," hired a bunch of ex-jocks to extol the virtues of "less-filling" beer, and sales history was made. So now it's all right to drink diet beer, because it's not diet beer, it's "lite" beer. We're dedicated to becoming a nation of lightweights (or is that liteweights?). We're watching what we eat. Even restaurant menus offer light meals and slim platters. No one really knows what a light meal in a restaurant is, except it seems to contain a lot of lettuce. We may not know what light foods really are or what makes them light, but when it comes to buying light foods in the supermarket we know one thing: They cost more. Today you can light up your life with any kind of food you want. There's light milk, light spaghetti sauce, light frozen dinners, light mayonnaise, light cookies, light potato chips, light ice cream, and even light ketchup. Legally, a manufacturer can call a food product "light" even if it contains only a few calories less than a comparable product. You probably didn't know it, but regular ketchup contains only fifteen or sixteen calories per serving. Now comes the light version, for more money, which offers eight to nine calories per serving.

The Cooperative Extension of New York State warned consumers in 1984 that, just because such words as "natural," "light," "life," "health," "nutrition," "country," "nature," "harvest," "fair," and "farm" appear on packages (along with pictures of sheaves of wheat, farms, green valleys, streams of clear running water, and farmers toiling in the field), it does not mean the contents are farm fresh, wholesome, organic, or healthy. After all, when was the last time you bought a loaf of bread that was anything less than "fresh baked"?

The Fine Print of Food Labels

The next time you wander through the supermarket, try reading the small print on the labels of a few products. You'll find Wrigley's Orbit chewing gum is, according to its wrapper, "not non-caloric," that Lance's "naturally flavored" spice drops contain natural and artificial flavors, and that Original New York Seltzer claims on its label "no sucrose" but does contain "fructose syrup." (By the way, it's not made in New York, it's not seltzer, and it's not original, but just another soda pop.)

Nabisco's 100% Bran contains wheat bran, sugar, malted barley flour, salt, fig juice, prune juice, and other stuff. So just what does "100%" in the name of this cereal mean? Or try Armour Potted Meat Food Product. Do you have any idea what a "meat food product" is? What does "potted" mean—that it comes in a can? The word "product" reminds me of those famous "meat by-products" in dog food. Take a close look at the label on this "meat food product" and you'll find that it's made of cooked beef fat tissue, partially defatted beef fatty tissue, and sodium erythorbate flavorings. Just like mom used to make.

The label on the Kraft Deluxe Macaroni & Cheese Dinner proclaims, "Complete with rich, creamy cheese sauce. Made with a blend of natural cheeses and other fine ingredients." Those "other fine ingredients" include milkfat, sodium phosphate, sodium alginate, and artificial flavor. According to its label, Durkee Grandee Spanish Olives are "stuffed with minced pimentos." However, the list of ingredients includes not minced pimento but "pureed pimento." Thus it is hardened pimento mush that is stuffed into the olives.

You can always try Café Français, an instant coffee that captures the famous flavor of the French recipe by using vegetable oil, corn syrup solids, sugar, instant coffee, sodium caseinate solids, trisodium citrate, dipotassium phosphate, mono- and diglycerides, silicon dioxide, artificial flavors, lecithin, and tetrasodium pyrophosphate. Of course, if you take "cream" in your coffee, there's always your choice of Coffee-Mate, Cremora, Coffee-Rich, Coffee Dream, or any number of other brands of "non-dairy creamers" containing such nondairy ingredients as corn syrup, partially hydrogenated vegetable oil, and one or more of the following oils: coconut, cotton seed, palm, and soybean. They also throw in some mono- and diglycerides, sodium caseinate, disodium phosphate, sodium citrate, and potassium stearate. But, don't worry; your fake cream has been "ultrapasteurized." I wonder when plain old pasteurization stopped being good enough?

The side panels on the package of Arnold Italian Crispy Croutons explains how, in the early 1800s, the French made croutons by cutting long loaves of bread into small pieces, drying the pieces, and then frying them in butter or oil. Then you read that "The delicious crunchy-crisp croutons in this package are directly derived from the original French dish, but the method of preparation has been adapted to modern lifestyles and standards." The modern method of preparation includes adding such tasty ingredients as ethoxylated mono- and diglycerides, calcium propionate, potassium bromate, disodium phosphate, artificial flavor, and other touches to improve on the classic French recipe.

But at least bread is bread, you think, and the label on a loaf of bread is pretty straightforward. You'd better think again. According to the *Code of Federal Regulations* there are twenty-seven chemicals that can be added to bread, but the food manufacturer doesn't have to list any of them on the label. Even for the ingredients that do have to be listed on the label, the manufacturer can use a little doublespeak. In 1985, the Center for Science in the Public Interest revealed that the source of "fiber" in a number of popular "high-fiber" breads was nonnutritional wood pulp. To reduce the number of calories and increase the amount of fiber in the bread, some companies had replaced some of the flour with alpha cellulose, which was sometimes listed as "powdered cellulose" among the ingredients on the package. None of the companies listed wood pulp among the ingredients. All of the companies defended their labeling as "not deceptive."

The food companies have never let up in their efforts to use words that mislead. On the NBC-TV "Today" program on September 9, 1987, Richard Frank, speaking for the Committee for Fair Pizza Labeling, a food industry lobbying group, argued for the use of a "low-cholesterol cheese alternate" on frozen pizza. In other words, Mr. Frank wanted Congress to approve the use of fake cheese on frozen pizza, and he wanted to use it without calling it fake cheese.

At least you don't have to read a list of all those ingredients on a bottle of wine. In 1981 the Wine Institute convinced the U.S. Bureau of Alcohol, Tobacco and Firearms to adopt a regulation that allows wine companies not to list all the ingredients in a bottle of wine. Now they can omit mention of such additives as grape juice, grape must, grape concentrate, yeasts, water, eggs (albumen or yolks), gelatin, casein, isinglass and pectolytic enzymes as clarifiers, ascorbic acid or erythodbic acid to prevent darkening, and sulfur dioxide and potassium salt of sorbic acid as sterilizing and preservative agents. Anyone for a glass of wine?

You can't even say you're getting a lemon when you buy foods like lemon pudding or lemon cake mix, because the lemons in these products are fake. In fact, you don't need any lemons to make lemonade. In 1982 the Food and Drug Administration denied a petition asking that the word "lemonade" be restricted to products containing real lemon juice. Howard N. Pippin, speaking for the FDA, said that "we don't know how much lemon juice it takes to make lemonade." He conceded that, under FDA regulations, a product could appear with a label reading "lemonade," yet contain no lemon juice. That's just what's happened, because General Foods' Lemonade Flavor Drink contains no lemon pulp, lemon peel, or lemon juice. It does contain citric acid, gum acacia, and "nutritive sweetener." When a consumer wrote to General Foods and asked how they could make lemonade without lemons, the company wrote back that "the aromatic or essential component of all citrus fruits is also referred to as 'natural flavor' and is derived from the oil sacs in the peel and not from the juice." Anyone want to buy "lemon oil sac component pudding and pie filling"?

If you look at all those products that use the word "lemon" on their packages, you'll find few if any lemons were used to make any of them. General Foods' Lemon Deluxe Cake Mix contains citric acid, while Royal Gelatin Lemon Dessert has fumaric acid, and Jell-O Lemon Pudding Mix contains fumaric acid and adipic acid for tartness. You also won't find any lemons in any of those lemon-scented ammonia cleaners, oven cleaners, furniture polishes, furniture waxes, air deodorizers, toilet bowl fresheners, or detergents that have the word "lemon" in big letters or a big picture of a lemon on their packages. Search as hard as you can, but you won't find a lemon in the whole bunch. How does Lemon Freshened Borax or Lemon Fresh Joy differ from non-lemon products? Since they don't contain real lemons, we are left guessing what ingredient they do contain that makes them different.

Fake Food

One of the fastest growing segments of the food industry is fake food. What, you ask, is fake food? Fake food looks and tastes like the real product (or so the manufacturers claim), but it is made from a cheaper substitute and sells for a fraction of the cost of the real thing. To be more accurate, the fake-food industry sells its products to the retailer for a fraction of the cost. Consumers usually end up paying as if the fake food were the real thing.

Some "food technologists" (as fake-food inventors like to be called) don't even call their products food; they call them "food systems." Food technologists develop such things as "cheese analogs" (fake mozzarella) and "restructured muscle products" (fake steaks). When these "food systems" are used in restaurants, there's no requirement that customers be told what they're buying and what they're eating.

The U.S. Department of Agriculture allows food processors to combine 135 parts of water with one part meat stock and still use the words "beef stock" instead of water on their ingredient labels. You can buy such fake foods as California Foolers, which are nonalcoholic versions of alcoholic drinks; and fake flavors (known as flavorgeins and flavor enhancers) such as butter, Mexican, Oriental, and Italian flavors. You can even get combinations such as nacho-flavored fortune cookies. Companies are even developing a fake barbecue sauce flavor and a fake mesquite smoke flavor. Soon you will be able to buy barbecue-flavored and mesquite-flavored food without the food ever having been near a real grill.

A number of Japanese companies ship large amounts of fake frozen crab meat (or, more precisely, a "surimi-based crab analog") to the United States. Surimi is a fish paste made by pressing and repeatedly washing deboned fish. The fake crab comes in the form of sticks or shredded meat and is made from cheap cod plus starch, salt, chemical seasoning, "essence of crab" (which is derived from boiling down crab shells), and polymerized phosphate. Sales of imitation crab meat exceeded $100 million a year in 1984 and were growing rapidly.

There are many other fake foods. Fake scallops are made from codfish with "essence of scallop," then compressed into cylinders and sliced to look like scallops. Canned red salmon is produced by using 30 percent real salmon plus cod with starch, salt, chemical seasoning, and synthetic red coloring added. Fake salmon roe consists of little orange-red colored balls made from seaweed gelatin, filled with salad oil.

Japanese fake-food manufacturers have also gone beyond fake seafood to fake beef. Using cod or sardines, the fake-food makers add salt and knead the mass until it takes on a gluey consistency. This mass is then put through an extruder and ethyl alcohol is added so that the protein becomes a mixture with the elasticity of natural beef. Meat flavoring and coloring are added so that the final product appears to be minced beef which can be used in hamburgers and other products.

Another process used to make fake beef takes internal organs, diaphragms, and waste meat from real beef and glues them together with adhesives made from egg white, starch, and gelatin. After a strip of real beef fat is glued along the edges, the product is frozen into the shape of a sirloin steak, a filet mignon, or a similar product. Food technologists boast that these products have the "mouthfeel" of real steaks. Ah, yes, beef is real food for real people.

You can also get surimi versions of lobster and shrimp, and the fake-food makers are busy working on surimi-based cheese, hot dogs, potato chips, and luncheon meat. The idea of fake hot dogs and fake luncheon meat is right up there with real virgin vinyl and genuine imitation leather. Surimi manufacturers protest that their products are not imitations. "Surimi isn't an imitation anything," says James Brooker of the National Maritime Fisheries Service. "It's a seafood. It's a blended-seafood product."

One triumph of "food technology" (as the fake-food business is discreetly called) is the "gourm-egg," developed by Ralston Purina and now ten years old (the technology, not the egg). A "gourm-egg" is a foot-long rod of hard-cooked egg suitable for slicing into seventy-five perfect center slices. Through the genius of food technology, the yolks of these slices do not slip out of the white rims, even if the slices do have the texture of gelatinous rubber and a vague, sulfurous near-egg aftertaste. But then think of all the work involved in shelling seventy-five real hard-boiled eggs.

Then there are "seafood curls," developed by Griffith Laboratories. Using fake shrimp fried in "microwavable" batter, Griffith serves them crisp with a spicy dipping sauce. Such mouth-watering treats will soon be outdone, if Professor Endel Karmas, a food chemist at Rutgers University, has his way. He is developing "fish chewies," a chocolate-flavored fish-based concoction with the texture of a soft Tootsie Roll. And you thought the greatest tragedy to befall American cooking was the death of the real hamburger.

Food technologists are not a humorless group. According to an article in *The Wall Street Journal* in 1986, a group of food technologists once concocted what they called "trash soups," just for fun. The soups were made almost entirely of by-products: minced cod, scallop mantels (which are the greenish, rubbery protective lips found in scallop shells), and a broth made from the effluent of a clam-processing plant that, after using the water to clean the clams, had simply dumped the water as sewage. The soups, called New England and Manhattan Clam Chowders, were a big hit in taste tests and sold very well. In fact, the soups sold so well that the clam company, after the food technologists were finished with their little experiment, bottled the water it used to clean the clams and sold it as clam juice for $8 a bottle.

The fake-food business is so big that even the Riverfront State Prison in Camden, New Jersey has a program in which inmates produce "restructured beef," which turns beef chuck into pieces looking like strip steak, chuck roast, and other cuts. The inmates process fifty tons of meat a month.

How successful are these fake foods? Japanese manufacturers claim that consumers are convinced they are eating the real thing. There may be some truth to this claim, since fake crab exports to the United States went from over twenty-two hundred tons in 1981 to more than forty-five thousand tons in 1986. Fake crab and other fake foods are used by U.S. restaurants in salads, sandwiches, soups, casseroles, and other dishes. So, the next time you dine in a restaurant, you might ask, Where's the crab?

FOOD LABEL QUIZ

Now it's time to test your taste buds, and your ability to read a food label. Take this short quiz and see whether you can identify some popular food products just by reading the list of their ingredients. Match the number of the product with the letter of the list of ingredients.

___ 1. Cool Whip Topping

___ 2. Country Time Lemonade Drink

___ 3. Gaines Burgers

___ 4. Carnation Instant Breakfast

A. Meat By-Products, Soybean Grits, Sucrose, Soybean Meal, Propylene Glycol, Wheat Flour, Corn Syrup, Soybean Hulls, Chicken Digest, Salt, Dried Whey Product, Calcium Carbonate, Water, Beef, Vegetable Oil, Monocalcium Phosphate, Iron Oxide, Potassium Sorbate, Animal Fat (with BHA), Ethoxyguin, Zinc Oxide, Ammoniated Glycyrrhizin, Vitamins, Calcium Pantothenate, Ethylenediamine Dihydriodide.

B. Water, Sugar Syrup, Citric Acid, Sodium Citrate, Vegetable Gum, Natural Flavors, Potassium Sorbate, Sodium Benzoate, Vitamin C, Glycerol Abietate, Artificial Color, BHA.

C. Live Yeast Cell Derivative, Shark Liver Oil, Phenylmercuric Nitrate.

D. Hydrolyzed Vegetable Protein, Salt, Sugar, Onion, Autolyzed Yeast, Beef Fat, Maltodextrin, Celery, Caramel, Beef Extract, Disodium Inosinate, Disodium Guanylate.

___ 5. Hartz Hamster
      & Gerbil
      Munch

___ 6. Coffee-Mate
      Non-Dairy
      Creamer

___ 7. Fresh
      Horizons
      White Bread

___ 8. Herb-Ox Beef
      Bouillon
      Cubes

___ 9. Pepsodent
      Toothpaste

___ 10. Preparation H
      Ointment

E. Nonfat Dry Milk, Sugar, Cocoa, Corn Syrup Solids, Lactose, Isolated Soy Protein, Sodium Caseinate, Lecithin, Magnesium Hydroxide, Ammonium Carrageenan, Artificial Flavors, Sodium Ascorbate, Ferric Orthophosphate, Vitamin E Acetate, Vitamin A Palmitate, Niacinamide, Copper Gluconate, Zinc Oxide, Calcium Pantothenate, Thiamine Mononitrate, Pyridoxine Hydrochloride, Folic Acid.

F. Water, Hydrogenated Coconut and Palm Kernel Oils, Sugar, Corn Syrup, Sodium Caseinate, Dextrose, Natural and Artificial Flavors, Polysorbate 60, Sorbitan Monostearate, Xanthin Gum, GUAR Gum, Artificial Color.

G. Corn Meal, Vegetable Oil, Artificial Meat Flavors, Salt, Artificial Coloring.

H. Corn Syrup Solids, Partially Hydrogenated Vegetable Oil, Sodium Caseinate, Mono- and Diglycerides, Dipotassium Phosphate, Artificial Flavorings and Colors.

I. Sorbitol, Water, Alumina, Hydrated Silica, Glycerin, PEG 32, Sodium Lauryl Sulfate, Dicalcium Phosphate, Cellulose Gum, Flavor, Titanium Dioxide, Sodium Saccharin, Sodium Benzoate.

J. Water, Flour, Powdered Wood Cellulose, Wheat Gluten, Brown Sugar, Salt, Sugar, Yeast, Lactalbumin, Calcium Sulfate, Sodium Stearoyl-2-Lactylate, Mono- and Diglycerides, Polyglycerate 60, Polysorbate 60, Potassium Bromate, Artificial Flavor, Vitamins, Calcium Propionate.

(Answers: 1–F; 2–B; 3–A; 4–E; 5–G; 6–H; 7–J; 8–D; 9–I; 10–C.)

The Doublespeak of Everyday Things

I still haven't learned to call "Directory Assistance" when I need a telephone number that's not in the telephone book. I want to call information. But then I still use a toothbrush, and not an "oral hygiene appliance" or a "home plaque removal instrument." In our everyday lives we encounter more and more doublespeak like these examples.

Plain thermometers have become "digital fever computers," while the bathroom scale has become an "ultra-thin microelectric weight sensor." The modern bathroom doesn't have a bathtub, sink, and toilet, it has a "body cleaning system," a "pedestal lavatory," and a "water closet tub." Should your "water closet tub" become clogged, you can always use a "hydro blastforce cup" (or plunger) to clear it.

Pacific Gas & Electric Company doesn't send you a monthly bill these days, now it sends you "Energy Documents." Hallmark doesn't sell greeting cards, but "social expression products," while Sony sells blank videotapes that come in the "Extra Standard Superior Grade." Videotape stores will sell you "previously viewed videos" or used videotapes. You don't buy ink, you buy "writing fluid." A calendar is now a "personal manual data base," while a clock is a "personal analog temporal displacement monitor" and a used wristwatch is a "pre-owned vintage watch classic, an estate quality timepiece." Seiko sells "Personal Time Control Centers" not wristwatches. What was once a vacuum cleaner is now Hoover's "Dimension 1000 Electronic Cleaning machine with quadraflex agitator."

Automobile junkyards have become "auto dismantlers and recyclers," and they sell "predismantled previously owned parts." Secondhand or used furniture stores now sell "second-choice furnishings." Spoiled fruits and vegetables are now "distressed produce," while discount stores have become "valued oriented" stores. When you buy popcorn at the Strand movie theater in Madison, Wisconsin, you go to the "Patron Assistance Center," not the refreshment or candy stand. And if you want to exercise, you can always go, not to the gym, but to the "fitness center."

A company advertises that you can place your order by "electronic information transfer." What they really mean is that you can telephone your order to them. Undertakers, some of whom now call themselves "perpetual rest consultants," will sell you an "underground condominium" or cemetery lot, or an "eternal condominium" or mausoleum. Graves, by the way, are never dug but are "prepared" by those specializing in "internment excavation." You can even make "pre-need arrangements."

Beware of the Polls

Statistical doublespeak is a particularly effective form of doublespeak, since statistics are not likely to be closely scrutinized. Moreover, we tend to think that numbers are more concrete, more "real" than mere words. Quantify something and you give it a precision, a reality it did not have before.

We live in an age where people love numbers. Computer printouts are "reality." You identify yourself with your Social Security number; your American Express, MasterCard, or Visa number; your driver's license number; your telephone number (with area code first); your zip code. Three out of four doctors recommend something, we are told; a recent poll reveals 52.3 percent are opposed; Nielsen gives the new television program a 9.2; the movie grossed $122 million.

Baseball produces not just athletic contests but an infinity of statistics, which all true fans love to quote endlessly. Crowds at football and basketball games chant, "We're number one!" while the Dow Jones index measures daily our economic health and well-being. Millions of people legally (and illegally) play the daily number. Millions of pocket calculators are sold every year. The list could go on to include the body count of Vietnam and the numbers of nuclear warheads and intercontinental ballistic missiles cited as the measure of national security.

The computer scientist, the mathematician, the statistician, and the accountant all deal with "reality," while the poet, the writer, the wordsmith deal with, well, just words. You may find, however, that the world of numbers is not as accurate as you think it is, especially the world of the public opinion poll.

If you believe in public opinion polls, I've got a bridge you might like to buy. Depending upon which poll you believed just before the New Hampshire primary in February 1988, you would have known that Robert Dole would beat George Bush 35 percent to 27 (Gallup); or Dole would win 32 percent to Bush's 28 percent (*Boston Globe*); or that Dole and Bush were even at 32 percent each (ABC-*Washington Post*); or Bush would win 32 percent to Dole's 30 (WBZ-TV); or Bush would win 34 percent to Dole's 30 percent (CBS-*New York Times*). Of course, George Bush won the actual vote 38 percent to 29 percent.

Things weren't much better on the Democratic side, either. While most primary polls were correct in identifying Michael Dukakis as the winner, the margin of victory varied from 47 percent to 38 percent. Dukakis won with 36 percent of the vote. For second place, though, the polls really missed the call. Two had Paul Simon ahead of Richard Gephardt for second place, while a third had the two tied and the others had Simon behind by a thin margin. In the actual vote, Simon finished third with 17 percent of the vote, while Gephardt finished second with 20 percent. No one predicted Gephardt's 20 percent of the vote, *not even the surveys of voters leaving the polling places after they had voted.* This last point should not be overlooked, for it reminds us that no poll is worth anything unless people tell the pollster the truth. Since no pollster can ever know whether or not people are telling the truth, how can we ever be sure of any poll?

Things didn't improve during the presidential campaign either. In August, 1988, before the Republican National Convention, seven polls gave seven different answers to the question of who was ahead. The CBS-*New York Times* poll had Dukakis leading Bush 50 percent to 33 percent, while a poll taken by KRC Communications/Research had Dukakis ahead only 45 percent to 44 percent. When the ABC News poll came out with Bush ahead 49 percent to 46 percent, many people in the polling business discounted the results. ABC promptly took another poll three days later which showed Dukakis ahead 55 percent to 40 percent. That was more like it, said the other professional poll takers.

Even as presented, such polls are deceptive. Any poll has a margin of error inherent in it, but pollsters don't discuss that margin very much. They like their polls to have an air of precision and certainty about them. The KRC polls just mentioned had a margin of error of plus or minus 4 percent. This means that, in the first poll KRC took Dukakis really had anywhere from 49 to 41 percent, while Bush had anywhere from 48 to 40 percent. In other words, Dukakis could have been ahead 49 to 40 percent, or Bush could have been ahead 48 to 41 percent. The poll didn't tell you anything.

Polls have become important commodities to be sold. Television news programs and newspapers use polls to show that they have the inside information, thus boosting their ratings and their circulation. Also, the more dramatic or unexpected the results of a poll, the better the chances the poll will be featured prominently on the evening news program. In addition to all this hype and use of polls as news, politicians, corporations, special-interest groups, and others have vested interests in the results of particular polls. Such people and groups have been known to design and conduct polls that will produce the results they want. In other words, polls can be and are a source of a lot of doublespeak.

How do you read a poll? Actually, it's not all that hard, but the problem is that most poll results don't give you enough information to tell whether the poll is worth anything. In order to evaluate the results of a poll, you need to know the wording of the question or questions asked by the poll taker, when the poll was taken, how many people responded, how the poll was conducted, who was polled, how many people were polled, and how they were selected. That's a lot of information, and rarely does a poll ever give you more than just the results.

In 1967, two members of Congress asked their constituents the following question: "Do you approve of the recent decision to extend bombing raids in North Vietnam aimed at the strategic supply depots around Hanoi and Haiphong?" Sixty-five percent said yes. When asked, "Do you believe the U.S. should bomb Hanoi and Haiphong?" however, only 14 percent said yes. In 1973, when Congress was considering articles of impeachment against President Nixon, a Gallup poll asked the question, "Do you think President Nixon should be impeached and compelled to leave the Presidency, or not?" Only 30 percent said yes to this question. They were then asked, "Do you think the President should be tried and removed from office if found guilty?" To this, 57 percent said yes.

The most popular form of polling these days is the telephone poll, where a few hundred people are called on the telephone and asked a couple of questions. The results are then broadcast the next day. The two ABC polls mentioned earlier were based on telephoning 384 and 382 people, respectively. Just remember that the U.S. population is over 245 million.

According to Dennis Haack, president of Statistical Consultants, a statistical research company in Lexington, Kentucky,

most national surveys are not very accurate measures of public opinion. Opinion polls are no more accurate than indicated by their inability to predict Reagan's landslide in 1980 or Truman's win in 1948. The polls were wrong then and they have been wrong many other times when they tried to measure public opinion. The difference is that with elections we find out for sure if the polls were wrong; but for nonelection opinion polls there is no day of reckoning. We never know for sure how well surveys measure opinion when elections are not involved. I don't have much confidence in nonelection opinion surveys.

The Doublespeak of Graphs

Just as polls seem to present concrete, specific evidence, so do graphs and charts present information visually in a way that appears unambiguous and dramatically clear. But, just as polls leave a lot of necessary information out, so can graphs and charts, resulting in doublespeak. You have to ask a lot of questions if you really want to understand a graph or chart.

In 1981 President Reagan went on television to argue that

citizens would be paying a lot more in taxes under a Democratic bill than under his bill. To prove his point, he used a chart that appeared to show a dramatic and very big difference between the results of each bill (see Figure 1). But the presi-

Figure 1

President Reagan's misleading and biased chart, compared with a neutral presentation regarding the same tax proposals.

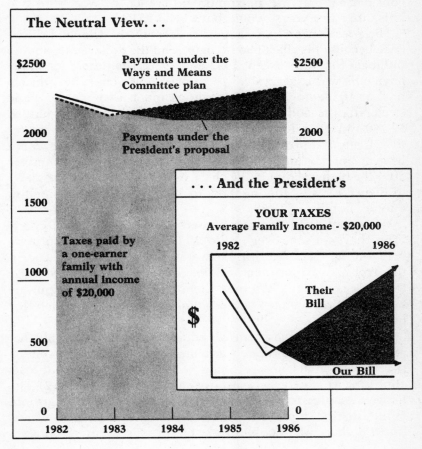

dent's chart was doublespeak, because it was deliberately designed to be misleading. Pointing to his chart, President Reagan said, "This red space between the two lines is the tax
money that will remain in your pockets if our bill passes, and
it's the amount that will leave your pockets if their bill is
passed. On the one hand, you see a genuine and lasting commitment to the future of working Americans. On the other, just
another empty promise." That was a pretty dramatic statement,
considering that the maximum difference between the two
bills, after five years, would have been $217.

The president's chart showed a deceptively dramatic difference because his chart had no figures on the dollar scale and no
numbers for years except 1982 and 1986. The difference in tax
payments was exaggerated in the president's chart by "squash-
ing" or tightening the time scale as much as possible, while
stretching the dollar scale, starting with an oddly unrounded
$2,150 and winding up at $2,400. Thus, the chart had no perspective. Using the proper method for constructing a chart would
have meant starting at $0 and going up to the first round number
after the highest point in the chart, as done in the "neutral view"
in Figure 1. Using that method, the $217 seems rather small in
a total tax bill of $2,385.

What happened to the numbers on the president's chart?
"The chart we sent over to the White House had all the numbers on it," said Marlin Fitzwater, then a press officer in
the Treasury Department. Senior White House spokesperson
David Gergen said, "We took them off. We were trying to get
a point across, not the absolute numbers." So much for
honesty.

In 1988 the Department of Education issued a graph that
seemed to prove that there was a direct connection between the
rise in elementary and secondary school spending and the decline in scores on the Scholastic Aptitude Test (see Figure 2). The
Reagan Administration had been arguing that spending more
money doesn't improve education and may even make it worse.
But the chart was doublespeak. First, it used current dollars

Figure 2

Misleading graph from the Department of Education, showing school spending relative to SAT scores.

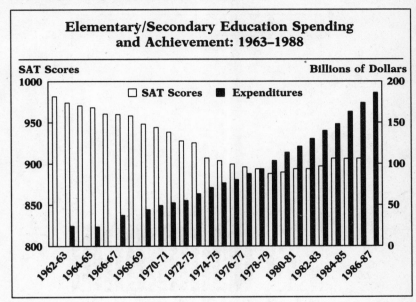

rather than constant dollars, adjusted for inflation. Because each year it takes more money to buy the same things, charts are supposed to adjust for that increase so the measure of dollars remains constant over the years illustrated in the chart. If the Department of Education had figured in inflation over the years on the chart, it would have shown that the amount of constant dollars spent on education had increased modestly from 1970 to 1986, as Figure 3 on page 50 shows.

Second, scores on the Scholastic Aptitude Test go from 400 to 1,600, yet the graph used by the Education Department (Figure 2) used a score range of only 800 to 1,000. By limiting the range of scores on its graph, the department showed what appeared to be a severe decline in scores. A properly prepared

Figure 3

*Elementary/secondary education
spending in constant dollars (billions).*

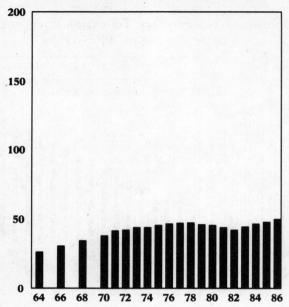

graph, shown in Figure 4 on page 51, shows a much more gradual decline.

The Department of Education's presentation is a good example of diagrammatic doublespeak. Without all the information you need in order to understand the chart, you can be easily misled, which of course was the purpose of the chart. You should always be skeptical whenever you see a graph or chart being used to present information, because these things are nothing more than the visual presentation of statistical information. And as for statistics, remember what Benjamin Disraeli is supposed to have said: "There are three kinds of lies—lies, damn lies, and statistics."

Figure 4

SAT scores, 1963–1986.

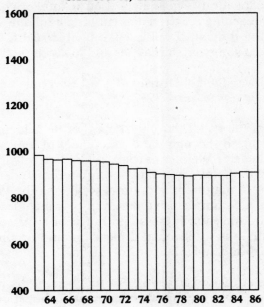

More Education Doublespeak

In 1977 the Houston *Chronicle* reported that the father of a high school student received the following note from the school principal, inviting him to a meeting:

> Our school's Cross-Graded, Multi-Ethnic, Individualized Learning Program is designed to enhance the concept of an Open-Ended Learning Program with emphasis on a continuum of multi-ethnic academically enriched learning, using the identified intellectually gifted child as the agent or director of his own learning. Major emphasis is on cross-graded, multi-ethnic learning with the main objective being to learn respect for the uniqueness of a person.

Two more paragraphs of similar language followed.

As noted in Chapter I, the doublespeak flows pretty thick in the world of education, where it is used to make what is pretty ordinary—teaching children and running a school—sound very complex and difficult. Doublespeak in this realm can also be used to avoid some harsh realities and to soothe some hurt feelings.

The Parkway School District of West St. Louis County, in its *Report to the Community 1987–88,*

> expresses the belief that the success of its students can be maximized through the development of a comprehensive Wellness Program targeted toward assisting the total community—employees, students and parents—in maintaining optimal wellness. The Wellness model is a comprehensive program that includes the physical dimension (fitness and nutrition), the social dimension, the intellectual dimension, and occupational, emotional and spiritual consideration.

I would be surprised if anyone in that school district had the faintest idea what all this verbiage meant, but it sure sounds impressive, doesn't it?

Sometimes it seems as if schools are competing with each other for the thickest doublespeak. The St. Vrain Valley School District in Longmont, Colorado published a booklet titled *Blueprint for Excellence,* in which it announced, "Our mission is to educate students so they may approach their full potential in: Pursuing post-secondary educational endeavors. Achieving economic self-sufficiency. Continuing their personal pursuit of learning throughout life. Relating successfully to people, institutions and value systems in all aspects of life."

Once they had impressed everyone with this education doublespeak, the writers of the booklet translated it for their readers. In clear language, they stated that what their schools tried to do was make sure that "Students were prepared to succeed in college, business or vocational school. Students are able to support themselves financially. Students are eager to learn wherever they go. Students are able to get along with people." Now, why didn't they just say that in the first place?

Simple, clear language just isn't impressive enough for many people in education. It seems they want to impress others with how hard their jobs are and how smart they have to be in order to do their jobs. After all, if anyone can understand it, then it can't be very special. So the doublespeak flows, especially when it comes time to write a grant proposal. After all, in order to get the government or a foundation to give you money, you've got to convince officials that what it is you're going to do with their money is worth doing and only you can do it.

As part of its proposal for a Title III grant from the federal government, a community college in Washington stated this as one of its major goals: "To organize a comprehensive process of assessment, teaching strategies, learning support, and intervention which effectively promotes student success in acquiring the skills and knowledge leading to satisfying and productive lives." Of course, they would never have gotten their grant if they had written something like, "We're going to teach these kids so they learn what they need to know to get along in life."

Education doublespeak, especially among academics who want to impress everyone with how intelligent they are, has been around for a long time. Even W. S. Gilbert (of Gilbert and Sullivan fame) commented on it, as you can see in these lyrics he wrote in 1881 for a song in the opera *Patience:*

If you're anxious for to shine in the high aesthetic line as
   a man of culture rare,
You must get up all the germs of the transcendental
   terms, and plant them everywhere.
You must lie upon the daisies and discourse in novel
   phrases of your complicated state of mind,
The meaning doesn't matter if it's only idle chatter of a
   transcendental kind.
And everyone will say,
As you walk your mystic way,

*"If this young man expresses himself in terms too deep
  for me,
Why, what a singularly deep young man this deep young
  man must be!"*

A glance at most academic journals would leave readers over-
whelmed by academic doublespeak and nodding their heads in
agreement with Gilbert's lines. But this is to be expected, says
Professor Scott Armstrong of the Wharton School of Business at
the University of Pennsylvania. According to Armstrong, there
are some important rules to follow if you want to publish an
article in a scientific or medical journal. In an article in a 1982
issue of the *Journal of Forecasting,* Armstrong recommends that
the aspiring scholar choose an unimportant topic, agree with
existing beliefs, use convoluted methods, withhold some of the
data, and write the article in stilted, obtuse prose. Armstrong
reports that, in one study, academics reading articles in scientific
journals rated the authors' competence higher when the writing
was less intelligible than when it was clear. Other studies conclude that obscure writing helps those who have little to say. In
other words, in academia, as in most professions, doublespeak
pays.

A recent issue of the *American Sociological Review* carried an
article that stated,

In effect, it was hypothesized that certain physical data
categories including housing types and densities, land
use characteristics, and ecological location, constitute a
scalable content area. This could be called a continuum
of residential desirabilities. Likewise, it was hypothesized
that several social strata categories, describing the
same census tracts, and referring generally to the
social stratification system of the city, would also
be scalable. This scale could be called a continuum of
socio-economic status. Thirdly, it was hypothesized that
there would be a high positive correlation between the
scale types of each continuum.

In cther words, rich people live in big houses in nice neighborhoods.

Not to be outdone by the sociologists, the prestigious journal *PMLA* (for *Publications of the Modern Language Association,* a major organization of scholars of English and foreign languages and literature) published an article in its October 1981 issue that contained this gem:

> We have now come to see, however, that the partitioning of art and history derives from a false dichotomy. Historical awareness is a construing of records already encoded, which can only be interpreted according to a historical poetics. And fictive ideologies are the stuff of history, which must be comprehended by linguistic and dramatistic analysis. All cultural phenomena are artifacts, at once real and fictive. This binocular perspective enables us to restore enacted courtesy, courtesy as lived, to the realm of poetic performance and to consider anew what such a way of living would have been like.

The entire article and most of the issue were written in similar prose, as is every issue of the journal.

A 1972 issue of the *Antioch Review* carried a review that contained such typical scholarly prose as this: ". . . Monod is constrained to use the word 'teleonomy,' which stands for living 'objects endowed with a purpose or project,' and which includes the genetic replication of such purpose. Yet in no way is this to be confused with 'teleology' *à la* Aristotle, or with final causation, and certainly not with 'animism,' which is the projection of organic teleonomy into the universe itself. This is the author's *bête noir,* and his stable extends from Plato through Leibnitz and Hegel, down to dialectical materialism. . . ." After reading these examples of scholarly prose, we can better understand "the germs of the transcendental terms" Gilbert was writing about over one hundred years ago. As we have seen, scholarly prose hasn't changed much since then.

In their article, "Needs Assessment and Holistic Planning," published in the May 1981 issue of *Educational Leadership*, authors Roger Kaufman and Robert Stakevas point out that "in order to achieve products, outputs, and outcomes through processes, inputs are required." An article titled "The Collection of Data About the Nature and Degree of Curriculum Implementation," published in the January 1985 issue of the *CCSEDC Quarterly*, states that "the significantly lower scores of implementers in their informational, personal, and management concerns suggest the wisdom of investigating means to raise these concerns, perhaps through increasing curriculum visibility."

Drop into any meeting of just about any academic society, organization, or group, and you'll find even the titles of the papers being presented incomprehensible. At the 1984 meeting of the Association for Education in Journalism and Mass Communications, there were papers on "Visual Complexity in Television News: A Times Series Analysis of Audience Evaluations of an Electronically Estimated Form Complexity Variable" and "Elaborating the Relationship Between TV Viewing and Beliefs About the Real World: Possible Contingent Variables." Or, if you had attended the 1988 meeting of the Academy of Management, you could have heard this paper presented: "Enter and Die: Effects of Incumbents' Waiting Periods on the Duration of Industry Entrants' Participation in 5 Subfields of the Medical Diagnostic Imaging Industry (1959–1986)."

At the annual meeting of the Mid–South Educational Research Association in 1985, a paper on reading comprehension among Navy recruits included this sentence: "The inferential analysis on high school graduation status indicates that higher percentages of high school graduates are included among the recruits during and immediately following the periods of enlistment restrictions to primary high school graduates."

At the 1988 conference of the American Sociological Association, one panelist said that "In the emphasis on diversity, the notion of a hegemonic sexual discourse is deconstructed, even among those who claim to have one." The speaker then went on to say that the "exploration of sexuality within feminism is attentive to the postmodern concern with the multiplying mutations of the self." Other phrases that popped up were "democratic hegemony," "distributionally conservative notions," "inequalities in the sex-gender system," and the "discourse of status ambivalence in clothing and fashion."

In 1987 Princeton University Press published *The State and Social Transformation in Tunisia and Libya, 1830–1980,* by Lisa Anderson, a book whose prose is illustrated by this sample sentence:

> It is also an argument for taking the variation in the periphery as a starting point for investigation and, more importantly, for examining the historical interaction of indigenous and foreign notions of political authority, structures of domination and mechanisms of appropriation as they combine to create the unprecedented circumstances and institutions of politics in the modern periphery.

It's probably not surprising to learn that teachers *like* that kind of writing. Although English teachers like to say they prefer the clear, simple style in writing, when given a choice they tend to choose the heavy, ponderous style. In the September 1981 issue of *College English,* a journal read by a great number of college writing teachers, Professors Rosemary Hake of Chicago State University and Joseph Williams of the University of Chicago reported on research in which they asked English teachers in high schools and colleges to judge groups of student essays. In each group of essays, Hake and Williams included several pairs of essays that differed only in their style.

The results were depressing. The teachers consistently preferred the essays that had sentences such as, "The absence of priorities and other pertinent data had the result of the preclusion of state office determinations as to the effectiveness of the committee's actions in targeting funds to the areas in greatest need of program assistance." The teachers consistently gave lower ratings to the essays that were written with sentences such as this: "Because the state office set no priorities and did not have pertinent data, it could not determine how effectively the committee targeted funds to those areas whose programs most needed assistance." Both of these sentences say the same thing, only the second says it more directly and more clearly. It has all the attributes teachers say good writing should have. Yet teachers overwhelmingly chose the first sentence over the second. Even those of us who should know better can be lured by the siren song of doublespeak.

At times it seems as if everyone involved in education lives on doublespeak, which starts at the top and flows downward. The Omnibus Education Act, passed by the Florida State Legislature in 1984, changed some terminology in the Florida statutes dealing with remedial education. In place of "remedial and developmental instruction" there is now "college preparatory instruction," while "remediation" has become "additional preparation" and "remedial courses" has become "college preparatory adult education" or "college preparatory instruction." At its October 1986 meeting, the State Board of Education in Ohio adopted a series of recommendations presented by its literacy committee, including these: "As early as a student is identified as an underachiever, an individualized intervention program with multiple teaching approaches should be developed" and, "An ongoing marketing approach should be implemented to provide the outreach necessary to find the unserved adult illiterate population."

The Troy, New York School Board passed the following resolution at one of its meetings in 1983: "Resolved, that the Superintendent be authorized to engage a consultant in public school administration for the purpose of assisting the Superintendent to plan a study to make specific recommendations in regard to the planning for management use and allocation of personnel and material resources particularly in the following areas. . . ." In 1984 the Amarillo, Texas Independent School District Board of Trustees hired two consultants to help in the search for a new school superintendent. The consultants wrote a public opinion survey that contained such sentences as these: "Each item in the instrument is productivity-oriented. Pupil Products expected are itemized first. Production Systems present in the district are itemized second." The National Testing Service Research Corporation of Durham, North Carolina prepared a report in 1980 on the results of a program designed to attack functional illiteracy among adults. The quality of this report can be illustrated by this sample of the prose used in the report: "The conceptual framework for this evaluation posits a set of determinants of implementation which explains variations in the level of implementation of the Comprehensive Project. . . ."

The doublespeak flows also into the classroom, with textbooks, lectures, and course materials filled with it. The following is the description of a graduate course in anthropology at the City University of New York:

As macro-processual interpretations come increasingly to seem, to historians, to falsify the complex multidirectionalities of local-level phenomena, and as community-based ethnographies come increasingly, in anthropology, to be situated within these same macro-processes, the framework for a synthesis between anthropology and history that has been building over the past twenty years, and that has achieved some substantial success, is starting to come apart, and is doing so in ways that can not be remedied by a return to earlier, more particularistic concerns.

Potsdam College of the State University of New York offers a course called "Clinical Techniques in the Human Services," which is described as focusing on "Theory and issues regarding clinical practice with major processes in human services including contingency management, supportive therapy, assertiveness training, systematic desensitization and cognitive restructuring." The description for the "Nursing II" course at Rutgers University, Camden, New Jersey states that the course "focuses on the care of clients throughout the life cycle who have basic alternations in health status. Stresses a multidimensional approach and encompasses . . . the amelioration of the health status of the client. The restoration of health a major focus."

At least the people in the St. Vrain Valley School District could translate their doublespeak. Most users of education doublespeak don't have the faintest idea what they're talking about when they use doublespeak. They sure sound impressive, though, enough so that you would never dare question what it is they're saying lest you appear ignorant and uninformed. Many of those who use doublespeak hope for this reaction. When one school board voted to deny funds for a new swimming pool, the high school principal simply submitted a proposal for an "Aquatic therapy department" for handicapped children and promptly got his new swimming pool.

Remember the old days when there were physical education classes? Well, physical education is out of date; it's now called "human kinetics" or "applied life studies." Sports are called "movement exercises." In 1988, officials of the University of Minnesota School of Physical Education wanted to rename their school the School of Human Movement and Leisure Studies. Michael Wade, the school's director, defended the proposed name change by explaining that other universities call their phys ed schools by such impressive names as "School of Kinesiology" or "School of Sport Exercise Science." (After all, Colorado State University changed the name of its phys ed department to the "Exercise and Sports Science Department" in 1986.) Wade noted that the old name put his faculty at a disadvantage when seeking grants, since the name of his school was not as impressive as the names used by those other schools. Wade also noted that there are two "journals of human movement" read and respected by professionals in the field. At last report the board of regents wasn't too keen on the idea, but Wade planned to continue his efforts.

Colleges no longer raid each other's faculties for big-name scholars. "Raiding isn't the right phrasing; it's selective development," said George Johnson, president of George Mason University. In Indiana they have a program called "quality recovery," while in Minnesota it's called "preventive retention." Colleges don't talk of looking for students to boost their enrollment. Instead, they talk about "posturing ourselves aggressively and positively to enhance our position in the enrollment marketplace" and "aggressively enhancing retention through positive recruitment and advisement programs."

Parents are told "there will be a modified English course offered for those children who achieve a deficiency in English." Children who talk to themselves "engage in audible verbal self-reinforcement," while children who disrupt class have an "attention deficit disorder." And children who have poor "graphomotor representation" just have lousy handwriting. Kids don't even cheat on tests anymore. According to a 1985 report by the Chicago Board of Education, an audit of scores on a reading test showed that "something irregular happened that can't be explained by chance."

Teachers are "educators" these days, or "classroom managers," or "learning facilitators" who possess effective "instructional delivery skills" which they demonstrate in "microteaching sessions." Teaching is called the "learning process" and learning is called "adjusted behavior." Students don't study, they spend "time on task" in their "learning environment." Students who skip school don't have to worry about the truant officer. If they live in New York they worry about the "attendance teacher." My eight-year-old stepdaughter has already become so imbued with education doublespeak that she insisted she did not take swimming lessons. It's "instructional swim," she informed me and her mother.

Teachers rarely test students these days. Instead they "implement an evaluation program," "conduct a needs assessment," (or, better yet, "implement a needs assessment strategy"), or prepare an "analysis of readiness skills" using an "evaluation tool (or instrument)." At Taft Junior High School in San Diego, California, students don't pass a grade, they "articulate." When students select the subjects they want to take in the next grade, it's called "articulation." Students ride to school on a "transportation component" which is operated by a "certified adolescent transportation specialist." When teachers go on a camping trip, it becomes an "outdoor education interdepartmental articulation conference." Even the coaches get in on the doublespeak when they call a stopwatch an "ascending timing device" or a "descending timing device."

The best schools are up on all the latest theories in education. First, you should remember that the very best schools aren't schools at all but "primary or secondary educational institutions" where "empirical-rational," "normative-re-educative," or "power-coercive" strategies of learning address the "situational parameters" through a variety of "implementation approaches," taking into account "multidisciplinary methodologies" in an "ecocultural framework," as educators develop "brain-based programs" of "content-specificity." Dedicated teachers, while worried about the burden of "excessive horizontal job enlargement," will still engage in a "healthy interface" in a "dual-communication mode of highly interactive student-oriented teacher methodology" designed to promote and enhance a child's "learning style" in "life-coping skills."

Teachers have learned to translate the doublespeak of educational researchers, administrators, and public officials. When the Illinois Board of Higher Education said "internal reallocation," "institutional self-help," "negative base adjustment," "productivity increases," and "personal services," teachers knew that the board meant budget cuts. Teachers knew also that "financial exigency" meant layoffs, and "institutional flexibility" meant administrators can do whatever they want without consulting the faculty as to the effect their decisions will have on the quality of the education offered to students. And "deferred maintenance" meant not doing needed painting, cleaning, and minor repairs, while "substantial deferred maintenance" meant not doing major repairs.

In Rochester, New York, a memorandum was sent to all teachers in independent school district no. 535 in 1983 offering "Staff Development Workshops" for those "who are considering, or would like to investigate a change of careers." The workshops were designed for those teachers who were being laid off and to encourage others to leave the teaching profession voluntarily. That's one way to develop the staff. The school board in the

Cleveland, Ohio school system did not lay off 141 administrators in 1982, it "nonrenewed" them.

Wherever teachers turn, they are confronted with doublespeak. A research report published by the Educational Testing Service in 1985 on how children learn to read said that "The children's preference for strategy was most clearly evident when they were near the limits of their capacity and needed to allocate their resources to optimal advantage." The Wharton Executive Education Program at the University of Pennsylvania Wharton School of Business does not make a profit but runs a "negative deficit." Educational researchers write of "knowledge-base possessors" and "knowledge-base non-possessors." When Texas passed a law in 1985 preventing students who have grades of "F" from participating in such extracurricular activities as football, Eddie Joseph, president of the Texas High School Coaches' Association, said of such students, "They're not failing; they're deficient at a grading period."

Doublespeak permeates all areas of society, so there is no reason why education shouldn't be infected as well. However, education doublespeak is particularly depressing because, more than anyone, teachers should be aware of doublespeak. They should be leading the fight against doublespeak by teaching their students how to spot it, how to defend themselves against it, and how to eliminate it in their own writing and speaking. Unfortunately, too many in education have found that using doublespeak can advance their careers and their pay, so they have decided to give in to it.

Doublespeak in Medicine

You may have a gall bladder operation, but to the surgeon it's a cholecystectomy. You come down with a cold, but the doctor calls it simple acute rhinitis, or coryza. You have a black eye or a shiner, but the doctor calls it hematoma of the eyelid. Medical doublespeak? No, not at all. Just because doctors talk in that technical language of theirs doesn't mean they're using doublespeak. The foregoing examples are simply precise medical terms, and there's nothing wrong with them, as long as doctors use them among themselves. But there is plenty of other language used in the medical profession that is pure doublespeak.

After developing a new machine that uses sonic waves to crush kidney stones, researchers at Massachusetts General Hospital called the machine the "extracorporeal shockwave lithotripter," which makes you want to ask if this tripter was necessary. Then there's the article in the *American Journal of Family Practice* that called fleas "hematophagous arthropod vectors." Try using that in the song, "My Dog Has Fleas." If you leap off a tall building you will, in the words of the medical profession, suffer "sudden deceleration trauma" when you hit the ground.

In today's medical doublespeak, aging is called "cell drop out," or the "decreased propensity for cell replication." There are hospitals that don't treat sick people anymore; instead, the patient is called "a compromised susceptible host." At Madison General Hospital in Madison, Wisconsin, members of the clergy who are on the staff belong to the "Human Ecology Department," while janitorial services are performed by the staff of "Environmental Services." At Memorial Hospital in South Bend, Indiana, the shop for wheelchair repairs is called the "Assistive Devices Resource Center." In another hospital, the sign posted over the microwave oven in the nurses' lounge lists the "rethermalization times" for different foods.

Patients aren't constipated anymore, they just suffer from "wheelchair fatigue," or an "alteration in self-care ability," or an "altered elimination status." Hospitals don't treat VD (for venereal disease) or even STD (for sexually transmitted disease), they treat "STI" (for sexually transmitted infection). No one is addicted to drugs these days; now it's just a "pharmacological preference." If you're not sure whether the problem is alcoholism or drug addiction, you can just use the term "chemical dependency" or "substance abuse." Researchers talk of the "pharmacological reward" that cocaine induces. But then maybe Timothy Leary doublespoke it better when he said he preferred to call the war on drugs "a war on neurotransmitters." With language like that he should go far in the medical profession.

Even psychiatry is getting in on the act. Now, the language of psychologists and psychiatrists has always been pretty bizarre, but, just when we catch on to one of their terms, they change it. Take, for example, "neurosis." Psychiatrists no longer use the word. Has it become a dirty word? "No," says Dr. Robert L. Spitzer. "It's just not a very salient concept anymore." Instead, psychiatrists speak of "vulnerability," so some of us are simply more "vulnerable" than others.

Medical doublespeak is often used to make something ordinary sound complicated. After all, it's easier to charge those big fees if what you're doing sounds really difficult. After giving President Reagan a routine physical examination, Dr. Daniel Ruge said that "previously documented decrement in auditory acuity and visual refractive error corrected with contact lenses were evaluated and found to be stable." That sounds a lot more technical than saying the president's hearing and eyesight haven't changed since his last examination and he doesn't need new contacts or a stronger hearing aid.

Operating on President Reagan after the president had been shot, Dr. Benjamin Aaron said he had located the bullet lodged in the president's lung by "very concentrated tactile discrimination." In other words, he let his fingers do the walking. When the president underwent a medical examination in 1988, he was given a pain-killing drug and a sedative. When asked if the president had been unconscious during the examination, one doctor said no, but such patients are generally in "non-decision-making form for two or three hours after the injection."

In 1982 it was reported that Supreme Court Justice William Rehnquist had, under a doctor's prescription, been taking a sleeping pill called Placidyl for severe back pains. When doctors cut the dosage he was taking, Rehnquist suffered severe withdrawal symptoms, including some perceptual distortions and hallucinations. Dr. Dennis O'Leary of the George Washington University Medical Center said, however, that Rehnquist had not been addicted to the drug. "Addiction is a buzz word, as you know. It carries a negative connotation." Rather, Dr. O'Leary said, the drug had "established an interrelationship with the body, such that if the drug is removed precipitously, there is a reaction."

In the doublespeak of the medical profession, hospitals that are in business to make money are called "proprietary" or "investor owned." Hospitals and doctors don't charge for their services, but ask for "reimbursement." Radiology and orthopedics are called "product lines," and those services that require physical contact with patients are called "high-touch products." Patients are called "consumers," patients who pay with private insurance are called "retail customers," and getting patients is called "patient accrual." Any medical treatment that requires cutting, puncturing, or jabbing is called a "procedure" (as in "invasive procedure" for surgery), while treatment requiring talking, thinking, or counseling is called a "cognitive service." Even general medicine is a specialty now.

The big word in the medical business these days is "wellness," as in "Patient failed to fulfill his wellness potential," a notation made by a doctor on the hospital chart of a patient who had died. *The University of California, Berkeley Wellness Letter* defines wellness as "optimum physical and mental health. A positive, on-going approach to a robust lifestyle. A preventative way of living that reduces—sometimes eliminates—the need for remedies."

Doublespeak can and is used to avoid those harsh realities the medical profession prefers not to acknowledge. At Creedmore Psychiatric Center in New York, a mental patient in a straitjacket died of "inappropriate physical abuse," said Irene Platt, acting chair of the New York State Commission on Quality of Care for the Mentally Disabled. Don't you wonder what might constitute appropriate physical abuse?

Medical doublespeak can have political and moral implications, as well as life-and-death consequences. In his 1987 book, *And the Band Played On: Politics, People, and the AIDS Epidemic,* Randy Shilts discusses AIDSpeak, "a new language forged by public health officials, anxious gay politicians, and the burgeoning ranks of 'AIDS activists.'" Shilts points out that AIDSpeak was designed to be "politically facile and psychologically reassuring." AIDSpeak goes to great lengths never to offend the moral or political sensibilities of the public, politicians, and members of the gay community. AIDSpeak never refers to AIDS sufferers as victims. They're called "People With AIDS," or "PWAs." That unpleasant word, "promiscuous," becomes in AIDSpeak "sexually active," because gay politicians decided that the word "promiscuous" was "judgmental" and AIDSpeak could never be judgmental. The most used phrase in AIDSpeak is "bodily fluids," an expression that avoids troublesome words like "semen."

But the most pernicious word in AIDSpeak, according to Shilts, is the term "exposed." Persons who had the HTLV-III antibodies were told they had been "exposed" to the virus, and the term soon became beloved by health workers around the country because it avoided so many problems. Yet this word is doublespeak of the most serious kind, because people who have the antibodies to a virus have been infected by it. They haven't simply been exposed. As Dr. Bruce Voeller, a San Diego research microbiologist, said, "When people say 'expose,' I get the feeling that they think the virus floats around the room, like the scent of gardenias, and somehow they get exposed. That's not how it works. If you've got an antibody, that virus has been in your blood." AIDSpeak is the doublespeak of life and death.

In the doublespeak of medicine, doctors addicted to drugs are "impaired physicians." At least that's what the American Medical Association says. The doctor who charged Blue Shield for services that were either medically unnecessary or were never performed had "inappropriately received" $750,000. Others might call it theft. Patients don't experience pain anymore, just "discomfort." But then, as noted earlier, people don't die in hospitals anymore, there's just "negative patient care outcome," a "terminal episode," or "terminal living." In the emergency room, "systems fail." And when the surgeon at a Philadelphia hospital perforated the patient's colon during an examination resulting in complications which caused the patient's death the hospital attributed death to a "diagnostic misadventure of a high magnitude." Such is the doublespeak of death in the medical world.

CHAPTER III

Virgin Vinyl, Real Counterfeit Diamonds,
and Genuine Imitation Leather:
With These Words I Can Sell You Anything

You settle back in your comfortable chair to watch some of the big events in the 1988 Summer Olympics. After the usual vacuous comments by some faceless commentator, there's a commercial. Actually, there are about eight commercials during the two-minute break, because each commercial is fifteen seconds long. Eight different products dance across the television screen, and then you're whisked back to Seoul. After watching a few minutes of women's basketball you're hit with another commercial break, and once again you're besieged by another six to eight different products. This pattern repeats itself again and again. You grab the remote control and change the channel, only to find another commercial. You try again, another commercial. Again. More commercials. You're getting desperate now. You start hitting the channel buttons with a sense of panic. You need a program to watch, any program, and all you can find are commercials. All of a sudden you find a channel with a program, not commercials. You breathe a little easier, the panic begins to recede, you relax and settle back. So what if it's the shop-at-home channel? At least this is a channel without commercials.

Perhaps this description is a little exaggerated, but not by much. If you watched the 1988 Olympics, you did see a lot of commercials. You saw an average of 10.2 minutes of commercials every hour, as a matter of fact, and that doesn't include the "promotions" NBC ran for its own programs. (The three networks normally average 7 minutes of commercials during prime time.) NBC paid $243 million for the rights to broadcast the Olympic games, and the only way it could get its money back was to run a lot of commercials (or thirty-five hundred "commercial units" as NBC called them) at $330,000 per thirty-second spot. NBC won the rights to broadcast the 1992 Summer Olympics in Barcelona with a bid of $401 million. Add to that about $100 million for production costs, and you can plan on watching a lot of commercials during the next Olympics, too.

The Superbowl of Advertising

Any football fan knows that watching a game on television means paying the price of watching lots of commercials. Games are regularly halted in order to run more commercials. While the fans in the stands freeze and the teams stand around on the field, the fans at home get to watch four to eight commercials.

The biggest football game (as far as advertisers are concerned) is the Superbowl, which probably got its name not from the quality of the game but from the advertising revenues it generates. If you wanted to advertise your product during the 1987 Superbowl, all you had to pay was $1.2 million for one sixty-second time slot. That's $20,000 per second, and you provided the commercial. CBS sold twenty-six minutes of advertising time for the game, for a total of $31.2 million. Then, of course, there were all the ads for the pre- and postgame shows, which added another $11.8 million to the take, for a grand total of $43 million. That's not bad for one afternoon, especially since CBS paid only $19 million for the rights to the game.

If nothing else, the Superbowl proves each year that advertising rates and revenues for blockbuster television programs just keep increasing. In 1983 the special two-and-one-half-hour final episode of the popular television series "M*A*S*H" commanded

$900,000 per minute of advertising, for a total of $15.75 million for this one program. Until the 1987 Superbowl, this program held the record for the most profitable program in television history.

Sometimes it seems as if the whole world is not just filled with advertising but dominated by it. You can't get away from ads. In the United States, every twenty-four hours you are exposed, on the average, to sixteen hundred commercial messages by one medium or another. Of these sixteen hundred ads, you notice eighty, but only twelve will get some kind of response from you. And it's not just radio, television, newspapers, and magazines that are filled with ads, but just about every part of your life. Ads are, of course, on all the products you buy. But then there are all the billboards, plus the signs on buildings, trucks, cabs, buses, subways, and anything else that moves or doesn't move. And don't forget all those coupons, flyers, and handbills, not to mention all the advertising junk mail. There are even ads on the inside of the doors in some public toilets now. Even public television has ads, although they're not called ads; they're called "enhanced underwriting" or "general support announcements."

But you are already painfully aware that advertising is all over the place. You also know that advertising is filled with doublespeak. You might even think that advertising is nothing but pure doublespeak. So why, you might ask, waste any time talking about the doublespeak of advertising? Analyzing advertising for doublespeak is like shooting fish in a barrel, or maybe even like analyzing political language for doublespeak. It's just too obvious, too easy to find.

However, it is exactly because advertising is so pervasive and so significant a part of our society that it is important to examine the doublespeak of advertising. After all, corporations don't spend billions of dollars on advertising if it doesn't work, if it doesn't get you to buy what they want you to buy, whether it's a product or an idea or a set of values. So, before examining the doublespeak of advertising, you might want to look briefly at the size, power, and influence of advertising and advertisers, so you can appreciate how important it is to understand as much as possible the doublespeak of advertising.

The Top Advertisers

Corporations spend a lot of money advertising their products. According to *Advertising Age*, the most important publication in the advertising industry, the top ten advertisers for 1987 spent over $8.3 billion, while the top 100 advertisers spent a total of $28.4 billion on all forms of advertising. The total amount spent on advertising by all advertisers during 1987 was over $120 billion. That's a lot of money, and a lot of advertising.

The big news for 1987 was that Philip Morris moved into first place as the number-one advertiser, replacing Procter & Gamble, which had been the leading advertiser for the preceding twenty-four years. For 1987, Philip Morris spent $1.557 billion (yes, that's *billion*) on all advertising, while Procter & Gamble spent a mere $1.38 billion. In third place was General Motors, spending $1.024 billion to gain a place as one of the three corporations to spend over $1 billion on advertising in a year. Sears, Roebuck and Company was in fourth place, spending $886.5 million, while RJR Nabisco was in fifth place with $839.6 million. PepsiCo took sixth place by spending only $704 million, while Eastman Kodak spent $658 million to gain seventh place. Ford Motor Company spent $639 million for ninth place, while Anheuser-Busch gained tenth place by spending $635 million. It is interesting to note that the U.S. government took twenty-ninth place on the top one hundred list by spending $311.3 million on advertising.

The top one hundred advertisers spent $6.67 billion of their $8.3 billion in advertising on network television, an amount that constituted over 75 percent of all advertising income for the three networks. Without this advertising income, the networks could not survive. If the networks are this dependent on so few advertisers, you have to wonder how independent the networks really are.

The Cost of Television Ads

Of all the media used by advertisers, television remains the most important, the most dominant, the most influential, and the most expensive. To reach the millions of people who watch television, advertisers are willing to pay big money. The numbers are pretty impressive. According to *Advertising Age,* the cost of running a thirty-second ad on each of the prime-time television programs for the 1987–1988 season averaged $121,860 (up from the previous year's $118,119) for the three networks combined. For the month of October 1987 (October usually sets the rates for the rest of the television season), CBS was in last place among the three networks, with an average of $103,130 per thirty-second ad. ABC was second with an average of $111,800, while NBC continued in first place with an average of $150,625.

The three networks made approximately $418 million from prime-time ads during October 1987, with total income from advertising during daytime programs coming to $946 million. (These figures do not include income from the World Series.) Thus, the three networks made $5 billion for the 1987–1988 broadcast year, just from prime-time advertising. With daytime revenues added in, the three networks made over $10 billion from advertising.

During the 1987–1988 television season, it cost $369,500 for just one thirty-second segment in which to run your ad on the "Cosby Show," and you had to provide the ad. The cost of a thirty-second ad on "Cheers" was $307,000, while a similar ad on "Magnum, P.I." was $140,790. Meanwhile, prices for such ads on "Dallas" and "Dynasty" were $139,470 and $113,540, while "Monday Night Football" charged $150,000. In case you're wondering, it cost $249,190 for a thirty-second spot on "Moonlighting," while an ad on "Miami Vice" went for $171,500.

For the first half of 1988, things just got better for the networks. Despite the writer's strike, television advertising revenue increased. *USA Today* reported that, for the first half of 1988, network television advertising totaled $4.7 billion, an increase of over 9 percent from the same period in 1987. Procter & Gamble was the leading television advertiser during this period, spending some $173 million, while General Motors was a close second with $171 million. They were followed by Philip Morris with $155 million, Kellogg with $140 million, and Chrysler rounding out the top five with $110 million. There are two sure things about television advertising: It keeps getting more expensive each year, and the television networks make lots of money from all those advertisements.

Why are corporations willing to pay such high prices to run their ads on television? It's really quite simple: That's where the people are. An ad on television reaches a lot of people, because a lot of people watch a lot of television. Advertisers were willing to pay $600,000 to run their thirty-second ad during the 1987 Superbowl because (if you believe A. C. Nielsen, and the networks and advertisers seem to) 122.6 million people watched the game.

Kids and Television

In 1988, the Center for Science in the Public Interest reported on a study it had conducted which revealed that children ages eight through twelve could identify more brands of beer than they could presidents of the United States. One girl could name fourteen brands of beer but only four presidents. The results of this study shouldn't be all that surprising.

The A. C. Nielsen Company claims that the television set is turned on an average of 7 hours and 38 minutes a day in American households. The Gallup Poll claims about the same. A study conducted by the American Academy of Pediatrics in 1987 claims that children between the ages of two and twelve spend an average of 25 hours per week watching television. (An A. C. Nielsen study in 1986 claimed that children between the ages of two and five spent 28 hours a week watching television.) By the time six-year-olds enter first grade, they will have seen over 100,000 ads on television; by the time they graduate from high school, they will have spent 11,000 hours in classrooms and 15,000 hours watching television, during which time they will have seen as many as 350,000 advertisements on television.

Nor does all this television watching and commercial viewing end when we become adults. According to author and television critic Dr. Jean Kilbourne, by the time we die we will have spent one and one-half years of our lives watching just television commercials.

Children eat, drink, and breathe television, which in many homes is on from the moment the newborn baby arrives from the hospital. Much of what children know about the world comes from television. "I call television the new religion," says George Gerbner, Dean of the Annenberg School of Communications at the University of Pennsylvania. "It's used more religiously than any religion has ever been," he claims. "By the time a child can speak, let alone read, a child will have absorbed a great deal of information about the world that will form a child's interests and will, in effect, represent the basic storytelling role in the child's life. It's the first time in human history that most of the stories told to most of the children are told, not by the parents, not by the church, and not by the school, but by a group of distant corporations. . . . Whoever can tell the stories has a large measure of control over future behavior."

What kind of a world do children see on television? In 1987 they saw a world in which men outnumbered women three to one, and on cartoons it was eight to one. White males in the prime of life comprised 45 percent of all prime-time characters. While prime-time shows averaged six to eight acts of violence per hour, children's shows averaged twenty to twenty-five acts of violence per hour.

Gerbner says that it doesn't matter whether people believe what they see on television. What is important is that they absorb what they see and hear on television. Television becomes the norm against which everything else in society is measured.

Teenagers and Television Advertising

Some people argue, however, that the influence of television advertising on children is exaggerated. They point, for example, to a 1987 study that claims that teenagers are dissatisfied with the content of television commercials. In a nationwide survey of teenagers between the ages of twelve and nineteen, 75 percent responded that television ads do not give them the information they want about a product; 65 percent said television commercials talk down to them. Sixty-six percent said they changed channels to avoid commercials, while 89 percent said they skipped commercials on a videotaped program. All of this sounds good until we discover that the study also reveals that 64 percent of the teenagers said they get information about new products from television, while 36 percent said they often buy products after seeing the commercials for them. Both advertisers and those who write the ads would find these figures very comforting and very reassuring, because, as this study also points out, teenagers are a significant force in the market. They spend $34.4 billion of their own money and $43.6 billion of their parents' money purchasing various products during the year, and 36 percent of that market comes to over $28 billion a year.

Television Advertising in Mexico

There is nothing unique to the power of television and television advertising in the United States. Studies conducted in other countries have revealed that television advertising works pretty much the same in any country that allows it. In 1981, the Mexican National Consumer Institute tested 1,800 primary school children in Mexico City on their comparative knowledge of "television reality" and "national reality." The results of the study read very much like similar studies conducted in the United States.

The children spent an average of 1,460 hours each year in front of the television, compared to 920 hours in school. They could answer 73 percent of the questions about television correctly, but they got only 38 percent of questions about their country correct. For example, while 92 percent knew that a duckling used to advertise chocolate cakes said "Remember me," only 64 percent could identify Father Miguel Hildago as author of the phrase "Viva la Independencia!" While 96 percent of the children could recognize television cartoon characters, only 19 percent could recognize the last Aztec emperors.

And so it went, with an amazing 98 percent of the kids recognizing Superman, while only 33 percent knew who Emiliano Zapata was. Although 74 percent could recognize Lopez Portillo, who was then president of Mexico, 96 percent recognized a local television character. The trademark of Adams Chiclets gum was recognized by more kids (77 percent) than the Monument to the Revolution (17 percent). In probably the most telling statistic, more children knew the times of television programs than the dates of religious festivals, including Christmas.

A Chinese View of Advertising

Sometimes outsiders provide the best insights to a society. The device of having strangers comment on the foibles of the world they have encountered is an old one in literature. We sometimes need the observations of an outsider to help us look anew at things that have become so commonplace that we no longer notice them. Although we may complain about advertising, we cannot really imagine a world without it, nor do we think that advertising has all that much of an effect on us as individuals. But we also fail to understand completely advertising and what its effects on us and our society might be. Perhaps the comments of an outsider might make us look differently at these issues.

In 1981 *The New York Times* reported the remarks of Hu Yun Huan, an English-language specialist from China who had spent a year teaching in a private high school in Boston. When asked about American television, he said,

The advertisements are pretty fantastic. Sometimes, I admire these advertisement makers. How can they imagine to make propaganda this way?

In China, the process of changing ideas reminds me very much of the television advertisements. The businessman doesn't force you to buy anything. But he gives you propaganda for his product. By and by, you believe you need this kind of thing.

Now, people talk about mind control in China. Actually, you are being educated to make you believe

what is good and what is evil. You are not controlled
any more than the businessman controls the consumer.

Some might take offense at these remarks and reply that in no
way does the American system of advertising begin to compare
with the Chinese system of government propaganda. But a close
look at these remarks and at advertising might make us recon-
sider the role of advertising in our society, its effects on us, and,
since it doesn't seem likely that we will ever ban advertising,
what we can do to protect ourselves from its propagandistic
effects.

The Influence of Advertising

Since we have been raised and live in an environment filled with
advertising, it is difficult for us to take an objective view of it.
Studies such as those cited earlier offer a lot of information
about the sheer size and influence of advertising in our lives, but
each of us usually protests that, while others may be and probably are affected by advertising, we know that advertising doesn't
really affect us. This is exactly what advertisers want us to think.
In 1985 the New York advertising agency of Rosenfeld, Siro-
witz & Lawson commissioned a study to find out who admits to
being influenced by advertising. According to this study, only 14
percent of the people questioned felt they were more affected by
advertising than other people. Half of the people in the study said
they were affected less than others, while 36 percent felt they
were influenced about the same as others. In other words, most
people feel that advertising affects everyone else as much as or
more than it affects them.
What is interesting about this study is that people felt that
women, younger people, and people in lower-income groups
were influenced by advertising more than the average person.
However, while women, young people, and low-income people
agreed that people like themselves were more influenced by advertising than other groups, individually they felt it didn't apply
to them. For example, 80 percent of the women agreed that

women in general were more affected by advertising, but only 13 percent of the women felt that they individually were influenced by advertising. The results were similar for young people and people in households with incomes under $20,000 per year.

So, if you believe that advertising doesn't affect you, then you believe what almost everyone else believes. It almost makes you wonder who's buying all those products that are so heavily advertised, and why corporations would waste so much money advertising if it didn't make people buy their products. Now, before you continue reading, look around you. Check what kind of toothpaste you use, what kind of shampoo, deodorant, laundry detergent, breakfast cereal, and dish-washing soap. What brands are in your house? Why did you buy them? Can you recall the ads used to promote any of them? The next time you go shopping, can you deliberately not buy any of these brands, but buy other brands instead? Does advertising affect you?

A very interesting situation regarding the effectiveness of advertising arose in 1988. Kraft, Inc. ran an advertising campaign saying that Kraft Singles cheese slices are made with five ounces of milk and are a good source of calcium. The Federal Trade Commission (FTC) charged that these ads wrongfully implied that one slice of Kraft Singles supplies as much calcium as five ounces of milk. Now comes the interesting part. In defending its advertising, Kraft said that the claim was true and that, even if it wasn't, it wasn't important to shoppers. Therefore, the advertising claim to which the FTC objected really didn't help sell cheese, so no consumer was misled and there was no case. Of course, you might want to ask why Kraft spent all those millions of dollars on advertising that doesn't work. Others in the advertising business were very upset with the argument against advertising made by Kraft.

Advertising and Reality

Rosser Reeves, a legendary ad man who worked for the Ted Bates advertising agency, once said that the basic problem advertisers had to solve was that most products were really the same:

"Our problem is—a client comes into my office and throws two newly minted half dollars onto my desk and says, 'Mine is the one on the left. You prove it's better.'" And that's the job of advertising: to make something out of nothing.

When Hicks B. Waldron was appointed president of Avon Products in 1983, his previous experience had been with the Heublein Corporation, directing the sales of Smirnoff vodka and Kentucky Fried Chicken. Mr. Waldron said he saw little difficulty in moving from a job directing the sales of vodka and fried chicken to a job directing the sales of beauty-care products. As Mr. Waldron noted, it's not the product that's being sold, it's fashion and style. He cited the vodka business as an example, where a colorless, odorless, tasteless liquid is sold at a higher price that depends on its fashionability as projected through advertising. "Advertising and positioning of the product are almost everything," Mr. Waldron was quoted as saying in an article in *The New York Times*. (All you vodka drinkers who insist on a special brand of vodka should read this paragraph three times.)

When many women stopped drinking rum and starting drinking white wine because they were concerned about the number of calories in rum, the makers of Bacardi rum mounted an advertising campaign comparing Bacardi mixed drinks with wine. The ads pointed out that a drink of Bacardi and Diet Coke had the same number of calories as an equal amount of white wine. As a result of this ad campaign, surveys of consumers revealed that they perceived rum in general as a more benign form of alcohol. "Not that we are more benign," said Paul Nelson, marketing director for Bacardi Imports, "but that is the way we are perceived." Any guesses how that perception was created?

In 1980 the Procter & Gamble and Colgate-Palmolive companies spent over $75 million to tout "new" toothpastes that didn't make teeth any whiter than the toothpastes the companies currently sold. Nor did the new toothpastes prevent cavities any better, nor did they even have new names. But the new toothpastes did taste different and have new colors. Most competing brands of everyday personal-care, household-cleaning, and food items are pretty much alike, according to *The Wall Street Journal* article that reported on this battle of the advertising giants. Therefore, manufacturers depend on minor changes in product appearances, packaging, scents, flavors, or other nonessential aspects of the product to sell it. So Procter & Gamble and Colgate-Palmolive spent millions of dollars to advertise the different taste and color of their toothpastes and to lure consumers with free samples, price discounts, coupons, and other promotions.

Procter & Gamble spent $28.6 million during 1980 to advertise Crest on television alone, while Colgate-Palmolive spent $17.9 million to advertise Colgate on television and $16 million to advertise Aim. All this money was spent to promote products which were essentially the same. It didn't make much difference which toothpaste you bought because both cleaned your teeth the same. So if you bought one of these toothpastes because of the ads promoting it, the advertiser won.

De Beers, the company that runs the world's diamond cartel and controls 80 percent of the world supply of gem diamonds, learned long ago that making something out of nothing through advertising can create huge profits. Each year the world's diamond mines produce over fifty times the number of gem diamonds (as opposed to industrial diamonds) needed for jewelry. In addition, it is conservatively estimated that the world's public holds more than five hundred million carats of gem diamonds. In short, there is and always was a glut of diamonds in the world. Why, then, do diamonds cost so much?

Early on, the men who ran De Beers realized that diamonds had little intrinsic value and their price depended almost entirely on their scarcity. After gaining control over production of all the important diamond mines in the world, they launched a campaign to stimulate the public's desire to buy diamonds. In 1938, De Beers hired the N. W. Ayer advertising agency to increase diamond sales in the United States. Ayer devised a campaign around the idea that diamonds were a gift of love, and the larger and finer the diamond the greater the expression of love. In 1948 Frances Gerety of Ayer came up with the caption "A Diamond Is Forever" on a picture of young lovers on a honeymoon—even though diamonds can be chipped, shattered, discolored, or incinerated. Sales of diamonds in the United States went from $23 million in 1939 to more than $2.1 *billion* (wholesale prices) in 1979, while during that same time advertising expenditures on diamonds went from $200,000 to $10 million. This campaign is considered one of the most successful in the history of advertising.

In 1976 the J. Walter Thompson advertising company began a campaign in Japan to popularize diamond engagement rings. It seems that in 1968 fewer than 5 percent of Japanese women getting married received a diamond engagement ring. De Beers was determined to change this situation and increase diamond sales in Japan. By 1981 some 60 percent of Japanese brides had diamond rings and Japan was the second largest market for diamond engagement rings.

When small diamonds from Russian mines threatened to flood the market, De Beers changed its advertising campaign. Women were told they should no longer equate the status and emotional commitment of an engagement with the size of the diamond. Instead, women were told that it was the quality, color, and cut of the diamond that were important, not the size. De Beers even invented the "eternity ring," which consisted of numerous small Russian diamonds and was advertised as the symbol of renewed love for married couples. Again the campaign was successful, and a new market was created. Russia joined the De Beers cartel, and profits for everyone continue to be quite handsome, averaging about 40 percent of sales. Not a bad profit margin for selling a commodity for which there is a glut in the world. Remember this when you think about buying a diamond ring.

Advertising often creates such attitudes and beliefs about products, but ads themselves can be just a little misleading. In 1986 the John Hancock Mutual Life Insurance Company ran a series of television ads featuring "real people in real situations." In each of the ads, a person revealed his or her complete financial status, discussing such information as income, savings, and mortgage payments and other expenses. The ads were presented as "slice-of-life" episodes with real people talking about their financial situation and how John Hancock could help them. One of the "real people" was Linda Fuller, who was divorced, worked as a librarian, and earned $20,000 a year plus $6,000 in child support. She talked about how worried she was that she wouldn't be able to afford college for her little boy. When asked how the company got all those people to reveal so much about their financial situation, Ralph Brunner, a spokesperson for the company, said that the people were actors and "in that sense, they are not real people." It makes you wonder what a real person is, according to the John Hancock Company.

Continental Airlines ran a radio ad in 1987 that featured a telephone conversation between a mother and her daughter in another city. The mother, upon discovering her daughter has a bad cold, says that, because of Continental's low MaxSaver fares, she will fly there right away to take care of her and the kids. As a voice in the background of the ad notes, however, Continental's MaxSaver fares require at least a seven-day advance purchase of tickets, which, once purchased, are nonrefundable. If the daughter is still sick a week later, the mom will be right there, but the ad doesn't note that little detail. Said Continental spokesperson Rick Scott, "I think that TV and radio commercials are not literal. I think we all know that. There's some creative license taken." Others might call "creative license" doublespeak for lying.

In 1989 the FTC accused Campbell's Soup Company of "overstating" the health benefits of its chicken noodle soup in ads which the FTC called "misleading." It seems Campbell's had run ads which said that the low-fat and low-cholesterol content of its chicken noodle soup was beneficial in reducing the risk of heart disease. However, the ads failed to note that the soup was also high in sodium. In fact, the soup contained almost one-third of the maximum recommended daily limit of sodium. The FTC charged that the ads "failed to disclose that Campbell's soups are high in sodium and that diets high in sodium may increase the risk of heart disease. . . . The failure to disclose these facts is deceptive." Campbell's, not too surprisingly, didn't agree with the FTC. "We don't believe the ad is misleading," said David

Hackney, manager of public relations for Campbell's. Maybe it was just a little "creative license" in the ads.

Puffing the Product and Truth in Advertising

It may come as a surprise to you, but advertisements do not have to be literally true. "Puffing" the product is perfectly legal. What is "puffing"? "Puffing" is an exaggeration about the product that is so obvious just about anyone is capable of recognizing the claim as an exaggeration. The most common examples of "puffing" involve the use of such words as "exciting," "glamorous," "lavish," and "perfect." However, when an advertising claim can be scientifically tested or analyzed, it is no longer "puffing."

Remember "puffing" and the De Beers, Continental Airlines, John Hancock, and other ads each time you see an ad on television, or hear one on the radio, or read one in a newspaper or magazine. Even with this inside information on advertising, though, you're still not equipped to deal with ads. You may think you are, but you're not. You need to know a little about the doublespeak of advertising, about how advertising uses words which you think you understand to say things without saying them, to make promises without promising anything, to make statements about products without saying anything, to pretend to communicate while saying nothing. The first rule of advertising is that nothing is what it seems, which brings us to the Rule of Parity.

The Rule of Parity

Products such as gasoline, cigarettes, toothpaste, soap, aspirin, cold remedies, cosmetics, deodorants, cereals, liquor, and others are called parity products. Parity products are simply products in which most if not all the brands in a class or category are pretty much the same. Most toothpastes, for example, are made the same way with pretty much the same formula. There is no essential difference among the dozens of toothpastes on the market today. Thus, all toothpastes are equal, which is what parity means. Now comes the interesting part. Follow this closely.

Since all toothpastes are equal, no one brand is superior to any of the others. Therefore, not only are all parity products "good" products, they are all the "best" products. Thus, you can advertise your toothpaste, gasoline, deodorant, or other parity product as the "best" and not have to prove your claim. However, if you claim your parity product is "better" than another parity product, you have to prove your claim because "better" is comparative and a claim of superiority, and only one product can be "better" than the others in a parity class. Did you get that? In the world of advertising doublespeak, "better" means "best," but "best" means only "equal to." So the next time you see a parity product advertised as the best, the ad simply means that the product is as good as any other in its class. It does not mean the product is better than any other product in its class.

If you're not confused by now over parity claims, there's even more. Follow this Humpty Dumpty logic: All parity products in one class (such as orange juice) are equal because they are essentially the same. But by definition they are also different from products in another parity class. Thus, you can make comparisons between products of different parity classes. So, you can claim your orange juice is better than a vitamin pill, because orange juice and vitamin pills belong to different parity classes.

The source of this redefinition of the words "better" and "best" as used in advertising, and the whole notion of parity products, does not lie entirely with the advertising industry. Advertisers were aided and abetted by the courts, which have through a series of decisions enshrined in law all this confusion of language.

Now that you know all about parity claims, you will no longer be taken in by ads that say, "Minute Maid. The best there is" or "Nestles' cocoa is the very best," or "Tests confirm one mouthwash best against mouth odor." Nor will you really believe the ads for the gasoline that claims to be "The best for your car," the razor that gives you the "best shave going," or the toothpaste that is "best for your teeth." All of these claims simply mean that each of these brands is as good as any other brand. As Humpty Dumpty said to Alice, "When I use a word, it means just what I choose it to mean—neither more nor less."

Advertisers can get just so much mileage out of parity claims, however. If such claims were all they used in their ads, the ads would soon be boring, and that is the one thing advertisers want to avoid at all costs. So, advertisers need other ways to make similar products seem unlike each other—even unique and special—or able to offer special benefits. When parity claims can't do the job, advertisers can always turn to those old standbys of advertising doublespeak, weasel words.

Weasel Words

One problem advertisers have when they try to convince you that the product they are pushing is really different from other, similar products is that their claims are subject to some laws. Not a lot of laws, but there are some designed to prevent fraudulent or untruthful claims in advertising. Even during the happy years of nonregulation under President Ronald Reagan, the FTC did crack down on the more blatant abuses in advertising claims. Generally speaking, advertisers have to be careful in what they say in their ads, in the claims they make for the products they advertise. Parity claims are safe because they are legal and supported by a number of court decisions. But beyond parity claims there are weasel words.

Advertisers use weasel words to appear to be making a claim for a product when in fact they are making no claim at all. Weasel words get their name from the way weasels eat the eggs they find in the nests of other animals. A weasel will make a small hole in the egg, suck out the insides, then place the egg back in the nest. Only when the egg is examined closely is it found to be hollow. That's the way it is with weasel words in advertising: Examine weasel words closely and you'll find that they're as hollow as any egg sucked by a weasel. Weasel words appear to say one thing when in fact they say the opposite, or nothing at all.

"Help"—The Number One Weasel Word

The biggest weasel word used in advertising doublespeak is "help." Now "help" only means to aid or assist, nothing more. It does not mean to conquer, stop, eliminate, end, solve, heal, cure, or anything else. But once the ad says "help," it can say just about anything after that because "help" qualifies everything coming after it. The trick is that the claim that comes after the weasel word is usually so strong and so dramatic that you forget the word "help" and concentrate only on the dramatic claim. You read into the ad a message that the ad does not contain. More importantly, the advertiser is not responsible for the claim that you read into the ad, even though the advertiser wrote the ad so you would read that claim into it.

The next time you see an ad for a cold medicine that promises that it "helps relieve cold symptoms fast," don't rush out to buy it. Ask yourself what this claim is really saying. Remember, "helps" means only that the medicine will aid or assist. What will it aid or assist in doing? Why, "relieve" your cold "symptoms." "Relieve" only means to ease, alleviate, or mitigate, not to stop, end, or cure. Nor does the claim say how much relieving this medicine will do. Nowhere does this ad claim it will cure anything. In fact, the ad doesn't even claim it will *do* anything at all. The ad only claims that it will aid in relieving (not curing) your cold symptoms, which are probably a runny nose, watery eyes, and a headache. In other words, this medicine probably contains a standard decongestant and some aspirin. By the way, what does "fast" mean? Ten minutes, one hour, one day? What is fast to one person can be very slow to another. Fast is another weasel word.

Ad claims using "help" are among the most popular ads. One says, "Helps keep you young looking," but then a lot of things will help keep you young looking, including exercise, rest, good nutrition, and a facelift. More importantly, this ad doesn't say the product will keep you young, only "young *looking*." Someone may look young to one person and old to another.

A toothpaste ad says, "Helps prevent cavities," but it doesn't say it will actually prevent cavities. Brushing your teeth regularly, avoiding sugars in food, and flossing daily will also help prevent cavities. A liquid cleaner ad says, "Helps keep your home germ free," but it doesn't say it actually kills germs, nor does it even specify which germs it might kill.

"Help" is such a useful weasel word that it is often combined with other action-verb weasel words such as "fight" and "control." Consider the claim, "Helps control dandruff symptoms with regular use." What does it really say? It will assist in controlling (not eliminating, stopping, ending, or curing) the *symptoms* of dandruff, not the cause of dandruff nor the dandruff itself. What are the symptoms of dandruff? The ad deliberately leaves that undefined, but assume that the symptoms referred to in the ad are the flaking and itching commonly associated with dandruff. But just shampooing with *any* shampoo will temporarily eliminate these symptoms, so this shampoo isn't any different from any other. Finally, in order to benefit from this product, you must use it regularly. What is "regular use"—daily, weekly, hourly? Using another shampoo "regularly" will have the same effect. Nowhere does this advertising claim say this particular shampoo stops, eliminates, or cures dandruff. In fact, this claim says nothing at all, thanks to all the weasel words.

Look at ads in magazines and newspapers, listen to ads on radio and television, and you'll find the word "help" in ads for all kinds of products. How often do you read or hear such phrases as "helps stop . . . ," "helps overcome . . . ," "helps eliminate . . . ," "helps you feel . . . ," or "helps you look . . . "? If you start looking for this weasel word in advertising, you'll be amazed at how often it occurs. Analyze the claims in the ads using "help," and you will discover that these ads are really saying nothing.

There are plenty of other weasel words used in advertising. In fact, there are so many that to list them all would fill the rest of this book. But, in order to identify the doublespeak of advertising and understand the real meaning of an ad, you have to be aware of the most popular weasel words in advertising today.

Virtually Spotless

One of the most powerful weasel words is "virtually," a word so innocent that most people don't pay any attention to it when it is used in an advertising claim. But watch out. "Virtually" is used in advertising claims that appear to make specific, definite promises when there is no promise. After all, what does "virtually" mean? It means "in essence or effect, although not in fact." Look at that definition again. "Virtually" means *not in fact.* It does *not* mean "almost" or "just about the same as," or anything else. And before you dismiss all this concern over such a small word, remember that small words can have big consequences.

In 1971 a federal court rendered its decision on a case brought by a woman who became pregnant while taking birth control pills. She sued the manufacturer, Eli Lilly and Company, for breach of warranty. The woman lost her case. Basing its ruling on a statement in the pamphlet accompanying the pills, which stated that, "When taken as directed, the tablets offer virtually 100% protection," the court ruled that there was no warranty, expressed or implied, that the pills were absolutely effective. In its ruling, the court pointed out that, according to *Webster's Third New International Dictionary,* "virtually" means "almost entirely" and clearly does not mean "absolute" (*Whittington* v. *Eli Lilly and Company,* 333 F. Supp. 98). In other words, the Eli Lilly company was really saying that its birth control pill, even when taken as directed, *did not in fact* provide 100 percent protection against pregnancy. But Eli Lilly didn't want to put it that way because then many women might not have bought Lilly's birth control pills.

The next time you see the ad that says that this dishwasher detergent "leaves dishes virtually spotless," just remember how advertisers twist the meaning of the weasel word "virtually." You can have lots of spots on your dishes after using this detergent and the ad claim will still be true, because what this claim really means is that this detergent does not *in fact* leave your dishes spotless. Whenever you see or hear an ad claim that uses the word "virtually," just translate that claim into its real meaning.

So the television set that is "virtually trouble free" becomes the television set that is not in fact trouble free, the "virtually fool-proof operation" of any appliance becomes an operation that is in fact not foolproof, and the product that "virtually never needs service" becomes the product that is not in fact service free.

New and Improved

If "new" is the most frequently used word on a product package, "improved" is the second most frequent. In fact, the two words are almost always used together. It seems just about everything sold these days is "new and improved." The next time you're in the supermarket, try counting the number of times you see these words on products. But you'd better do it while you're walking down just one aisle, otherwise you'll need a calculator to keep track of your counting.

Just what do these words mean? The use of the word "new" is restricted by regulations, so an advertiser can't just use the word on a product or in an ad without meeting certain requirements. For example, a product is considered new for about six months during a national advertising campaign. If the product is being advertised only in a limited test market area, the word can be used longer, and in some instances has been used for as long as two years.

What makes a product "new"? Some products have been around for a long time, yet every once in a while you discover that they are being advertised as "new." Well, an advertiser can call a product new if there has been "a material functional change" in the product. What is "a material functional change," you ask? Good question. In fact it's such a good question it's being asked all the time. It's up to the manufacturer to prove that the product has undergone such a change. And if the manufacturer isn't challenged on the claim, then there's no one to stop it. Moreover, the change does not have to be an improvement in the product. One manufacturer added an artificial lemon scent to a cleaning product and called it "new and improved," even though the product did not clean any better than without the lemon scent. The manufacturer defended the use of the word "new" on the grounds that the artificial scent changed the chemical formula of the product and therefore constituted "a material functional change."

Which brings up the word "improved." When used in advertising, "improved" does not mean "made better." It only means "changed" or "different from before." So, if the detergent maker puts a plastic pour spout on the box of detergent, the product has been "improved," and away we go with a whole new advertising campaign. Or, if the cereal maker adds more fruit or a different kind of fruit to the cereal, there's an improved product. Now you know why manufacturers are constantly making little changes in their products. Whole new advertising campaigns, designed to convince you that the product has been changed for the better, are based on small changes in superficial aspects of a product. The next time you see an ad for an "improved" product, ask yourself what was wrong with the old one. Ask yourself just how "improved" the product is. Finally, you might check to see whether the "improved" version costs more than the unimproved one. After all, someone has to pay for the millions of dollars spent advertising the improved product.

Of course, advertisers really like to run ads that claim a product is "new and improved." While what constitutes a "new" product may be subject to some regulation, "improved" is a subjective judgment. A manufacturer changes the shape of its stick deodorant, but the shape doesn't improve the function of the deodorant. That is, changing the shape doesn't affect the deodorizing ability of the deodorant, so the manufacturer calls it "improved." Another manufacturer adds ammonia to its liquid cleaner and calls it "new and improved." Since adding ammonia does affect the cleaning ability of the product, there has been a "material functional change" in the product, and the manufacturer can now call its cleaner "new," and "improved" as well. Now the weasel words "new and improved" are plastered all over the package and are the basis for a multimillion-dollar ad campaign. But after six months the word "new" will have to go, until someone can dream up another change in the product. Perhaps it will be adding color to the liquid, or changing the shape of the package, or maybe adding a new dripless pour spout, or perhaps a————. The "improvements" are endless, and so are the new advertising claims and campaigns.

"New" is just too useful and powerful a word in advertising for advertisers to pass it up easily. So they use weasel words that say "new" without really saying it. One of their favorites is "introducing," as in, "Introducing improved Tide," or "Introducing the stain remover." The first is simply saying, here's our improved soap; the second, here's our new advertising campaign for our detergent. Another favorite is "now," as in, "Now there's Sinex," which simply means that Sinex is available. Then there are phrases like "Today's Chevrolet," "Presenting Dristan," and "A fresh way to start the day." The list is really endless because advertisers are always finding new ways to say "new" without really saying it. If there is a second edition of this book, I'll just call it the "new and improved" edition. Wouldn't you really rather have a "new and improved" edition of this book rather than a "second" edition?

Acts Fast

"Acts" and "works" are two popular weasel words in advertising because they bring action to the product and to the advertising claim. When you see the ad for the cough syrup that "Acts on the cough control center," ask yourself what this cough syrup is claiming to do. Well, it's just claiming to "act," to do something, to perform an action. What is it that the cough syrup does? The ad doesn't say. It only claims to perform an action or do something on your "cough control center." By the way, what and where is your "cough control center"? I don't remember learning about that part of the body in human biology class.

Ads that use such phrases as "acts fast," "acts against," "acts to prevent," and the like are saying essentially nothing, because "act" is a word empty of any specific meaning. The ads are always careful not to specify exactly what "act" the product performs. Just because a brand of aspirin claims to "act fast" for headache relief doesn't mean this aspirin is any better than any other aspirin. What is the "act" that this aspirin performs? You're never told. Maybe it just dissolves quickly. Since aspirin is a parity product, all aspirin is the same and therefore functions the same.

Works Like Anything Else

If you don't find the word "acts" in an ad, you will probably find the weasel word "works." In fact, the two words are almost interchangeable in advertising. Watch out for ads that say a product "works against," "works like," "works for," or "works longer." As with "acts," "works" is the same meaningless verb used to make you think that this product really does something, and maybe even something special or unique. But "works," like "acts," is basically a word empty of any specific meaning.

Like Magic

Whenever advertisers want you to stop thinking about the product and to start thinking about something bigger, better, or more attractive than the product, they use that very popular weasel word, "like." The word "like" is the advertiser's equivalent of a magician's use of misdirection. "Like" gets you to ignore the product and concentrate on the claim the advertiser is making about it. "For skin like peaches and cream" claims the ad for a skin cream. What is this ad really claiming? It doesn't say this cream will give you peaches-and-cream skin. There is no verb in this claim, so it doesn't even mention using the product. How is skin ever like "peaches and cream"? Remember, ads must be read literally and exactly, according to the dictionary definition of words. (Remember "virtually" in the Eli Lilly case.) The ad is making absolutely no promise or claim whatsoever for this skin cream. If you think this cream will give you soft, smooth, youthful-looking skin, you are the one who has read that meaning into the ad.

The wine that claims "It's like taking a trip to France" wants you to think about a romantic evening in Paris as you walk along the boulevard after a wonderful meal in an intimate little bistro. Of course, you don't really believe that a wine can take you to France, but the goal of the ad is to get you to think pleasant, romantic thoughts about France and not about how the wine tastes or how expensive it may be. That little word "like" has taken you away from crushed grapes into a world of your own imaginative making. Who knows, maybe the next time you buy wine, you'll think those pleasant thoughts when you see this brand of wine, and you'll buy it. Or, maybe you weren't even thinking about buying wine at all, but now you just might pick up a bottle the next time you're shopping. Ah, the power of "like" in advertising.

How about the most famous "like" claim of all, "Winston tastes good like a cigarette should"? Ignoring the grammatical error here, you might want to know what this claim is saying. Whether a cigarette tastes good or bad is a subjective judgment because what tastes good to one person may well taste horrible to another. Not everyone likes fried snails, even if they are called escargot. (*De gustibus non est disputandum,* which was probably the Roman rule for advertising as well as for defending the games in the Colosseum.) There are many people who say all cigarettes taste terrible, other people who say only some cigarettes taste all right, and still others who say all cigarettes taste good. Who's right? Everyone, because taste is a matter of personal judgment.

Moreover, note the use of the conditional, "should." The complete claim is, "Winston tastes good like a cigarette should taste." But should cigarettes taste good? Again, this is a matter of personal judgment and probably depends most on one's experiences with smoking. So, the Winston ad is simply saying that Winston cigarettes are just like any other cigarette: Some people like them and some people don't. On that statement R. J. Reynolds conducted a very successful multimillion-dollar advertising campaign that helped keep Winston the number-two-selling cigarette in the United States, close behind number one, Marlboro.

Can It Be Up to the Claim?

Analyzing ads for doublespeak requires that you pay attention to every word in the ad and determine what each word really means. Advertisers try to wrap their claims in language that sounds concrete, specific, and objective, when in fact the language of advertising is anything but. Your job is to read carefully and listen critically so that when the announcer says that "Crest can be of significant value . . ." you know immediately that this claim says absolutely nothing. Where is the doublespeak in this ad? Start with the second word.

Once again, you have to look at what words really mean, not what you think they mean or what the advertiser wants you to think they mean. The ad for Crest only says that using Crest "can be" of "significant value." What really throws you off in this ad is the brilliant use of "significant." It draws your attention to the word "value" and makes you forget that the ad only claims that Crest "can be." The ad doesn't say that Crest *is* of value, only that it is "able" or "possible" to be of value, because that's all that "can" means.

It's so easy to miss the importance of those little words, "can be." Almost as easy as missing the importance of the words "up to" in an ad. These words are very popular in sale ads. You know, the ones that say, "Up to 50% Off!" Now, what does that claim mean? Not much, because the store or manufacturer has to reduce the price of only a few items by 50 percent. Everything else can be reduced a lot less, or not even reduced. Moreover, don't you want to know 50 percent off of what? Is it 50 percent off the "manufacturer's suggested list price," which is the highest possible price? Was the price artificially inflated and then reduced? In other ads, "up to" expresses an ideal situation. The medicine that works "up to ten times faster," the battery that lasts "up to twice as long," and the soap that gets you "up to twice as clean" all are based on ideal situations for using those products, situations in which you can be sure you will never find yourself.

Unfinished Words

Unfinished words are a kind of "up to" claim in advertising. The claim that a battery lasts "up to twice as long" usually doesn't finish the comparison—twice as long as what? A birthday candle? A tank of gas? A cheap battery made in a country not noted for its technological achievements? The implication is that the battery lasts twice as long as batteries made by other battery makers, or twice as long as earlier model batteries made by the advertiser, but the ad doesn't really make these claims. You read these claims into the ad, aided by the visual images the advertiser so carefully provides.

Unfinished words depend on you to finish them, to provide the words the advertisers so thoughtfully left out of the ad. Pall Mall cigarettes were once advertised as "A longer finer and milder smoke." The question is, longer, finer, and milder than what? The aspirin that claims it contains "Twice as much of the pain reliever doctors recommend most" doesn't tell you what pain reliever it contains twice as much of. (By the way, it's aspirin. That's right; it just contains twice the amount of aspirin. And how much is twice the amount? Twice of what amount?) Panadol boasts that "nobody reduces fever faster," but, since Panadol is a parity product, this claim simply means that Panadol isn't any better than any other product in its parity class. "You can be sure if it's Westinghouse," you're told, but just exactly what it is you can be sure of is never mentioned. "Magnavox gives you more" doesn't tell you what you get more of. More value? More television? More than they gave you before? It sounds nice, but it means nothing, until you fill in the claim with your own words, the words the advertiser didn't use. Since each of us fills in the claim differently, the ad and the product can become all things to all people, and not promise a single thing.

Unfinished words abound in advertising because they appear to promise so much. More importantly, they can be joined with powerful visual images on television to appear to be making significant promises about a product's effectiveness without really making any promises. In a television ad, the aspirin product that claims fast relief can show a person with a headache taking the product and then, in what appears to be a matter of minutes, claiming complete relief. This visual image is far more powerful than any claim made in unfinished words. Indeed, the visual image completes the unfinished words for you, filling in with pictures what the words leave out. And you thought that ads didn't affect you. What brand of aspirin do you use?

Some years ago, Ford's advertisements proclaimed "Ford LTD—700% quieter." Now, what do you think Ford was claiming with these unfinished words? What was the Ford LTD quieter than? A Cadillac? A Mercedes Benz? A BMW? Well, when the FTC asked Ford to substantiate this unfinished claim, Ford replied that it meant that the inside of the LTD was 700% quieter than the outside. How did you finish those unfinished words when you first read them? Did you even come close to Ford's meaning?

Combining Weasel Words

A lot of ads don't fall neatly into one category or another because they use a variety of different devices and words. Different weasel words are often combined to make an ad claim. The claim, "Coffee-Mate gives coffee more body, more flavor," uses Unfinished Words ("more" than what?) and also uses words that have no specific meaning ("body" and "flavor"). Along with "taste" (remember the Winston ad and its claim to taste good), "body" and "flavor" mean nothing because their meaning is entirely subjective. To you, "body" in coffee might mean thick, black, almost bitter coffee, while I might take it to mean a light brown, delicate coffee. Now, if you think you understood that last sentence, read it again, because it said nothing of objective value; it was filled with weasel words of no specific meaning: "thick," "black," "bitter," "light brown," and "delicate." Each of those words has no specific, objective meaning, because each of us can interpret them differently.

Try this slogan: "Looks, smells, tastes like ground-roast coffee." So, are you now going to buy Taster's Choice instant coffee because of this ad? "Looks," "smells," and "tastes" are all words with no specific meaning and depend on your interpretation of them for any meaning. Then there's that great weasel word "like," which simply suggests a comparison but does not make the actual connection between the product and the quality. Besides, do you know what "ground-roast" coffee is? I don't, but it sure sounds good. So, out of seven words in this ad, four are definite weasel words, two are quite meaningless, and only one has any clear meaning.

Remember the Anacin ad—"Twice as much of the pain reliever doctors recommend most"? There's a whole lot of weaseling going on in this ad. First, what's the pain reliever they're talking about in this ad? Aspirin, of course. In fact, any time you see or hear an ad using those words "pain reliever," you can automatically substitute the word "aspirin" for them. (Makers of acetaminophen and ibuprofen pain relievers are careful in their advertising to identify their products as nonaspirin products.) So, now we know that Anacin has aspirin in it. Moreover, we know that Anacin has twice as much aspirin in it, but we don't know twice as much as what. Does it have twice as much aspirin as an ordinary aspirin tablet? If so, what is an ordinary aspirin tablet, and how much aspirin does it contain? Twice as much as Excedrin or Bufferin? Twice as much as a chocolate chip cookie? Remember those Unfinished Words and how they lead you on without saying anything.

Finally, what about those doctors who are doing all that recommending? Who are they? How many of them are there? What kind of doctors are they? What are their qualifications? Who asked them about recommending pain relievers? What other pain relievers did they recommend? And there are a whole lot more questions about this "poll" of doctors to which I'd like to know the answers, but you get the point. Sometimes, when I call my doctor, she tells me to take two aspirin and call her office in the morning. Is that where Anacin got this ad?

Read the Label, or the Brochure

Weasel words aren't just found on television, on the radio, or in newspaper and magazine ads. Just about any language associated with a product will contain the doublespeak of advertising. Remember the Eli Lilly case and the doublespeak on the information sheet that came with the birth control pills. Here's another example.

In 1983, the Estée Lauder cosmetics company announced a new product called "Night Repair." A small brochure distributed with the product stated that "Night Repair was scientifically formulated in Estée Lauder's U.S. laboratories as part of the Swiss Age-Controlling Skincare Program. Although only nature controls the aging process, this program helps control the signs of aging and encourages skin to look and feel younger." You might want to read these two sentences again, because they sound great but say nothing.

First, note that the product was "scientifically formulated" in the company's laboratories. What does that mean? What constitutes a scientific formulation? You wouldn't expect the company to say that the product was casually, mechanically, or carelessly formulated, or just thrown together one day when the people in the white coats didn't have anything better to do. But the word "scientifically" lends an air of precision and promise that just isn't there.

It is the second sentence, however, that's really weasely, both syntactically and semantically. The only factual part of this sentence is the introductory dependent clause—"only nature controls the aging process." Thus, the only fact in the ad is relegated to a dependent clause, a clause dependent on the main clause, which contains no factual or definite information at all and indeed purports to contradict the independent clause. The new "skincare program" (notice it's not a skin cream but a "program") does not claim to stop or even retard the aging process. What, then, does Night Repair, at a price of over $35 (in 1983 dollars) for a .87-ounce bottle do? According to this brochure, nothing. It only "helps," and the brochure does not say how much it helps. Moreover, it only "helps control," and then it only helps control the "*signs* of aging," not the aging itself. Also, it "encourages" skin not to *be* younger but only to "look and feel" younger. The brochure does not say younger than what. Of the sixteen words in the main clause of this second sentence, nine are weasel words. So, before you spend all that money for Night Repair, or any other cosmetic product, read the words carefully, and then decide if you're getting what you think you're paying for.

Other Tricks of the Trade

Advertisers' use of doublespeak is endless. Remember the explanation of advertising's function given by Rosser Reeves earlier in this chapter: to make something out of nothing. The best way advertisers can make something out of nothing is through words. Although there are a lot of visual images used on television and in magazines and newspapers, every advertiser wants to create that memorable line that will stick in the public consciousness. I am sure pure joy reigned in one advertising agency when a study found that children who were asked to spell the word "relief" promptly and proudly responded "r-o-l-a-i-d-s."

The variations, combinations, and permutations of doublespeak used in advertising go on and on, running from the use of rhetorical questions ("Wouldn't you really rather have a Buick?" "If you can't trust Prestone, who can you trust?") to flattering you with compliments ("The lady has taste." "We think a cigar smoker is someone special." "You've come a long way baby."). You know, of course, how you're *supposed* to answer those questions, and you know that those compliments are just leading up to the sales pitches for the products. Before you dismiss such tricks of the trade as obvious, however, just remember that all of these statements and questions were part of very successful advertising campaigns.

A more subtle approach is the ad that proclaims a supposedly unique quality for a product, a quality that really isn't unique. "If it doesn't say Goodyear, it can't be polyglas." Sounds good, doesn't it? Polyglas is available only from Goodyear because Goodyear copyrighted that trade name. Any other tire manufacturer could make exactly the same tire but could not call it "polyglas," because that would be copyright infringement. "Polyglas" is simply Goodyear's name for its fiberglass-reinforced tire.

Since we like to think of ourselves as living in a technologically advanced country, science and technology have a great appeal in selling products. Advertisers are quick to use scientific doublespeak to push their products. There are all kinds of elixirs, additives, scientific potions, and mysterious mixtures added to all kinds of products. Gasoline contains "HTA," "F-310," "Platformate," and other chemical-sounding additives, but nowhere does an advertisement give any real information about the additive.

Shampoo, deodorant, mouthwash, cold medicine, sleeping pills, and any number of other products all seem to contain some special chemical ingredient that allows them to work wonders. "Certs contains a sparkling drop of Retsyn." So what? What's "Retsyn"? What's it do? What's so special about it? When they don't have a secret ingredient in their product, advertisers still find a way to claim scientific validity. There's "Sinarest. Created by a research scientist who actually gets sinus headaches." Sounds nice, but what kind of research does this scientist do? How do you know if she is any kind of expert on sinus medicine? Besides, this ad doesn't tell you a thing about the medicine itself and what it does.

ADVERTISING DOUBLESPEAK QUICK QUIZ

Now it's time to test your awareness of advertising doublespeak. (You didn't think I would just let you read this and forget it, did you?) The following is a list of statements from some recent ads. Your job is to figure out what each of these ads really says.

DOMINO'S PIZZA. "Because nobody delivers better."
SINUTAB. "It can stop the pain."
TUMS. "The stronger acid neutralizer."

MAXIMUM STRENGTH DRISTAN. "Strong medicine for tough sinus colds."

LISTERMINT. "Making your mouth a cleaner place."

CASCADE. "For virtually spotless dishes nothing beats Cascade."

NUPRIN. "Little. Yellow. Different. Better."

ANACIN. "Better relief."

SUDAFED. "Fast sinus relief that won't put you fast asleep."

ADVIL. "Advanced medicine for pain."

PONDS COLD CREAM. "Ponds cleans like no soap can."

MILLER LITE BEER. "Tastes great. Less filling."

PHILIPS MILK OF MAGNESIA. "Nobody treats you better than MOM (Philips Milk of Magnesia)."

BAYER. "The wonder drug that works wonders."

CRACKER BARREL. "Judged to be the best."

KNORR. "Where taste is everything."

ANUSOL. "Anusol is the word to remember for relief."

DIMETAPP. "It relieves kids as well as colds."

LIQUID DRĀNO. "The liquid strong enough to be called Drā-no."

JOHNSON & JOHNSON BABY POWDER. "Like magic for your skin."

PURITAN. "Make it your oil for life."

PAM. "Pam, because how you cook is as important as what you cook."

IVORY SHAMPOO AND CONDITIONER. "Leave your hair feeling Ivory clean."

TYLENOL GEL-CAPS. "It's not a capsule. It's better."

ALKA-SELTZER PLUS. "Fast, effective relief for winter colds."

The World of Advertising

In the world of advertising, people wear "dentures," not false teeth; they suffer from "occasional irregularity," not constipation; they need deodorants for their "nervous wetness," not for sweat; they use "bathroom tissue," not toilet paper; and they don't dye their hair, they "tint" or "rinse" it. Advertisements offer "real counterfeit diamonds" without the slightest hint of embarrassment, or boast of goods made out of "genuine imitation leather" or "virgin vinyl."

In the world of advertising, the girdle becomes a "body shaper," "form persuader," "control garment," "controller," "outerwear enhancer," "body garment," or "anti-gravity panties," and is sold with such trade names as "The Instead," "The Free Spirit," and "The Body Briefer."

A study some years ago found the following words to be among the most popular used in U.S. television advertisements: "new," "improved," "better," "extra," "fresh," "clean," "beautiful," "free," "good," "great," and "light." At the same time, the following words were found to be among the most frequent on British television: "new," "good-better-best," "free," "fresh," "delicious," "full," "sure," "clean," "wonderful," and "special." While these words may occur most frequently in ads, and while ads may be filled with weasel words, you have to watch out for all the words used in advertising, not just the words mentioned here.

Every word in an ad is there for a reason; no word is wasted. Your job is to figure out exactly what each word is doing in an ad—what each word really means, not what the advertiser wants you to think it means. Remember, the ad is trying to get you to buy a product, so it will put the product in the best possible light, using any device, trick, or means legally allowed. Your only defense against advertising (besides taking up permanent residence on the moon) is to develop and use a strong critical reading, listening, and looking ability. Always ask yourself what the ad is *really* saying. When you see ads on television, don't be misled by the pictures, the visual images. What does the ad *say* about the product? What does the ad *not* say? What information is missing from the ad? Only by becoming an active, critical consumer of the doublespeak of advertising will you ever be able to cut through the doublespeak and discover what the ad is really saying.

Professor Del Kehl of Arizona State University has updated the Twenty-third Psalm to reflect the power of advertising to meet our needs and solve our problems. It seems fitting that this chapter close with this new Psalm.

The Adman's 23rd

The Adman is my shepherd;
I shall ever want.
He maketh me to walk a mile for a Camel;
He leadeth me beside Crystal Waters
   In the High Country of Coors;
He restoreth my soul with Perrier.
He guideth me in Marlboro Country
For Mammon's sake.
Yea, though I walk through the Valley of the
   Jolly Green Giant,
In the shadow of B.O., halitosis, indigestion,
   headache pain, and hemorrhoidal tissue,
I will fear no evil,
For I am in Good Hands with Allstate;
Thy Arid, Scope, Tums, Tylenol, and Preparation H—
They comfort me.
Stauffer's preparest a table before the TV
In the presence of all my appetites;
Thou anointest my head with Brylcream;
My Decaffeinated Cup runneth over.
Surely surfeit and security shall follow me
All the days of Metropolitan Life,
And I shall dwell in a Continental Home
With a mortgage forever and ever.

                                        Amen.

CHAPTER IV

Negative Deficits and the Elimination of Redundancies in the Human Resources Area: Business Communication, Sort Of

It's been a tough day shopping, but you're almost finished. Just a couple more things to get and you can head for home. Loaded down with bags, you struggle into the last store. Looming before you is the "Courtesy Desk," with the sign that firmly states, "For Your Convenience Please Check All Packages At the Desk." You wait in line to unload your pile of packages into the hands of the "Customer Service Representative," who stacks them behind the counter and gives you your check number. After finding two of the four things you need and standing in line for what seems like hours waiting to pay, you reclaim your packages and wearily fight your way through the traffic to get home.

Sorting through your packages at home, you discover something's missing. But you distinctly remember paying for that electric hamburger flipper and taking it with you. Then you realize that they must have forgotten to give it to you at the last store, when you reclaimed your checked packages. So, fighting the traffic yet again, you drive back to the store to pick up the package you checked for your convenience. It dawns on you then that you didn't check your packages for your convenience at all. In fact, it was very inconvenient for you to check your packages. You checked those packages for the store's convenience. And you checked them because the store is trying to control its "inventory shrinkage," not because it's providing a service for you.

You have just been introduced to business doublespeak. Since business permeates so much of our lives, business doublespeak can have serious and far-reaching consequences. Because business doublespeak is so prevalent, however, you tend to ignore it, and you end up paying for your ignorance, whether you realize it or not. While some business doublespeak, such as job titles, is often obvious and humorous, other business doublespeak is subtle and serious. You need to be aware of business doublespeak, for your own economic survival if for no other reason. And there is plenty to keep you busy.

These days, banks don't offer second mortgages on rental property, they offer "non-owner occupied equity recovery." When fewer policyholders died during the year than the insurance company expected, it reported a bigger than anticipated profit due to "positive mortality experience." When the Wilson Sporting Goods Company decided to close its U.S. plant where baseball gloves were made and import foreign-made gloves instead, it announced that it had "decided to foreign-source its glove needs." In its catalog of products for 1986, Sears offered a ceramic mug that was "made in USA and imported from England." Credit companies no longer have collection departments or billing departments, they have "Fulfillment Offices."

After the psychedelic sixties, which were followed by the silent seventies, we hit the greedy eighties, a time when making lots of money was not only socially and morally acceptable but required. Yuppies with their lives of hard work, big bucks, and fancy cars, clothes, and habitats made the cover of *Newsweek*. "Greed is good," said Michael Douglas in the movie *Wall Street*, and we all knew what he meant. The Peace Corps was out and business school and investment banking were very much in. Then the "fourth quarter equity retreat" hit in October 1987.

Business, like most areas of our lives, has always had double-speak, but, with the increased popularity of business, the double-speak has not just been given wider circulation, it has increased dramatically. When Thomas Murphy, chair of the board of General Motors, was interviewed on "Meet the Press" in 1980, he was asked why the automobile business was so bad. Said Mr. Murphy without hesitation, "We are in a period of negative economic growth." This was one way of saying that because so many workers were laid off during the recession few people could afford to buy a new GM car. And when the GAF Corporation announced in 1981 that it was selling nearly half of its subsidiary companies, a Wall Street investment banker praised the company for its "enterprise restructuring," a term that sounded a whole lot better than the previously popular term, "downsizing."

The Doublespeak of Avoidance

With doublespeak, companies can discuss subjects they would prefer to avoid. Pacific Gas and Electric Company no longer sends its customers monthly bills. Now it sends them "Energy Documents." At United Parcel Service, no driver is the worst driver. Instead, a driver is the "least-best" driver. At CBS-TV, the "Program Practices Department" is the name given to the censor. Kirk Willison of the American Banking Association denied in 1988 that interest rates on bank credit cards were too high. "Don't call it an interest rate. Call it a service rate. It's not just a credit card, it's a payment mechanism," protested Mr. Willison. In 1982 federal investigations into widespread fraud in the heart pacemaker industry revealed that "kickbacks" were called "rebates" or "fees for product testing."

When General Motors wanted to avoid a recall of 5.3 million cars in 1984, it tried to persuade the federal government that it "isn't dangerous for a car's rear wheel and axle to fall off." Rockwell International had a slight problem in 1984 when, after more than five years of research and $12 million worth of engineering, the space shuttle's toilet still did not work. On ten of eleven trips into space, the toilet failed. Rockwell, however, insisted that the toilet had not failed but had just suffered "a number of different problems." For Mark Carter of Austin, Texas, the doublespeak used by his savings and loan association was financially painful. When Mr. Carter handed over his automatic teller machine card and access code at gunpoint, the robber's $500 withdrawal was an "authorized transaction," according to Texas Federal Savings and Loan officials. A letter to Mr. Carter stated that "Texas Federal has established a policy to consider a robbery of an ATM to be an authorized transaction." Willie Sutton would have loved to have heard that.

Doublespeak and Product Development

Through doublespeak, corporations can change the products and services they sell, without spending a cent on product development. Hallmark no longer makes plain, ordinary greeting cards. Now Hallmark makes "social expression products." In 1985, officials of the Quaker State Oil Refining Corporation were reported in the *Wall Street Journal* as urging reporters to stop describing their corporation as an oil company and instead to call it "a consumer marketing company serving the automotive aftermarket." Once upon a time, North American Van Lines was a moving company, but in 1988 it became "North American Relocation Services." Doesn't the four-syllable "relocation" sound more impressive than the two-syllable "moving"?

No longer is it an automobile junkyard, nor junk, nor even used car parts. Now it's "auto dismantlers and recyclers" who sell "predismantled, previously owned parts." New Jersey junkyard operator Richard Montaldo insisted, "We're not a wastepaper business. We're a secondary-fiber business." To Camden Zoning Board of Adjustment officials, however, "a secondary-fiber business is a waste-paper business is a junkyard." In Burlington, New Jersey, gravedigger Newton Johnson has the words "Internment Excavation" on his truck, and he points out that he "prepares" graves, he does not dig them.

Sometimes companies don't want people to know what it is they really do, so doublespeak helps. The Nuclear Engineering

Company of Louisville, Kentucky, a company that disposes of radioactive and chemical wastes, changed its name in 1981 to "U.S. Ecology, Inc." because the firm wanted a name "that would make people feel comfortable."

Business Schools and Doublespeak

Even business schools get in on the doublespeak. The Wharton School of the University of Pennsylvania runs a program called the Wharton Executive Education Program, which provides intensive instruction for senior executives at corporations around the world, for a nice fee, of course. Does the program make a profit? No, but it does run a "negative deficit."

In 1979, the *Wall Street Journal* reported that students taking the "Competitive Decision Making" course at the Harvard Business School (which calls curriculum "learning technology") learned that negotiating in the real world involves "strategic misrepresentation," or lying. They were taught that hiding certain facts, bluffing, or even outright lying often gets them a better deal. The purpose of the course isn't to teach them to lie (or to use "strategic misrepresentation"), but to learn that they may be lied to.

The *Harvard Business Review* contributes its share to the doublespeak of business by publishing prose such as this:

> If competitive advantage can be achieved from
> just-in-time participatory management styles, then
> bottom-line oriented organizations can better facilitate
> their gain-sharing systems to network for the new global
> technologies. At my company, for example, detected
> casualties fluctuate between generic niche discontinuities
> and complementary enculturative yield functions.

If this writing reflects the kind of clear thinking prevalent among senior executives of American corporations, we should have little trouble meeting the challenge of foreign competition. They'll just roll right over us while we flounder in our prose.

The Doublespeak of Job Titles

As H. L. Mencken noted in his classic work, *The American Language*, Americans are always trying to make their jobs sound more dignified, more important, more prestigious, more complicated than they really are. Both employers and employees cooperate in creating doublespeak to describe, name, or classify jobs. New doublespeak terms for jobs are created faster than you can keep up with them.

Janitors, of course, are no longer called janitors. They're "custodians" or "building superintendents." Going a step further, these days hospitals have "environmental technicians" who work for the "Environmental Services Department." The person in the office at the hospital who takes care of the patients' insurance forms is called the "Director of Patient Financial Account Analysis." Car salesmen are now called "New Car Accountants," while automobile mechanics are called "automotive internists." Some gas stations even employ "petroleum transfer engineers."

Bars now have "doormen" or "entertainment coordinators," not bouncers, while the doorman in an apartment building is called an "access controller." Bodyguards are called "personal protection specialists" and work for an "executive protection agency." Guards in department stores are called "Loss Prevention Specialists," while guards in other businesses are called "protective service workers." Even night watchmen are called "Night Entry Supervisors." Beauticians, who were once hairdressers, are now called "estheticians" or "estheticiennes," while manicurists are called "nail technicians." Some exterminators now are called "sanitarians," who "deroach" buildings. Even newspaper delivery boys have been upgraded to the status of "media courier." Those who were once potato chip delivery truck drivers are now "Executive Snack Route Consultants."

Repairmen have become "service technicians" or "field service representatives," while nurses are called "patient care specialists." There are no secretaries anymore, just "executive assistants" or "office automation specialists." These days it seems as if everyone who works in an office is an assistant, associate, or an executive something or other.

Stock salesmen became stock brokers, but now they're called "portfolio managers" or "registered representatives." Insurance salesmen have become "field underwriters," while bill collectors are now called "portfolio administrators" or "experts in the management of the accounts-receivable asset." The Internal Revenue Service hires "forms facilitators," not clerks, while IBM employs "advisory marketing representatives," not sales representatives. Some companies call their salesmen "territory managers." The television weatherman prefers to be called a "meteorologist." The Honda plant in Marysville, Ohio, has two thousand "associates" and not one "employee."

In fact, many companies now avoid using the word "employee" altogether. Since the hot topic in business these days is "participative management," the word "employee," with all its negative connotations, just won't do. So the search is on for words that mean employee but don't say it. "Associate" is one of the most popular, but other words include "partner," "junior partner," "team member," "internal customers," and "stakeholder." Some companies use "family" and "people" when talking about their employees as a group.

Domino's Pizza doesn't use any of these. At Domino's there are only "team members," "team leaders," and the "coaching staff." The word "employee" is never used. Domino's is organized into thirty "commissaries," each of which consists of a plant, warehouse, and distribution system.

The Doublespeak of Accounting

You may think that, since accounting deals with numbers, not words, accounting is free from doublespeak. You couldn't be more wrong. If you think accounting is a value-free, exact, objective science, you'd better stay out of the stock market, because one of the most creative areas for accounting is that pride of industry, the corporate annual report.

A corporation's annual report supposedly presents a clear, precise picture of the financial status or health of the company. After all, numbers don't lie. Moreover, a corporate annual report is examined before publication by an outside accounting firm to insure its accuracy. An annual report must therefore be a good guide to a company's financial position. If you believe that, I have some retirement land in Florida and a vacation lot in Arizona I'd like to sell you, and to get you to these places I'll sell you the car my sainted grandmother drove only on Sundays to church.

The numbers in a corporate report do not imply precision, nor do the numbers represent reality. The world is not the way the numbers in a corporate report tell you it is. What the numbers do represent, according to Adam Smith in his book, *Supermoney,* is a lot of imagination at work, the combined imaginations of corporate executives and very bright and high-priced accountants. Those bean counters really earn their big salaries. When an outside accounting firm examines the corporation's report and certifies it, the accounting firm states only that they have examined the books of the corporation and that the books conform to "generally accepted accounting principles." As Smith notes, "It is safe to say that for a generation no one knew what those four words meant."

Smith quotes Leonard Spacek, senior partner and chairman emeritus of Arthur Andersen & Company, one of America's biggest and most prestigious accounting firms. Here, according to Adam Smith, is what Mr. Spacek has to say about generally accepted accounting principles:

How my profession can tolerate such fiction and look the public in the eye is beyond my understanding. I suppose the answer lies in the fact that if your living depends on playing poker, you can easily develop a poker face. My profession appears to regard a set of financial statements as a roulette wheel to the public investor—and it is his tough luck if he doesn't understand the risks that we inject into the accounting reports.

Accounting doublespeak provides a number of ways for the financial status of a company to be reported so that one dollar of earnings can become 50¢ or $1.50, depending on the way that dollar is reported on the financial statement. Depreciation can be changed from accelerated to straight line, the valuation of inventories can be changed, adjustments can be made in the charges for the pension fund, the costs of a new project can be deferred until the project produces revenue, or research can be capitalized instead of listed as an expense. The list is endless. The numbers in an annual report may not be what they seem. There can certainly be a little bit (or a lot) of the creative writer in the accountant.

In 1981 a corporation called O.P.M. Leasing Services not only went into bankruptcy but its founders, Mordecai Weissman and Myron S. Goodman, were sentenced to long prison terms. From its founding in 1971 to its demise in 1980, O.P.M. was without funds and lost money every year of its existence, yet it continued to grow and borrow large amounts of money ($500 million at one time). How was this possible? Having a good accounting firm doing the annual reports really helped. Mr. Goodman said that he shopped around for an accounting firm that would be "flexible," one that would certify financial statements that painted a rosy picture but would not detect the lease frauds in which the company was engaging. He found his accounting firm, one of the twelve largest in the country, which miraculously changed losses and deficits into profits and a positive net worth. As the story goes, however, they needed some encouragement.

At first the accounting firm came up with a financial statement that showed large losses and a negative net worth for the company. In other words, the company was losing money and owed more than it was worth. Undaunted, Mr. Goodman told the accountants to "get back to the grindstone and try to figure out a way to show a profit," and the accountants did.

After a number of rather large companies went bankrupt right after issuing annual reports that showed them to be solvent and profitable, a lot of people became concerned with the practices of the accounting firms that were certifying such reports. Accounting firms themselves became concerned. In 1986, for example, the accounting firm of Leventhal & Horwath issued a booklet that informed the public that audited financial statements aren't 100 percent correct; they're simply not wrong by a "material amount." Auditors don't tell clients what to report; they just cooperate to make accounting "meaningful," according to this booklet. Leventhal & Horwath's booklet cautions that an audit can detect fraud "only if it's major." I guess the fraud of O.P.M. Leasing Services, involving $225 million, wasn't major enough to be detected.

What constitutes major fraud is a good question. In 1989, the Federal Home Loan Bank Board filed suit against some of the biggest accounting firms in the United States. It seems these firms had audited some savings and loan associations and had failed to uncover large losses, fraud, and mismanagement, all of which led to the bankruptcies of many of the associations. On more than one occasion an accounting firm had audited a savings and loan and given it an "unqualified opinion," meaning the auditing firm found nothing wrong and that the financial statement prepared by the savings and loan association fairly represented its financial condition. However, within days after the audits were conducted, the savings and loan association went under and had to be rescued by the Federal Home Loan Banking Board. Some had losses in the neighborhood of $2 billion. But, then, $2 billion in fraud isn't major enough to detect, I guess, so the accounting firms aren't to blame.

Banks and Nonperforming Assets

Banks are certainly not adverse to using accounting doublespeak. Just look at the way in which banks deal with bad loans these days. When people borrow money from a bank, they are supposed to pay it back, with interest. That's how banks make money. When people borrow money from a bank and don't pay it back, the bank loses money. When people don't pay back the money they've borrowed, the bank had a bad debt, right? Wrong. An accountant would never say something as negative as "bad loan" or "bad debt." When the First National Bank of Chicago had $23 million in overdrafts by a currency exchange and gold dealer in Jordan in 1986, the overdrafts were classified as "nonperforming assets" in the bank's fourth-quarter financial statement. What do you think the odds are that those "nonperforming assets" will ever start performing again? When the Continental Illinois Corporation, the sixth largest bank holding company in the country in 1982, reported that its "nonperforming credits" increased 44 percent in the fourth quarter to $653 million, it was really reporting that it had $653 million in bad loans and might never see any of that money ever again.

In an article for *The New York Times* in 1985, John Kenneth Galbraith commented on the use of doublespeak by banks. Once upon a time, Galbraith wrote, loans that were not paid in full were in default. Now, however, such loans are "rolled over. Or rescheduled. Or they become problem loans. Or, best of all, they are nonperforming assets." Galbraith went on to add a personal story. It seems that the son of a banker had a bad accident with the family car. The son reported to his banker father that the car wasn't totally destroyed, only "rendered permanently nonperforming." Using such doublespeak can avoid reporting a very unpleasant reality, and maybe even prevent bringing the wrath of stockholders down on the bank officers who made all those bad loans. It may even be that banks learned this doublespeak from their corporate clients—you know, the corporations that are never in the red, but just experience "negative cash flow."

The Wonders Wrought with Accounting Doublespeak

Accounting doublespeak allows corporations to do all kinds of wonderful things. In 1985 the Penrod Drilling Company, an oil company owned by the famous and very wealthy Hunt brothers of Texas, made money despite posting losses of $100 million. In 1986 Tenneco announced that it would change its accounting methods and would take $988 million in charges against prior years' earnings. "It's not misleading, but it's a cleverly timed change," said Lee Seidler, an accountant at Bear, Stearns & Company, the Wall Street investment banking and brokerage company. "It is quite creative accounting, and other oil companies may want to do the same," said Norman Strauss, a partner at Ernst & Whinney, a national accounting firm.

If you think charging present expenses to past earnings is a neat accounting trick, follow this one closely. A study in 1986 revealed that, during one four-year period, ten corporations had combined total domestic profits of $39.67 billion and not only had paid no income tax but had received tax rebates totaling $1.5 billion. One of those ten corporations making all that money but paying no taxes was AT&T, which disputed the conclusion that it had paid no taxes. AT&T pointed out that, under special provisions of the tax code, a growing company may defer paying taxes until later years. Thus, a company that continues to grow may defer paying taxes forever. (AT&T was formally organized in 1899 and has been growing ever since.) AT&T contended that deferred taxes should be counted as taxes actually paid. Now isn't that a neat trick? Don't pay the taxes, but count them as an expense as if you had paid them. (And you thought that magicians performed their tricks only on stage in Las Vegas.) AT&T defended its accounting practices by pointing out that many corporations like itself use various accounting styles in different reports to shareholders and government agencies, in which they sometimes count taxes owed as having been paid, depending on the point they are trying to make. In other words, AT&T keeps two sets of books: one for the shareholders, in which the taxes are recorded as paid, and one for the government, in which the taxes aren't paid. See what creative accounting can do?

Not to be outdone, General Dynamics, the nation's largest military contractor, paid no federal income tax from 1972 to 1986, a period during which the company reported making more than $2 billion in profits. By using an accounting method called "completed contract accounting," General Dynamics was able not only to avoid all federal income taxes but to pay over $100 million in dividends to its shareholders, dividends that were not taxable. Really creative accounting can be very profitable.

You may not have realized it, but IRS regulations and those

famous "generally accepted accounting principles" allow corporations like AT&T and General Dynamics to report their profits two ways: as low as possible for the IRS and as high as possible for shareholders and the public. The effect of this accounting wizardry, of course, is a lower tax bill and a rosier annual report. Now that's real doublespeak.

Upping the ante on their colleagues at the IRS, the Securities and Exchange Commission approved a creative accounting change in 1984 called "in-substance defeasance." This method allows a corporation to pay off large amounts of old, cheap debt with smaller amounts of new bonds that pay high interest rates, and then through the magic of accounting report extra profit on its balance sheet. That's how you "defease" a debt.

When corporations use accounting doublespeak to make money, they often use doublespeak to explain their actions—when they have to explain them, that is. See if you can figure out what Pacific Gas & Electric Company is trying to conceal in this notice, which it sent to all its customers in April 1982:

> One item of expense included in the rate increase recently granted to PG&E by the Public Utilities Commission, amounting to $177.4 million, was attributable to President Reagan's Economic Recovery Tax Act of 1981, which requires the Public Utilities Commission to charge ratepayers for the expense of taxes which are not now being paid to the Federal Government and which may never be paid. This expense may increase in the future.

If you can figure this out, you should consider a career in business, maybe even accounting. You would go far.

The Corporate Annual Report: Making Bad News Look Good

When corporations have a bad year or something goes wrong, the corporate report is filled with doublespeak. Warner Communications had an eventful year in 1982, but you would never know it from reading the company's annual report. Somehow, Warner forgot to mention that one of its top officers was convicted in a stock fraud case and another officer had pleaded guilty in 1981. When asked why those little details were not in the company's annual report, a Warner spokesperson said, "We did not think it was relevant to the operations of the company."

The Manville Corporation faced the biggest challenge in preparing a corporate report in 1982. Manville had filed for protection from creditors under Chapter 11 of the Federal Bankruptcy Act, as a legal strategy to handle the thousands of lawsuits filed against it by victims of asbestosis, a disease linked to the products the company manufactured. So Manville had to figure out a way to tell its shareholders that it was not really bankrupt, it just appeared to be. After noting that 1982 was a year "of significant changes and accomplishments," the report went on to say that "the following discussion of capital resources and liquidity presents a somewhat unusual position of availability of funds compared to that normally associated with many bankruptcy filings."

In 1984, Colgate-Palmolive saw its earnings plunge from $2.42 to 86¢ a share, while its working capital shrank drastically and shareholder equity and book value sank to their lowest levels since 1979. How did the company handle this bad news in its report? Simple. Chief Executive Officer Reuben Mark's letter to the shareholders began in big, bold lettering by claiming that "Colgate-Palmolive today sells over 3,000 products in 135 countries." The letter went on to overwhelm the reader with loads of similar glowing but irrelevant comments before revealing in paragraph six the disastrous news, in small, light-faced type.

When the news is really bad, a report will use doublespeak to face the news head on—sort of. In its 1985 report, Koppers Company of Pittsburgh was faced with explaining a $30-million loss, a decline of the per-share value of its stock from 79¢ to a *negative* $3.72, and a $138-million charge against pretax income. Chairman Charles R. Pullin simply said that "What may seem at first to be less than good news turns out, in the long run, to be the best of news for shareholders. Consider how [the writeoff] improves our resources for profitable redeployment."

You really have to know how to figure out the true meaning behind the doublespeak in a corporate report, if you want to have any chance at all of protecting your money. "Nineteen eighty-four brought a new beginning for Continental Illinois Corp," stated the annual report. Indeed it did. The Chicago banking company had a net loss of $1.1 billion, fired five directors and a bunch of top officers, and was taken over by federal regulators so the bank wouldn't go under. "AM International Inc. enjoyed a year of significant accomplishment in fiscal 1986," boasted the report. How significant do you think it is when income drops from $25.5 million to $5.7 million in one year? Sambo's Restaurants boasted in its 1981 annual report that the company had "achieved national prominence and publicity." The company sure had; the national press reported that the company had filed under Chapter 11 of the Federal Bankruptcy Act.

During a recession, the doublespeak flows thick in corporate reports. Instead of being active, dynamic, aggressive forces acting on behalf of their shareholders, corporations become helpless and hapless victims of economic forces beyond their (or anyone's) control. With this perfectly reasonable and understandable loss of control goes any responsibility for the bad news in the annual report. Companies are "impacted" by the recession because of the "climate of high interest rates" which produces a "cloudy future." Management, however, remains "cautiously optimistic" and "performance" (doublespeak for profit) for the year, given the "atmosphere of recession," was "reasonable," "acceptable," or "satisfactory," even if the company had disastrously lower profits than the year before, or even lost money.

In its annual report for 1981, Mirro Corporation claimed it had a "milestone year." Indeed it did. Mirro lost $1.2 million and announced plans to sell off more than half the company. One more milestone year like that, and the company would be out of business. According to its 1981 report, Ceco Corporation "enjoyed another good year" with net income "second only to the record achieved in [1980.]" This is one way of saying earnings fell 13 percent. Indianapolis Power & Light Company proudly stated that earnings in 1981 "reached" $2.81 a share. That is, they reached downward from the $3.68 a share of the previous year. Fairchild Industries noted in its 1981 report that, "despite the chilling effect of the recessionary climate on many American businesses, Fairchild has succeeded in maintaining and, in many cases, improving its position for future growth." In other words, Fairchild didn't make any money.

Public Service Electric and Gas (PSE&G) of New Jersey had a bad year in 1981, but not through any fault of management, because "weaknesses in the economy, accompanied by high inflation and interest rates, continued to exact a toll on the utility industry." This was a toll that for some reason was not exerted on Utah Power and Light, Minnesota Power, and Public Service Company of Colorado, among others, all of whom did quite well. PSE&G, however, saw earnings decline "as a consequence of the bleak economic climate and erosion of the rate relief received in 1980." PSE&G promised to attempt to cope with the "continuing unfavorable economic atmosphere," even though "high inflation and money costs continue to plague the utility industry."

It would seem that business should be expected to make a profit only in a favorable economic atmosphere. The message in these corporate reports seems to be that when the company makes money it's because of the skill of management, but when the company loses money it's because of outside forces beyond the control of management.

Often annual reports are simply filled with a lot of seemingly impressive language that says nothing. This is the doublespeak of gobbledygook or bureaucratese. The 1982 annual report of the Standard Oil Company (Ohio) contained a lot of sentences like this one: "The realities of 1982, as well as the ordinary changes which inevitably result in ongoing planning processes, have caused some modifications of refinements—which is probably a more accurate description—dealing with timing and degree that do not constitute any significant deviation from past thinking." Reynolds Metals Company's report for the same year contains this gem of perfectly meaningless prose: "Indeed, we have put renewed emphasis on aggressive and resourceful market development efforts throughout the company, targeting those market segments where aluminum's unique advantages will give us a competitive edge and optimal profit opportunities. Our research and development effort has also been reorganized, with product and process development keyed closely to strategic planning."

Clear Corporate Annual Reports

Not all corporate annual reports are filled with doublespeak. Many are quite straightforward accounts of the company's financial and business position. Some are even models of clarity, honesty, and plain talk. In the 1982 report of Marshall & Illsley, a bank holding company based in Milwaukee, Wisconsin, Chairman J. A. Puelicher's letter to the stockholders simply stated, "Your company had a very good year in 1982. Some of it was due to luck; some of it was due to good planning and management. We hope you enjoy the numbers and the pictures." That was the complete letter.

Writing a clear, simple, direct, doublespeak-free annual report is easy when all the news is good. But writing such a report when the news for the stockholders is bad is another matter. One of the best examples of such a doublespeak-free report revealing bad news was published by Teradyne, Inc., in 1986. Written by Frederick Van Veen, vice-president corporate relations, the report began, "Most of Teradyne's 26 years have been very good, and many of them have been spectacular. A small number—five to be exact—have been bad, if you define bad as meaning a year of no growth. 1986 was definitely one of the bad ones." The report went on to discuss the company's problems in blunt language: "Overall, our sales were down by about 9 percent, which doesn't sound so bad when you say it fast, except that it followed a 14 percent drop in 1985, for our first two-year decline ever. The fact that most of our competition did even worse is some consolation. But not much, frankly."

The report noted that Teradyne had "always believed in keeping score in dollars, and it's hard to put a bright face on a year in which net profits fell 99 percent. . . . A P&L [profit and loss] statement with no 'P' is lamentable, but it is certainly survivable." The report also discussed Teradyne's slow growth in Japan, despite fifteen years of effort. "The language is a big problem. In Europe, an American can at least read the street signs and dredge up some French or German learned in high school. In Japan, it's all Greek, so to speak." There is no attempt in the report to place the blame for slow growth in Japan on Japanese efforts to exclude foreign competition from their domestic market, an excuse used by many companies: "It is tempting to lay the blame for this on some dark Japanese conspiracy to exclude us, but the truth is more complicated than that. First of all, the Japanese competition is competent. . . . Life would be so much simpler if everyone else were incompetent."

Teradyne's report is evidence that some subjects are not too technical to be discussed in clear language. The report also shows how financial bad news can be communicated not just clearly and simply, but with style, grace, and wit. Corporate reports are filled with doublespeak only because those writing them want to make negative news appear positive, shift responsibility, conceal information, and pretend to communicate when in fact they want to avoid communicating.

Profits and Losses in the Insurance Industry

The accounting practices of insurance companies are a great and wondrous mystery. In few lines of business is it possible to make lots of money while losing money at the same time. When it comes to understanding insurance accounting, by comparison understanding Einstein's theory of general relativity, translating Etruscan texts, or deciphering the Mayan alphabet is child's play.

In the early 1980s, property and casualty insurance companies claimed they were losing money—lots and lots of money. (These are the insurance companies that cover damage to or theft of your property, or protect you in case you damage someone else's.) Medical malpractice rates (casualty insurance) suddenly went up so much that some doctors gave up practicing medicine.

Day-care centers, small towns, and small businesses couldn't afford the rates for liability insurance any more. This was all because the insurance companies said they were losing so much money. In fact, the property and casualty insurance industry claimed that in 1985 the industry as a whole lost $5.6 billion. The big rate increases, the industry claimed, were not only justified but absolutely necessary if the industry were to survive.

So, after losing money for years, the property and casualty insurance companies started making money again in 1986. But how much money the companies had been losing, and how much money they were making depended on how you figured profits. You'd think that something like profits should be easy enough to figure out. Profits are what's left after all the bills have been paid—unless you run an insurance company.

Insurance companies don't talk about "profits." They like to talk about "operating income," an amount that includes all the income from insurance premiums plus interest and dividends earned on investments. From this amount the insurance company subtracts all claims that are paid, plus general expenses, taxes, and dividends paid to stockholders. According to this method of determining profits, the property and casualty insurance industry as a whole had an operating profit of $4.5 billion in 1986, a welcome improvement over the operating loss of $5.6 billion the industry suffered in 1985.

But you need to remember that you are dealing with accounting when it comes to determining profits, and what you think is plain and simple is never the case with accounting, and especially with accounting in the insurance business. If insurance companies were to use another method for determining their profits, there would be an entirely different picture of their profitability.

Net income, or that famous bottom line we hear so much about these days, is the final profit or loss figure carried on a company's books and on its report to stockholders. Net income for an insurance company is determined by taking the operating profit after federal taxes and adding realized capital gain. For example, if an insurance company bought stock at $10 per share and the stock is now worth $20 per share, the company has a capital gain of $10 per share. However, this gain is a "realized" gain only when the insurance company sells the stock and actually pockets the profit it makes on the sale of the stock. Until the company sells the stock, the gain is "unrealized" because the company has only the stock and not the money. (Since the value of a stock goes up and down regularly, insurance companies don't count their profits from stocks because they don't know how much profit, if any, they'll make from the stock until they sell it.)

Now, if you add in realized capital gains to get the net income for the property and casualty insurance industry in 1986, you get a profit not of $4.5 billion but $11.5 billion. If you use the net income method for figuring profits, you discover that, instead of losing $5.6 billion in 1985, the property and casualty insurance industry *made* $1.9 billion. See what the doublespeak of accounting can do? It turns profits into losses and losses into profits. The doublespeak of accounting is some of the most powerful and influential (not to mention profitable) doublespeak there is.

The Doublespeak of Depreciation

The Economic Recovery Act of 1982 provided all kinds of tax breaks for companies that invested in certain kinds of new plants and equipment. One goal of the act was to encourage business investment in order to increase productivity and stimulate the economy, which was in a deep recession at that time. Then the accountants got their hands on the act and went to work in their own creative way when they figured the tax bills for their clients.

In 1982 the Internal Revenue Service, that bastion of clarity in language, charged the accounting firm of Ernst & Whinney with intentionally using "false, misleading and deceptive" terms, of engaging in "a word game—a verbal sleight of hand." According to the suit filed by the IRS against the firm in civil court, the following are some of the terms they had used "to improperly qualify property for investment tax credits on portions of new buildings": A fire alarm bell was called a "combustion enunciator," doors were called "movable partitions," a manhole became an "equipment access," windows were "decorative fixtures," a wood-covered wall was a "cedar decoration," and toilet stalls were called "movable partitions-privacy," which was a phrase also used for a continuously locked door. But the accountants at Ernst & Whinney really outdid themselves when a paved road was called a "truck accessway," fifty-foot-high shopping center signs became "identifying devices," an entire refrigerator warehouse was termed a "freezer," and thirty-two tons of gravel and ninety-two cubic yards of topsoil were called a "planter." Wouldn't you really like to see the window—I mean, decorative fixture—on which that planter was hung?

In the court papers Ernst & Whinney filed in answer to the charges by the IRS, the accounting firm said that the vocabulary is used "to put the client's best foot forward," otherwise the IRS may pick a "carelessly chosen word or phrase" as support for "denying the tax-credit claim." Federal Judge Robert H. Hall dismissed the suit, saying that the issue should be resolved on an administrative basis within the IRS, rather than through the courts. Think about that for a minute. The IRS, producer of so many unreadable forms, pamphlets, and regulations, was told to guide an accounting firm in formulating clear language.

Investment Doublespeak

A major purpose of the corporate annual report is to present the company in such an attractive light that you (hereinafter called the "investor") will buy (or "invest in") the company's stock. Annual reports, though, are not enough to get you to buy any company's stock, so investment doublespeak becomes very important.

Investors must always see companies in a positive light, so no matter how bad the news, there's always something positive to be said. After all, if you already own the stock, they don't want you to sell it; and if you're thinking about buying it, they don't want you to decide to put your money someplace else, such as in a savings account. In investment doublespeak executives never "spend" the company's money; they "invest" in plant and equipment, or "expend" what is necessary to maintain market share or a competitive position. While at first there may be "deficit enhancement," corporate officials will have every confidence that ultimately the program they have developed will contribute to a "positive cash flow." You should always be careful when executives of a company claim to be very proud of their "production values" and "unusually high standards of manufacturing," because it usually means that the product is overpriced, losing money, or not selling.

In 1982, the Wall Street firm of Smith Barney Harris Upham and Company issued a report titled, "Economic Investment and Strategy XXI, No. 32," which stated, among other sparkling gems of advice for the investor, that "One of the biggest technical problems now is the current negative-decline breadth divergence." It makes you want to run right out and buy some stock, doesn't it? Indeed, brokerage firms approach gingerly the delicate problem of recommending that investors sell a stock. No broker wants to be accused of starting a run on a stock, and no broker wants to be accused of hyping a stock. No broker wants to be sued for misrepresenting a stock, either. As a result, clients have to learn how to interpret the language brokers use to discuss a stock. If your broker rates a stock as a "weak hold," you should probably sell the stock as fast as you can, unless you enjoy losing money. Or if your broker says a stock "has limited upside potential," you might consider putting your money in something with more promise of profit, like that new gold mine in Florida.

Investment doublespeak is language designed to give the appearance of certainty to matters of almost pure chance. More importantly, investment doublespeak is the language of sales: Someone is trying to sell you something. Trust the doublespeak of investing as much as you trust the language of a person trying to sell you a used car, insurance, or a vacuum cleaner.

In November of 1982, *The Arizona Republic* newspaper quoted the considered opinions of two economists on investment prospects for the coming year. The first offered investors the following explanation:

> In 1983, we can tell you definitely there will be an easing up at the rate at which business has been easing off. Put another way, there will be a slowing up of the slowdown. By way of explanation, the slowing up of the slowdown is not as good as an upturn in the downturn. But it's a good deal better than either speeding up the slowdown or easing the downturn. I might suggest the climate's about right for an adjustment of this readjustment.

You have to wonder how anyone could say that seriously and with a straight face.

The other economist offered this advice:

> The indicators indicate a leveling off, commonly referred to as bumping along rock bottom. This will be followed by a general pickup, then a faster pickup, then a slowdown of the pickup and finally a leveling off again. At any rate, the climate's about right for a pickup sometime in 1983, if we don't have a decline.

If you read the materials put out by investment firms, you will find investment doublespeak filled with such sentences as these: "If positive decisions are forthcoming, the shares could approach double current levels. However, even without such positive news the shares are inexpensive. Little of the major project earning potential is currently factored in the stock price." When you cut through the doublespeak here, you end up with the suggestion that the stock could go up or it could go down, but either way you probably won't lose money. Or, how about this one? "Historical precedent would indicate that the $1 dividend is vulnerable but it is our belief that if earnings per share are $10 then the dividend will be maintained." In other words, the company earns so little that the dividend may be cut, but if earnings go a little higher there won't be any cut in the dividend.

Investment doublespeak is particularly useful when market analysts want to appear to make a definite statement while saying nothing at all, merely stating the obvious, or trying to cover something up. "Silver is in the normal recessionary over-supply situation" simply means that, because of the recession there's more silver available than there are buyers. "Copper could reach the 82 cents level if prices do not close below 72 cents" means, in other words, the price of copper may go up or it may go down. "The downside risk is far less than the upside potential" means the stock could go up or it could go down. "Business has slumped badly but as a result of a highly favorable product-mix operations are still making money." These folks are asking, What are you complaining about? At least we haven't declared bankruptcy. Finally, there's the company that said, "We forecasted short-term weakness and long-term strength. The short-term weakness materialized but the long-term strength hasn't yet." This means that they were wrong.

What these examples show is that the successful investor must be a very good translator of investment doublespeak.

How to Fire Workers Without Firing Them

No one gets fired these days, and no gets laid off. If you're high enough in the corporate pecking order, you "resign for personal reasons." (You're never unemployed; you're just in an "orderly transition between career changes.") Even those far below the lofty heights of corporate power are not fired or laid off. Firing workers is such big business in these day of "restructuring" and "downsizing" that there are companies whose business is helping other companies fire their workers. (Think about that for a minute.) Michael McKee, for example, is president of Corporate Consultants, Inc. Mr. McKee does most of his work in "termination and outplacement consulting" for companies involved in "reduction activities." In other words, he teaches companies how to fire or lay off workers.

How do companies do this? Let us count the ways. Some companies have "workforce adjustments," "headcount reductions," or "negative employee retention." A television station in Philadelphia didn't fire one of the anchorpersons on its evening news program, it was just "rearranging the anchor configuration." In 1985, Peak, Marwick, Mitchell and Company, one of the largest accounting firms, said that a number of partners in the firm had been "asked to take early retirement." In the past, said the firm, about fifteen partners a year were asked to leave, but this year "requested departures" would be increased. At a very large oil company, the vice-president never said "laid off" at the staff meeting; he called it "downsizing our personnel," meaning that five hundred people, or 20 percent of the workforce, would be laid off. The advantage of this "downsizing," he said, was that "We'll have the opportunity to selectively improve operational capacity."

Layoffs are always good for the company and never a sign that the company may be in trouble. When Ramada Inn laid off a large number of workers, a company official said, "Our objective in making these changes is to streamline our organization and to focus our human resources on priority areas of our business." Spokesperson Kurt Van Vlandren of the Sun Oil Company denied the company was laying off five hundred people at its headquarters. "We don't characterize it as a layoff," he said. "We're managing our staff resources. Sometimes you manage them up, and sometimes you manage them down." Congratulations; you've just been managed down, you staff resource, you.

Some companies are not as sophisticated as others in their use of doublespeak when announcing layoffs. Mobil Oil Corporation announced that it had "surplussed [sic] 27 mechanics," while AT&T sent out a notice headed "AT&T Announces Force Management Plan." And what is a "Force Management Plan"? Well, it's a plan where certain divisions are identified as having "surpluses," so a new "force management plan" will be implemented to correct "force imbalances" that now exist. (Are you still with me on this one?) "Surplus managers" will be offered "separation payments" as incentives to leave. If a "surplus" still exists after these incentives, "additional managers will be given a separation payment to leave." How's that for sophisticated doublespeak to announce the firing of a lot of workers?

Sometimes the doublespeak of layoffs is impenetrable, usually because the reality it is masking is particularly upsetting. In 1987 General Motors issued the following statement: "General Motors Corporation today reported a volume-related production schedule adjustment at its Chevrolet-Pontiac-Canada (CPC) Group Framingham (Mass.) assembly plant." This sentence meant that General Motors was closing down an entire automobile assembly factory. Not to be outdone by its rival, Chrysler did not lay off over five thousand workers at the American Motors plant in Kenosha, Wisconsin. Chrysler simply "initiated a career alternative enhancement program."

Companies also use doublespeak when laying off workers because the doublespeak has clear economic benefits. During a strike at Continental Airlines in 1983, Continental denied that it was firing striking workers. Bruce Hicks of Continental said that "strikers haven't been fired." However, Continental did begin hiring "permanent replacements" for striking mechanics who had been warned they would be replaced if they failed to return to their jobs. The LTV Corporation did not lay off six hundred workers at its Aliquippa, Pennsylvania, steel plant in 1985. Instead, LTV called the layoffs an "indefinite idling" rather than a permanent shutdown so that it wouldn't have to pay severance or pension benefits to the workers who were left without jobs. Doublespeak can pay, for the company, but usually not for the workers who are laid off or fired.

The Car We Sold You Is Broken

The automobile recall notice has become a regular feature of American life. Every once in a while you read a small article in the newspaper reporting how an automobile manufacturer is recalling a few million cars because the wheels might fall off, or the gas tank explode, or some other little thing might go wrong. If you've never had to read one of those recall notices, you have missed one of life's really confusing and confounding experiences.

You would think that since the automobile companies have

been recalling cars for so many years now they would know how to write a letter telling you what's wrong with the car and how to get it fixed. But reading a recall letter will convince you that the automobile companies write about as well as they make cars. After all, these are the same companies who write such wonderful sentences as, "Notice to consumer: The equipment described within this Service Guide may or may not be identified as either standard or optional." That's from the *1986 Taurus Sable Do It Yourself Service Guide*. With prose like that you won't be able to do much yourself, but then maybe that's the whole idea.

Sometimes, companies say more than they want to, or intend to. In 1985 the National Highway Traffic Safety Administration announced that it was investigating almost a half-million Ford light trucks because the rear wheels of the trucks could allegedly fall off. Ford promptly responded that the safety of its truck wheels were "equal to that of other manufacturers." Makes you want to run right out and buy a light truck, any light truck, doesn't it?

In 1982, the General Accounting Office recommended that car manufacturers "stop using circumlocutions, euphemisms, and engineering lingo" in notifications of safety defects sent to car buyers. In response to this recommendation, the National Highway Traffic Safety Administration said "it would work with auto makers to improve their writing skills." (Remedial recall-letter-writing courses for car company executives?) The agency said that "controlled experiments should be conducted to determine the effectiveness of various types of notifications." Maybe the General Accounting Office made its recommendation after it got around to reading that letter Ford sent out in 1972 recalling its Torino and Mercury Montego models. (That's the letter discussed in Chapter I.)

Whatever "controlled studies" the National Highway Traffic Safety Administation may have conducted, they sure didn't improve the writing in those recall letters. But then maybe all those car company executives flunked their remedial recall-letter-writing courses because here's a letter the Buick Division of General Motors sent to owners of some of their cars in 1988:

DEAR BUICK OWNER:

This notice is sent to you in accordance with the requirements of the National Traffic and Motor Vehicle Safety Act.

Reason for Recall:

General Motors has determined that some 1988 LeSabres fail to conform to Federal Motor Vehicle Safety Standard No. 209 which covers seat belt assembly usage.

The owner's manual information did not include instructions on the proper usage of the rear seat belt systems.

What We Will Do:

To correct this omission, new Owner's Manuals will be provided for each vehicle involved.

What You Should Do:

Please place the provided new Owner's Manual in your vehicle's 'glove box' and discard the old manual or take it to your dealer for installation at no charge to you.

Instructions for this service have been sent to your Buick dealer. The time to install the new Owner's Manual is approximately five (5) minutes.

Presentation of the provided Owner's Manual and this letter to your dealer will assist him in promptly making the necessary correction if you decide to seek the dealer's assistance.

Your Buick dealer is best equipped to obtain parts and provide service to ensure your vehicle is corrected as promptly as possible. However, if he does not remedy this condition on that date, or within five (5) days, we recommend you contact the Buick Customer Assistance Department. . . .

After contacting your dealer and the Buick Home Office, if you are still not satisfied that we have done our best to remedy this condition without charge within a reasonable time, you may wish to write the Administrator, National Highway Safety Administration. . . .

Now if you read through all that prose a few times you'll discover that what Buick wants you to do is replace the Owner's Manual you have with the new one they're sending you. But if that's too tough for you to do, then you can just go to your Buick dealer and the mechanic there will replace the manual for you.

A spokesperson for Buick explained that the wording of the letter was required by federal regulations: "According to our legal department, there is a certain wording that has to be used for any safety-related item. It is required by federal regulation," he said. A spokesperson for the federal agency agreed. This letter is an example of what can be written when three of the most powerful forces for the creation of doublespeak join together: corporate bureaucrats, government bureaucrats, and lawyers. Together they are an awesome juggernaut of doublespeak. Now all we need is an agency with the power to force the recall of the language in this letter. Better yet would be an agency with the power to force those who created this linguistic monstrosity to write it in clear, simple language, 100 times, right after remedial recall-letter-writing class.

Perhaps the most effective doublespeak in a letter from a car manufacturer is the doublespeak you never see. In 1986, General Motors Corporation acknowledged that it had told its dealers that all 1984 GM cars equipped with a 2.5-litre, four-cylinder engine might "experience engine failure." (I certainly hope it's a meaningful experience.) However, GM had no intention of telling its customers that the cars' engine blocks could crack and lose coolant, resulting in repairs that could cost up to $2,000 per car. While GM acknowledged that company bulletins issued to dealers specifically stated that "there will be no owner notification letters mailed on this special policy," the company insisted that "there's nothing secret about this special policy." In a statement, GM said that

> It's true—we did issue a dealer bulletin shortly after we discovered the engine block leak condition. But there's nothing secret about the policy. It's on file in all appropriate dealerships. Since 1983, information in each

new car's glove box specifically tells customers how they can find these policies [the dealer service bulletins] at their dealers or order them from GM. They certainly aren't secret.

Asked Clarence Ditlow of the Center for Auto Safety, "How can a person ask about a problem they don't know anything about, or even know exists?" Now that's doublespeak.

How to Be Less Than Candid with Doublespeak

When a speculator in the stock market buys up a large block of a company's stock and threatens to take over the company, but is then bought off by the company's board of directors, the term used is "greenmail," which sounds nicer than economic blackmail. Corporate raiders are called "takeover artists," while wheeler-dealers have become "deal makers." Companies "release surplus labor" who then become the "disemployed" or "involuntarily leisured." Some companies earn more money through "aggressive cash management," or crooked deals. And Carl Hahn, chairman of the Volkswagen Corporation, did not admit in 1983 that the company's plant in Pennsylvania was running at a loss, but he did say that "Profits on imports partly compensate for the current burden on the manufacturing side." Volkswagen later closed the plant because it was losing too much money.

In 1985 the First National Bank of Boston was charged with a failure to report $1.22 billion in 1,163 cash transfers with foreign banks, transfers that were suspected of being used to launder money made through illegal activities. The bank pleaded guilty to a felony charge of "knowingly and willfully" failing to report the cash transfers and paid a $500,000 fine, but said that its failure was merely a "systems failure," an "internal administrative glitch." Doesn't that give you confidence in the bank? After all, $1.22 billion is so easy to let slip through your fingers.

The Crocker National Bank of San Francisco had a similar problem in 1985 when it agreed to pay a record $2.25 million penalty to the federal government for failing to report almost $4 billion in large cash transactions between 1980 and 1985. Harold P. Reichwald, executive vice-president and general counsel for Crocker, said it wasn't a fine but a "settlement." John M. Walker, chief enforcement officer for the Treasury Department, said that, "although there is no evidence that the bank itself deliberately engaged in money laundering, Crocker's reporting failures were systemic and pervasive." If the bank didn't engage in money laundering, who did? After all, the investigation revealed that Crocker had violated the Bank Secrecy Act 7,877 times. That's a lot of reporting failures.

Using doublespeak, bad news can be magically transformed into good news. When Mattel, the toy company, reported lower earnings in 1986 than in 1987, it saw the reduction in earnings not as bad news but good news: "The moderation in sales growth in the third quarter from the first half of the year is a measure of our success at increasing year-round demand for toys and providing greater balance to our production and shipping schedules." More good news like that and the company can file for bankruptcy.

When Herbalife International agreed in 1986 to pay $850,000 to settle charges by authorities that it made false claims in promoting its nutritional and weight-loss products and agreed to change some of the claims it was making, President Mark Hughes wasn't flustered a bit. He issued this press release:

Today represents a milestone for Herbalife—a solid foundation that is built on the confidence given to us today by statements issued by state and federal regulatory agencies. I am pleased to announce that, after more than a year and a half of discussions and negotiations with the Food and Drug Administration, the California State Attorney General and the California Department of Health, all three agencies have independently determined that Herbalife products have been and still are safe for the American public. Furthermore, all of our product claims, labeling and

marketing materials are now in conformance with the
spirit and the letter of both federal and state law.

A few more such encounters with federal and state authorities,
and Herbalife will be ready for sainthood, if you believe this
press release.

Graphic Scanning Corporation issued a press release which
stated that, "To further enhance its inherent value Graphic Scanning Corp. has undertaken a series of transactions which consolidate its radio paging business around core markets, thereby
increasing the market strength and cash flow of this business
segment." Are you impressed? You won't be when you get to page
three of this doublespeak and discover that Graphic Scanning
Corp. had a $49.9 million net loss in 1986.

The Coca-Cola Company used lots of doublespeak trying to
explain its disastrous attempt to replace the old Coca-Cola with
a new-formula Coke. The company described the public's over-
whelming rejection of the new Coke by saying that consumers
"demonstrated unexpectedly strong loyalty" to the old brand of
Coke. In the process of correcting its mistake, the company reissued the old Coke under a new name, Coca-Cola Classic, and
declared that New Coke was no longer a "flagship brand" but was
instead a "fighting brand" within a "megabrand," possessing attributes that are a "strategic plank" in Coke's total marketing
scheme. That prose is almost as thick as Coke syrup.

In December of 1985, the General Electric Company sent a
letter with this heading: "Important Message to Users of GE
Multi-Vapor and Mercury Lamps." The message, over a page and
a half long of small type, included the following:

There exists the possibility with any of these lamp types,
regardless of wattage, that the arc tube may
unexpectedly rupture due to internal causes or external
factors, such as a systems failure or misapplication.
When this occurs, the glass outer jacket surrounding the
arc tube could break and particles of extremely hot
quartz from the arc tubes and glass fragments from the

outer jacket will be discharged into the fixture enclosure and/or the surrounding environment thereby creating a risk of personal injury or fire. Users must recognize that metal halide lamps and mercury lamps are not risk-free. Few products found in industry today could claim to be totally risk-free. This does not mean, however, that such products should be considered "unsafe."

These are some of the clearer sentences in the letter.

The Cost of Doublespeak

Doublespeak can cost a company money, sometimes a whole lot of money. In 1981 the Sixth U.S. Circuit Court of Appeals ruled that a loan agreement violated the Truth in Lending Act because of "indecipherable" language, especially this sentence: "A deferment charge may be made for deferred payments equal to the portion of the regular finance charge applicable by the sum of the digits method to the installment period immediately following the due date of the first deferred installment times the number of months deferred."

Sometimes a company may try to use doublespeak to avoid paying money but get caught. The A. H. Robins Company, which had devised the Dalkon Shield intrauterine contraceptive device, was told to simplify the notice it used to tell women about the time limit for filing claims against the company. U.S. District Judge Robert Merhige found that the notice was appropriate for lawyers but not for women whose native language is English. The following is an excerpt from the notice:

Any claims filed after December 30, 1985, shall be disallowed. Any person or entity that is required to file a proof of claim and that fails to do so by December 30, 1985, shall not be treated as a creditor for purposes of voting or distribution, and any claim of such person or entity shall be forever barred; provided, however, that a proof of claim for any claim against A. H. Robins

Company, Incorporated arising out of the rejection by
A. H. Robins Company, Incorporated of a voidable
transfer, as described in Bankruptcy Code Section 502(g)
and 502(h), must be filed on or before December 30,
1985 and 30 days after the entry of an order authorizing
the rejection of the executory contract or unexpired
lease, or 30 days after the entry of an order or judgment
avoiding the transfer.

Sometimes doublespeak can cost not just a lot of money but
things more important than money. In 1979 a memorandum
written by D. F. Hallman, a manager for Babcock & Wilcox
Company's Generation Group, was sent to staff members at the
Three Mile Island nuclear power plant. The memorandum was
supposed to alert the staff to the possibility of a malfunction at
the plant but was so confusingly written that it failed. The memo
suggested "a change in B&W's philosophy for HPI system use
during low-pressure transients. Basically, they recommend leaving the HPI pumps on, once HPI has been initiated, until it can
be determined that the hot leg temperature is more than 50°F
below T_{sat} for the RCS pressure. Nuclear Service believes this
mode can cause the RCS (including the pressurizer) to go solid."
Guess what went "solid"? This piece of prose is worth about $3
billion in expenses to clean up Three Mile Island. While doublespeak may make money for some people, it can also cost other
people a lot of money, if not their lives.

CHAPTER V

Protein Spills, Vehicle Appearance Specialists, and Earth Engaging Equipment: Doublespeak Around the World

You have to wonder sometimes how it is that government officials in so many different countries sound the same. When faced with the problem of explaining a tax increase, politicians around the world shift into doublespeak. Here's a statement from a government report explaining a recent 6.5-percent tax increase. Can you guess what country it's from?

Local Government is currently operating in a climate of expectation to constrain expenditure, increase productivity and improve the level of service to the community. At the same time it must face constraints from the State Government including rate pegging and load borrowing which is being reduced or terminated or not keeping pace with inflation. . . . These constraints however must not be seen by Council as a problem which cannot be solved but as an opportunity to become more efficient and effective in managing its resources and delivering its services. Improvement to Council's management systems and organisation structure have been implemented to take up this challenge together with a number of entrepreneurial initiatives to supplement traditional income sources.

This passage is from the Willoughby, Australia, Municipal Council's annual report, yet it sounds just like a justification for budget cutting and reduced public services given by politicians in the United States, or any number of other countries for that matter.

Doublespeak is not unique to the United States. Just as Greece in the time of Thucydides and Rome in the time of Caesar had doublespeak, so other countries in the world have their doublespeak today. Given the speed and coverage of modern communications, the doublespeak uttered in Moscow, London, Pretoria, or Washington, D.C. is quickly sent around the world. Because English is spoken by so many people (estimates run from 750 million to 1 billion people, with about half speaking English as a mother tongue), English doublespeak, or doublespeak translated into English from another language, can spread and have a significant influence well beyond the borders of the United States.

Some foreign doublespeak, like some of the doublespeak in the United States, is rather transparent and even amusing. Officials at Expo 86 in Vancouver, Canada, said that some of the amusement rides at the park were so exciting that they had planned for the "occasional protein spill." The park also had "security hosts" and "guest relations facilities," or guards and public lavatories. According to Ralph McKay Ltd. of Melbourne, Australia, its subsidiary, the Empire Plow Company of Cleveland, Ohio, does not make plows but "earth engaging equipment." But then in Australia the government called a tax increase "widening the revenue base." Even the Vatican gets into the act by naming its bank "Instituto per le Opere di Religione," or the Institute for Religious Works.

China and Russia don't have prostitutes. The Russian government has for years maintained that prostitution had been wiped out, so there are no legal regulations against it. While not admitting that there might be prostitution, government officials have acknowledged that there are "priestesses of love," "night stalkers," "ladies of easy virtue," and "ladies who take tips" walking the streets of Moscow and other cities. In China, the doublespeak for prostitutes is "the girls who sell their smiles."

But some foreign doublespeak, while still transparent, is more serious. Dr. Chu Cheng Gil of North Korea staunchly maintained that there were no prisons in his country because there was no crime. However, he did admit that there were some "labor reform camps for ideological re-education." According to Erich Honecker of East Germany, the Berlin Wall is not a wall but an "anti-fascist protective rampart." Meanwhile, the official name for West Germany's domestic counterintelligence agency is the "Office for the Protection of the Constitution." In the Philippines you don't pay ransom to kidnappers, you make a "contribution to cover abduction expenses." Turkey called its 1974 invasion of Cyprus a "peace operation." And after Soviet troops crushed the 1956 Hungarian rebellion, Beijing radio observed that from the invasion of Russian troops, "The Hungarian people can see that Soviet policy toward the people's democracies is truly one of equality, friendship and mutual assistance, not of conquest, aggression, and plunder."

Often the doublespeak used by foreign governments is very serious. Usually, the only information you get about other countries comes from radio and television news programs and from newspapers. Since the news media are concerned with other countries only when something exciting or unusual is happening—like a war, a riot, a revolution, a political crisis, a nuclear accident, or a natural disaster like a flood or an earthquake—the doublespeak you get from other countries usually concerns something serious, something that is often a matter of life and death. Often you get nothing but doublespeak from other countries, because their governments want to mislead public opinion in other countries, or cover up what's really going on in their countries. If you want to understand what's really going on in the world, you have to cut through the doublespeak.

Canadian Doublespeak

Maybe it's because Canada is so close to the United States that we hear a lot of Canadian doublespeak. Or maybe the Canadian government and Canadian business seem to produce as much doublespeak as their counterparts in the United States because they hear so much doublespeak being pumped out in the United States. Whatever the reason, Canada produces more than its share of doublespeak. And just as in the United States, government in Canada produces a lot of doublespeak.

In 1985 the Canadian government spent $8,500 for a public opinion survey to find a catchy name for its employment and job training program, which was once known as "labor market strategy." The new name, which "incorporates all of the highly favored words" that turned up in the survey, is "Canadian Jobs Strategy: Working Opportunities for People." Not to be outdone, a memorandum issued to auditors in the Sudbury, Ontario district office of the Revenue Department explains that production quotas are not quotas when they're "materiality of adjustments in relation to assigned workloads." On the local level of government, a Charlottetown alderman referred to vagrant alcoholics on the city streets as "chemically unfortunates."

Canadian government officials work up to their doublespeak, starting with relatively small matters so they're in shape for the doublespeak needed to discuss really important issues. In 1984, Fred Doucet, senior adviser to Brian Mulroney, prime minister of Canada, said that Elizabeth MacDonald, who was one of eleven household staff members at the prime minister's residence, was not a nanny to the three Mulroney children. She was only one of the staff who "interface with the children in a habitual way," said Mr. Doucet. After that doublespeak, the government was ready to move on to big-time issues like the trade agreement between Canada and the United States. Because a large number of people opposed the agreement, the Canadian government avoided the politically charged phrase "free trade" by first using the phrase "trade enhancement," then "security of access," then "freer trade," and finally ending with the statement that the purpose of the agreement was a "phased but virtually total removal of tariff and non-tariff barriers."

Such language is in keeping with the inherent urge of government to use language to cover up what it's really doing. Stephen Rogers, environment minister of British Columbia, announced the government's new strategy for disposing of "special wastes," which sounds so much better than hazardous wastes. The Canadian Ministry of Natural Resources proposed the "multiple use integrated resource management" of Ontario's forests, meaning campers could use the forests right along with the logging and mining companies. The same ministry also issues a "tree farm license," which is a permit to "harvest" trees on government land, and not just one or two trees but whole forests, or "overmature timber."

Rising to the challenge, the minister of labor for New Brunswick explained that his youth employment strategy will "provide assessment, counseling and employment for young people who are having difficulty achieving labor force attachment."

Jobs for Those Seeking Labor Force Attachment

Maybe when they seek labor force attachment some of the young people without labor force attachment might want to apply for the position of "Director, Indigenous Participation Programs," as advertised by the Public Service Commission. It seems the job requires "a top-notch executive" who can "guide government departments and agencies in introducing positive measures that will result in meaningful career development for indigenous people." The job also requires a person who "will encourage a climate conducive to employing relations between the government and indigenous organizations . . ." and who will obtain "data for ensuring sound decisions for . . . indigenous participation programs." At least they didn't ask for interfacing or interpersonal skills.

Well, if those seeking labor force attachment aren't qualified for that job, how about the job of "Senior Project Officer"? The duties are really quite simple, according to the description in the official announcement:

Leads project teams to implement Branch Plans;
co-ordinates selected horizontal administrative activities
and acts as a functional co-ordinator for cross sectoral
development initiatives; assists in Branch policy
formulation in response to horizontal issues impacting
on sector industries; identifies strategic issues impacting
on the sector development process and then formulates
and recommends strategies and initiatives to address
these issues; develops, delivers, administers and
monitors projects under Branch programs to foster
development of the sector; participates in investment,
marketing, trade missions, fairs and promotional
activities to encourage sector investment and trade
development.

If you can figure out what you're supposed to do in this job,
you're hired.

Since all those young people seeking labor force attachment
might not be qualified for that position (who is?), they could
always apply to the Greater Vancouver Regional District in British Columbia for the distinguished position of "Building Maintenance Coordinator," a position that requires that the successful
candidate "successfully liaises with the Building Services Supervisor to facilitate the forward planning of building maintenance
programs for the Recreation facilities." Maybe we need to concentrate on developing better liaising skills in those seeking
labor force attachment.

Those young people seeking labor attachment may not want
to be janitors, no matter what the people in Vancouver call the
job. Well, there's always the exciting and challenging position of
"Co-ordinator, Occurence [sic] Screening, Quality Assurance Department" at the Winnipeg Health Sciences Center. So, what
does an "Occurence Screener" do?

Occurence screening is an objective, criteria-based
review of medical records conducted concurrently and
retrospectively to identify and flag, confirm, analyze,
trend and report instances of suboptimal care

attributable to health care disciplines. Under the general direction of the Director, Quality Assurance, the incumbent will co-ordinate the development, implementation and maintenance of multidisciplinary and integrated systems of occurence screening; will assess and review adverse patient occurence data; will assist with the identification of existing and/or new resources required to conduct occurence screening.

Enter the exciting world of occurrence screening, where you get to report "adverse patient occurence data" attributable to "suboptimal care" caused by the "health care disciplines." And you get to learn a whole new language which carefully avoids unpleasant facts and disturbing reality.

Mel Couvelier, Prince of Doublespeak

When faced with tough questions, Canadian politicians prove that they can use doublespeak just as effectively as anyone to avoid answering simple questions. When Mel Couvelier, the minister of finance for the Province of British Columbia, was asked if the property purchase tax would be paid on the sale of the Expo 86 land, or whether the tax had been waived, he replied, "The negotiations went through many combinations and permutations, so that I'm happy to advise the member that to the best of my knowledge, tax will be paid. I will be happy to confirm that upon passage of a little more time. Let me study the documents."

That wasn't too bad, but Mr. Couvelier was only warming up. When he was asked what the sale price was on which the tax would be computed, Mr. Couvelier responded,

> Therein lies my hesitation, Mr. Speaker. In any event, to the best of my memory there were no particular arrangements provided in that respect. I think the honorable member, by virtue of his previous life, of all the individuals in this house, would be most aware of the fact that those lands had a very heavy cost associated

with them in order to reclaim them so that they were usable. This honorable member who asked the question would, by virtue of his peculiar knowledge, appreciate the enormity of that necessary reclamation. Therefore the issue of the pricing, of the terms, of necessity had to recognize those unusual aspects of the sale. To a large extent, much of this information has come to light during a relatively recent few years, and the member who asked the question would be one of the best able to understand the complexities of the issue I have described.

When he responded to other questions with this same kind of doublespeak, Mr. Couvelier was pressed to explain his answers. He replied, "The honorable member seems to have some difficulty following the perfectly lucid answers I've been providing on this question."

After reading this exchange, you have to wonder if double-speak is an infectious disease spreading across borders, whether politicians all over the world take lessons in doublespeak, or whether doublespeak is just the natural language of politicians in every country.

He Wasn't Dead, Just Non-Viable

Canadian doublespeak, like the Saskatchewan River, just keeps rolling along. The British Columbia Health Ministry replaced the term "sex change operation" with "sexual reassignment surgery," while Bill Kissan, the medical services coordinator for the Strathcona, Alberta Fire Department said that emergency personnel found the victim "in a non-viable condition—he had no pulse and was not breathing." That's about as non-viable as you can get. An official at the British Columbia Ministry of Education did not call them teachers; he called them "on-site facilitators of pupil learning," thus earning the gratitude of teachers all over Canada, especially English teachers, who had mistakenly believed for years that they were teachers. But, then, in some Canadian schools students who are kicked out of all their classes because of "anti-social behavior" are called "students who are difficult to serve."

Some Canadians know that doublespeak allows them to make things look a whole lot better. Roger Taylor, mayor of Elliot Lake, said that his community had no objections to a permanent dump for low-level radioactive wastes being located close to the town, since it's not a dump. It's a "containment initiative." *The Toronto Sun* calls the people who sell advertising space in the newspaper "Ad Counsellors," while the ABN Bank in Vancouver does not have loan officers but "Relationship Managers." Those folks at Espirit Auto Detailing in Vancouver are your "vehicle appearance specialists" and would never call their business a carwash. Federal Health Minister Jake Epp said that "a small ratio of mice in fact died" after they were injected with an extract from contaminated mussels. Six mice were injected and all six died. But then six is a small number, even if it is 100 percent. And Steve Strunk, who won a Mr. Universe amateur division title in 1987, called anabolic steroids "a pharmaceutical training aid."

Improving Mail Service by Reducing It

When Canada Post decided to save some money by doing such things as closing post offices in small towns and reducing the number of mailboxes in cities, officials just naturally turned to doublespeak. They announced plans to "streamline and enhance" mail collection in Vancouver and ran a newspaper ad announcing "more places to . . . post your mail" in reference to the removal of about one-fifth of the city's mailboxes and reductions in the number of collections per day from the remaining boxes. "We are not closing post offices—we are replacing them with something better . . ." said Gilles Herbert, Canada Post's director of rural services, in announcing plans to close or replace over five thousand rural post offices with stamp counters or substations. In addition, Canada Post improved mail service in cities by requiring that the people who move into new homes use remote lockboxes, called "super mailboxes," in place of home mail delivery. More improvements like these and Canadians will have a mail service that functions as smoothly as the U.S. Post Office functions for Americans.

Even England

Ah, England. Birthplace of Chaucer, Shakespeare, Milton, Keats, and Dickens. But having a tradition of great writers hasn't made the British immune to doublespeak. The United States has its "Internal Revenue Service," and England has its "Internal Revenue Department," and both avoid the dreaded term "tax collector." Readers of *The London Times* have reported such doublespeak in fair England as a dump being called a "Public Waste Reception Centre"; a gymnasium, a "human resource laboratory"; a janitor, an "environmental hygienist"; a plumber, an "environmental physicist"; and tracing paper, "simulator transparent." The London Zoo now has a "behavioral enrichment research fellow" whose job it is to cure the animals' boredom. While others might think a simple "Park at Your Own Risk" sign might be sufficient, officials of the British Museum in London obviously didn't think so. The sign in the parking lot of the museum states, "No responsibility is accepted for the safety of persons using or entering this car park or for their cars or other property and such persons are permitted to enter and use it only on the understanding that they do so at their own risk."

According to the person being interviewed on the BBC, people aren't worried about unemployment in England. "It's more a case of being concerned about the future." A memorandum sent to the staff at the BBC announced that the switchboard was to be closed on Saturday evenings "because of the very high non-utilization factor." When seventeen bakers staged a sit-in at a bakery, company officials used guard dogs to eject the protesters. The managing director of the company denied that the dogs were used to frighten the men into leaving, saying that "Five Alsatian dogs from a private security firm were brought in to impress on the men the seriousness of the situation, and in this they were most successful."

The Post Office in England has a way with words. A resident of Exeter wrote to the Post Office complaining of the delays in his correspondence with a town very close to Exeter. He enclosed one of his envelopes with his complaint. After several weeks he received this reply from the head postmaster: "After a thorough investigation, we are able to establish that the late arrival of your mail was due to delay in transit." When the pension fund for postal workers was found to be missing a large amount of money, the Post Office explained the discrepancy quite easily: "It was also pointed out that £725 million is not 'missing.' It is an actuarial deficiency representing a prospective excess of liabilities over assets which would have to be found to meet future pension obligations."

Each year the National Consumer Council and the Plain English Campaign in England give the Golden Bull Award for the best examples of doublespeak. In 1983, a government agency in Newark won for a letter that told welfare housing tenants: "Within the housing benefit granted to you there has been an amount of 'transitional addition,' this was granted to compensate for taper changes and higher non dependent charges." In 1988, the Department of Health and Social Security won an award for explaining to a widow, who had inquired about her pension, that a

> basic retirement pension based wholly or partially upon
> the contributions of her late husband cannot be paid in
> full to a widow who is getting such a benefit. She can
> only be paid the balance of basic retirement pension and
> increase for putting off retirement which is left after
> taking off her war widow's pension or, the part of the
> basic retirement pension which is based purely on her
> own contributions, plus any increase for putting off her
> retirement, whichever is the more favorable.

Such prose proves once again that doublespeak respects no geographical boundaries, including oceans.

British corporations use doublespeak much like their counterparts in other countries. At the Rolls Royce factory in Crewe, England, visitors are told that "our cars don't break down. They just fail to proceed." A stock prospectus issued by the British Gas Company told buyers that they "agree that without prejudice to any other rights to which you may be entitled, you will not be entitled to exercise any remedy of rescission for innocent misrepresentation at any time after acceptance of your application." Then there was the letter that Spooner Snacks, Ltd. sent to a customer who complained that the package of their potato chips she bought contained purple chips. Said the good people of Spooner's: "Potato varieties with pigmented skins owe their color to anthrocyanins dissolved in the cell sap of the periderm and cells of the peripheral cortex," thus solving the mystery of the purple potato chips.

George Orwell's lesson of increasing the chocolate ration by reducing it was not lost on some in the British business community. In a letter to customers, R. A. McLeod, manager of the John Lewis Bristol Branch of Lloyds Bank, said that "in order to improve service to customers in a highly competitive marketplace some change is necessary and desirable." Mr. McLeod goes on to say that "branch alterations will be made not only to improve our already good service but present a better environment for our customers in which to transact their business." Just what is included in the alterations that will make all these unspecified improvements? Why he's going to reduce the number of hours the bank is open, of course. Whoever said the British had lost their way with words.

During the 1982 Falklands-Malvinas War between Argentina and Britain, the British government and press demonstrated how efficient they were in using doublespeak to lessen the horrors of war while at the same time portraying British forces as the heroes and Argentine forces as the villains. The Union Jack was the "Flag of Freedom," British soldiers were "our brave boys," and British commandos were "our tough guys." British casualties were the "price of victory." British airplanes were "lost" or "shot down," while Argentine airplanes were "blown out of the sky." Britain's "brave planes" carried out bombing raids or strafed enemy ships, while Argentine planes carried out "desperate suicide missions" or "merciless air onslaughts." Argentine warships were "blasted to smithereens," while British ships were "lost" or "sunk." One British ship that was sunk was called a "brave little frigate." Orwell understood well the doublespeak of war, a tradition of language that prospers in England.

Some Russian Doublespeak

In 1982, when the United States government ordered an embargo on equipment that could be used in the construction of a natural-gas pipeline in Russia, the Russian government announced that the embargo would not disrupt construction of the pipeline. Soviet officials said that Soviet workers have "accepted new socialist obligations" in order to meet production targets. In other words, workers on the pipeline had to work overtime. In 1983, the official Soviet government statement on the downing of Korean Airlines flight 007 said that "the interceptor fighter plane of the anti-aircraft defenses fulfilled the order of the command post to stop the flight." He sure stopped it, didn't he? Such doublespeak is certainly not new in Russia. But as Russia opens up a little and lets the world in, and as Gorbachev practices the newly discovered art of public relations, you are going to hear a lot more Russian doublespeak. After all, Russia has to keep up with the rest of the world.

Oleg Peresypkin, the Russian ambassador to Libya, speaking of the accident at the Chernobyl nuclear power plant, said, "We can say that this is a normal incident, and there is nothing abnormal. There is bound to be a technical incident" in any factory or power plant. Now you know why he's ambassador to Libya; they wanted to keep this guy as far as possible from a nuclear power plant in the Soviet Union. But the Soviet Council of Ministers' official statement on the accident wasn't much better. In line with their counterparts in the nuclear power business around the world, the ministers' statement was designed to soothe and cover up. The statement said that the Chernobyl accident resulted in "a certain leak of radioactive substances." The statement went on to say that "priority measures have been taken to deal with the effects of the accident. The radiation situation ... has now been stabilized...." See, it wasn't so bad, and besides, they've got everything under control.

In the official report on the accident, Soviet officials described the massive explosion of the reactor core as "rapid fuel relocation." It sure did relocate—all over Eastern and Western Europe, and ultimately all over the world. Some time later, when the director of a nuclear power plant in Sweden needed to refer to the source of the radiation released by the Chernobyl accident, he said, "East of here, and east of Finland, if you know what I mean."

When Russian publishers produced a special Russian edition of the *Oxford Student's Dictionary of Current English,* they changed the definitions of several political words in the Russian edition. Among the words redefined were "communism," "imperialism," "Marxism," "fascism," "Bolshevism," "internationalism," "socialism," and "capitalism." For example, the Russian edition defines capitalism as "an economic and social system based on private ownership of the means of production operated for private profit, and on the exploitation of man by man, replacing feudalism and preceding communism." The Russian edition also defines socialism as "a social and economic system which is replacing capitalism." By comparison, the *Shorter Oxford Dictionary* gives the following definitions: "Capitalism: the condition of possessing capital or using it for production; a system of society based on this; dominance of private capital." "Socialism: a theory or policy of social organization which advocates the ownership and control of the means of production, capital, land, property, etc. by the community as a whole, and their administration or distribution in the interests of all." So much for looking up a word in the dictionary to find out what it really means.

Doublespeak Is Not New in Japan

During World War II, it was the policy of Japanese forces never to retreat. But as the war turned against the Japanese, their troops simply had to retreat. However, retreats were never called retreats. In 1944, one Japanese commander, faced with over-whelming odds, issued the following order to his troops: "A decisive battle is the only battle known to a Japanese soldier, or fitting to the Japanese spirit, but now other methods may have to be adopted." Those other methods employed by this commander included a retreat. When the emperor of Japan announced his country's surrender in 1945, he said that "the war situation has developed not necessarily to Japan's advantage." Given this history of doublespeak, and with their famous ability to work hard and develop the product, maybe the Japanese will corner the world market in doublespeak, just like they have in so many other areas.

The Japanese are quite familiar with doublespeak, and some Japanese, especially politicians, are quite good at using it. But like many people in the United States, the average people in Japan just don't know what some of the doublespeak used by their politicians means.

So much doublespeak is used in Japanese politics and so little of it is understood by the Japanese people that Kazuhisa Inoue, a member of the Japanese Diet, or Parliament, has asked the Japanese government to form a committee of linguists and other scholars to study ways to eliminate misleading language from parliamentary debate. Mr. Inoue has compiled a list of fifty-one expressions that are used regularly by Japanese politicians but that ordinary Japanese cannot understand. Moreover, Mr. Inoue is concerned that such phrases are used by Japanese officials in their dealings with foreign governments and can lead to serious international misunderstandings.

When a Japanese Cabinet minister says, "Eii doryoku shimasu," which means, "We shall make efforts," other politicians, including members of the Diet, know that he really means that he will do nothing. Or when a minister says he will accomplish something "kakyuteki sumiyaka" or "with the greatest expedition possible," he really means that he will go as slowly as possible. Then there are the bureaucrats who say they will take "shoyo no gutaitkei sochi" or "necessary concrete measures." Of course, that concrete isn't even mixed and certainly is never poured. And when a Japanese businessman says, "Kangai saesete kudasai" or "Let me think about it," he means no.

In 1969, Prime Minister Eisaku Sato visited the United States to assuage American anger over the flood of textile imports from Japan. During a meeting with Prime Minister Sato, President Nixon urged that the Japanese exercise restraint in their exports, to which Mr. Sato replied, "Zensho shimasu," which the translator dutifully rendered literally as, "I will do my best." What Mr. Sato meant, of course, was, "Not a chance." President Nixon, however, thought that Mr. Sato had agreed to limit Japanese textile exports to the United States. When Japan did not limit its textile exports, President Nixon was reportedly angry enough to call Mr. Sato a liar.

Given this background, how much of a chance does Mr. Inoue have for success with his campaign to eliminate such language? Well, Keizo Obuchi, the chief cabinet secretary and government spokesman, avoided comment on Mr. Inoue's proposal. But that's a good sign, because if Mr. Obuchi had said that it was difficult, he would really have been saying, "Forget it." As long as politicians in any country can use doublespeak and get away with it, they will; and Japanese politicians are no different from politicians in other countries.

Doublespeak and Japanese History

Just as Japanese politicians are not reluctant to use doublespeak, neither is the Japanese Education Ministry. In 1982, the ministry directed textbook publishers to "update" the accounts of Japan's invasion of China in 1931. In the new textbooks the Japanese invasion of China became the Japanese "advance." Accounts of the slaughter of an estimated 300,000 Chinese men, women, and children and the raping, looting, and arson by Japanese troops during the 1937 capture of Nanjing were deleted from all textbooks. The annexation of Korea in 1910 became an "advance" of Japanese forces, and the establishment of a "supervisory government," while the 1919 uprising of Koreans against the Japanese occupation forces became a "riot." Outlawing the Korean language became "education in the Japanese language" in the "updated" Japanese textbooks, while Korean civilians who were forced into work gangs for the Japanese forces were called "voluntary laborers." The last Korean king simply "resigned." The "updated" textbooks made no mention of the thousands of young Korean girls who were forcibly packed off to the front lines to serve as "wartime ladies of consolation" for Japanese troops.

When this official revision of history became known, Korean and Chinese officials protested. After much discussion, the Japanese announced some revisions in their revisions of history. The revised textbooks now refer to the "so-called Nanjing massacre," which was an episode of "mad confusion" during which innumerable soldiers and civilians were killed. Maybe when they were writing their "updated" accounts of these events, Japanese historians were thinking of the U.S. "incursion" of Cambodia and the U.S. "rescue mission" in Grenada.

South Africa and the Doublespeak of Apartheid

Among the governments in the world using doublespeak, the government of South Africa stands out. Indeed, it often seems that doublespeak is the only language known or used by the South African government, which uses doublespeak not only to justify its policy of apartheid but also to rationalize the elimination of freedom of speech, press, and assembly. After all, this is the country where the South African Broadcasting System announced in 1974, "It's not true that we have banned the Beatles. It's just that we don't play their records."

The doublespeak of South Africa begins with the national motto of the country, which is "Unity is Strength," and carries right on to the "Ministry of Cooperation and Development," which is the government agency responsible for apartheid. (Previous names for this ministry include "Department of Native Affairs," "Department of Non-European Affairs," "Department of Plural Relations," and "Department of Bantu Administration and Development.") But there is no apartheid in South Africa, just "self-determination," in the official language of the government. According to the government, the term "white minority regime" is incorrect since it implies a black majority, but there is no black majority, just many "black minorities."

Then there's Louis Nel, Deputy Minister for Information (a title which itself is a nice bit of doublespeak), who said to reporters in 1986, "To me, censorship means that every report must be approved before it can be published. We do not have censorship. What we have is a limitation on what newspapers can report." Mr. Nel would be right at home in Oceania.

In South African doublespeak, it was only a "scuffle" when police stormed into the Graaf Reinet Methodist Church in the eastern Cape during a commemorative service and killed two blacks. And it was only "isolated incidents" during which fifty-four blacks died over eight days.

How does Mr. Nel's lack of censorship affect the South African press? During an official briefing for the press, officials said the press conference wasn't going to be used "as a legal platform for information. . . . And you cannot report on your own questions." *The Star* and the *Weekly Mail,* two newspapers in South Africa, ran blank spaces where forbidden quotes or commentary would have appeared. South African authorities later advised newspapers that the blank spaces might be "subversive."

However, a few months later the South African government gave up all pretense at no censorship and announced that, for the sake of freedom of the press, there would be no freedom of the press. Stoffel van der Merwe, Deputy Information Minister, said that "The whole strategy of the revolution [is] to use the freedoms of democracy to destroy democracy; therefore, the revolutionary forces have to be denied the use of democratic facilities." Dave Steward, head of Pretoria's Bureau for Information, agreeing with Mr. van der Merwe, said that "the state has a right, and in fact a duty, to make sure that the opposition, the radicals, cannot use the media to bring about a situation where the freedom of the media would ultimately be destroyed." You cannot be free unless you give up your freedom. So much for freedom of the press in South Africa.

Doublespeak has allowed the South African government to announce changes in its policy of apartheid when in fact nothing has changed. In 1986 the government officially declared an end to forced removals of black townships. Indeed, the government calls them "locations" or "communities," not "townships." However, when the government now wants to move a black township farther away from a white neighborhood, all it has to do is "deproclaim" or "disestablish" the black neighborhood, meaning the town ceases to exist. Once the township ceases to exist, the government just starts a new township farther away and the blacks must move to it.

With doublespeak, the more things change the more they stay the same, or get worse. The "Extension of Universities Act" is the law that closed the established universities to blacks, "coloreds," and "Indians." The "Abolition of Passes Act" actually extended the pass system among blacks. The "Group Areas Act" allocates land to different racial groups and thus separates living areas.

The word "group" is doublespeak for racial group, which avoids the overt reference to the apartheid basis of the grouping. Thus, Gerrit Viljoen, Minister of Cooperation and Development, can say in 1986 that "Without group security and group protection we cannot bring about acceptable reform."

In 1985, President P. W. Botha proposed a plan designed to replace apartheid with "cooperative coexistence." The plan called for a "multiplicity of units" that would be recognized on a "geographical and group basis" and called for "power sharing." Once the doublespeak of the proposal had been translated, the intent of the plan became clear. President Botha was offering to the black majority a complex form of government that would not impinge on white power and economic privilege.

President Botha went ahead with his plan, and in 1986 the government declared that apartheid was dead. However, it continues to enforce the Population Registration Act of 1950, which requires that all newborn babies be registered according to their race: white, black, or colored. Con Botha, information director of the ruling National Party, said in 1987 that the Act "is part and parcel of the necessity to identify groups. It is an essential element in our whole philosophical approach to the racial mix in this country."

Meanwhile, the pass laws, which restrict the rights of blacks to move to townships set aside for them in urban areas, are officially known as "influx control measures." When discussing whether to restore citizenship to millions of blacks who lost it when the South African government created "tribal homelands," Mr. Chris Heunis, Minister of Constitutional Planning and Development, said that the restoration of citizenship to blacks "does not however mean they will exercise political rights in South Africa." And the doublespeak of apartheid continues in South Africa.

Doublespeak in the Middle East

Words are very important in discussing the continuing "conflict" (some call it "war") between Israel and Palestinian "demonstrators" (whom some call "rioters") in the "occupied" (or "administered") territories. The "unrest" in the Arab territories is called "revolution," "upheaval," "disturbances," "demonstrations," or "rioting," depending on who's doing the reporting. In Israeli government press releases, young Arabs are called "youths," while young Israelis are called "children"; Israelis are "murdered," while Palestinians are "killed." Palestinians always call those Palestinians who are killed "martyrs." The Palestinian press refers to the "1967 War," while the Israeli press refers to the "Six-Day War." "We don't like to emphasize how badly we lost," explained an Arab newspaper editor.

In the Middle East, one person's "terrorist" is another's "commando," "guerrilla," or "freedom fighter." Some use the word "gunman." A "terrorist attack" to some is a "military operation" to others. Dead women and children are "casualties" to some, "murder victims" to others. Israeli "settlements" are inhabited by "settlers." Palestinians call the "settlers" "combatants," not "civilians."

In the official vocabulary of the government of Israel, the West Bank is "Judea and Samaria," while the Arab residents of the

West Bank and Gaza, who make up 98 percent of the population, are referred to as "the minorities." Israeli settlements are not enlarged or expanded but "thickened." Annexation is referred to as "application of Israeli law," and Arab-owned lands are never seized but "closed." Radio Israel uses only the initials PLO or PFLP and never uses the terms Palestine Liberation Organization or Popular Front for the Liberation of Palestine, because the word liberation implies a legitimate claim to land Israel considers its own. The Israeli invasion of Lebanon was called "Operation Peace for Galilee," and Prime Minister Menachem Begin said that "Israel did not invade any country." Later, however, Israel called its policy in Lebanon "Iron First."

After killing five Israeli civilians and wounding eighteen Arabs and Jews in rifle attacks on civilians' buses, a band of Palestinian attackers was killed by Israeli security forces. *Al Fajr,* the English language newspaper in East Jerusalem, ran the following headline on its story of the fight: "Israel Kills Commandos."

Israel Radio's English language service gave this brief report in July of 1985: "Police are investigating two bombings and a grenade attack in the Tel Aviv area. The two bombings are suspected to be the work of terrorists, while the grenade attack on the Hassan Bek Mosque in Jaffa is believed to have been carried out by Jews."

In 1986, after two Arabs suspected of attacking a bus filled with civilian passengers "failed to survive interrogation" by the Shin Beth security agency (a subsequent investigation revealed the two men had been beaten to death), a commission headed by Israeli Supreme Court Justice Moshe Landau issued a report that justified the use of "physical pressure" in certain instances when interrogating suspects. The Israeli cabinet then formed a committee to consider the amount of "physical force" Israeli security agents may use in questioning Palestinians suspected of guerrilla actions. When Mubarak Awad advocated nonviolent resistance in Israeli-occupied territories, an Israeli official said, "This non-violence is a smart way to trigger Israeli violence and thus incite the uprisings." Words are important in the Middle East, the words of war and peace, life and death.

Doublespeak, Dictators, and Others

When General Augusto Pinochet, the military dictator of Chile who seized power in 1973 by overthrowing the elected government of Salvador Allende Gossens, imposed a state of siege in 1984, he said that "it is precisely to save democracy and liberty that now more than ever it is necessary to be inflexible with respect to the institutional order that rules us." Under the state of siege, the police could arrest suspects without charges or warrants, suspects could be held incommunicado indefinitely, and trials could be delayed indefinitely. And when the good general was asked about political philosophies that opposed his own, he said that "We have nothing against ideas. We're against people spreading them."

General Pinochet continues a long tradition of those who would overthrow democracy in order to protect it, those who would destroy democracy in order to save it. So many rulers seem to think that the people they rule are never quite ready for democracy and only a nondemocratic form of government can preserve democracy. Even those rulers who claim their goal is the establishment of democracy have a strange way of going about it.

General Joaõ Baptista Figueiredo said in 1979, upon being elected Brazil's next president, "I intend to open this country up to democracy, and anyone who is against that, I will jail, I will crush." After jailing or exiling virtually every opposition leader in Haiti, President-for-Life Jean-Claude Duvalier said in a public address from the balcony of the presidential palace, "Long live democracy. Long live human rights." President Ferdinand Marcos of the Philippines defended his suspension of civil liberties with imposition of martial law in 1981 by claiming that "When I proclaimed martial law, it was to protect human rights." And Mohammed Zia ul-Haq, Pakistan's military ruler, announced the end of press censorship in his country in 1983, but warned that newspapers should exercise self-restraint and continue to observe self-censorship.

Sometimes the doublespeak of dictators and other authoritarian and totalitarian governments isn't even subtle. After a coup attempt failed, President Lansana Conte of Guinea said that he planned to give the leaders of the failed coup a fair trial and then shoot them. Therefore, he added, "If anyone wants to intercede in the name of human rights, he had better do it today because tomorrow will be too late." The government of Uruguay built a maximum-security prison for political prisoners and called it "Penal Libertad"—"Liberty Prison"—and those who are held there as prisoners are later billed for room and board for the time they spent there.

Dictators are particularly good when using doublespeak to cover up their use of secret police to enforce their rule. In 1981, President Park Chung Hee of South Korea changed the name of the Korean Central Intelligence Agency to the "Agency for National Security Planning." Eric Gairy, when he was prime minister of Grenada, crushed all opposition using a group of gunmen he first named the Secret Police, then the Night Ambush Squad, and finally "Volunteers for the Defense of Fundamental Liberties." Idi Amin of Uganda called his secret police the "State Research Unit."

With doublespeak, a government can kill its citizens while still respecting their rights. After foreign journalists reported that Salvadoran army troops rounded up and shot to death more than one hundred people, including women and children, in three small towns in northern El Salvador, the army command acknowledged that soldiers had "caused about 100 casualties to . . . subversives during a military operation." In a television interview, Jose Garcia, defense minister of El Salvador, said that "human rights are being respected, but that's not to say they're not being violated." In 1981, President Jose Napoleon Duarte of El Salvador, in response to charges that government forces in his country were responsible for the deaths of over ten thousand civilians in a year, said that "We will not deny that there may have been certain abuses of authority by the security forces."

The Defense of the Indefensible

Often, political leaders are reduced to a kind of doublespeak absurdity when defending their position, or as Orwell put it, "the defense of the indefensible." Prince Narodom Sihanouk was asked in 1982 how he could form an alliance with Khieu Samphan, a leader of the Khmer Rouge faction that had slaughtered millions of Cambodians during the rule of Pol Pot. Replied Prince Sihanouk: "Cambodians prefer to be killed by the Khmer Rouge because they are Cambodians and not be wiped out by the Vietnamese or Soviets."

Somehow, dictators never see the killing of thousands of their citizens as anything but necessary for the good of those killed and those still alive. Such instances give rise to doublespeak that is used to make murder respectable. Although the official media in Iran reported the execution of several thousand people in 1981, Ayatollah Ruhollah Khomeini said that the prophet's wars were to purify nations and "those who prevent moral purification must be eliminated. In appearance this can seem like a mass killing to people, but in reality, it amounts to getting rid of obstacles to humanity—Iran purifies them if it can, or if not, it eliminates them."

War is Peace, or The We-Has-Met-the-Enemy-and-He-Is-Us Award

With doublespeak, enemies can kill each other while stoutly maintaining their only interest is peace. In 1975, Yasir Arafat, in response to the charge that the Palestine Liberation Organization wanted to destroy Israel, said that "They are wrong. We do not want to destroy any people. It is precisely because we have been advocating co-existence that we have shed so much blood." In 1982, Israeli Foreign Minister Yitsak Shamir, speaking at the funeral of an Israeli diplomat assassinated in Paris, said that Israeli forces would "strike at them [the PLO] without reservation, without end, because we have decided to live and to live in peace."

As Orwell wrote, war is peace.

CHAPTER VI

Predawn Vertical Insertions
and Hexiform Rotatable Surface Compression Units:
The Pentagon Word Machine Grinds On

There are three ways of doing things: the right way, the wrong way, and the military way, to paraphrase an old G.I. saying. So when it comes to doublespeak, the military has a way with words that is unmatched by other users of doublespeak. Only the military could call a tent a "frame-supported tension structure"; a parachute, an "aerodynamic personnel decelerator"; a life jacket, a "personal preservation flotation device"; and a zipper, an "interlocking slide fastener." It's not a toothpick, but a "wood interdental stimulator"; not a pencil, but a "portable, hand-held communications inscriber." Others may call it a bomb, but to the army it's a "vertically deployed anti-personnel device."

Military doublespeak often filters out to the civilian world, but some of the best is rarely exposed to civilian sunlight because it is found in those dull, dry documents called "military specifications." Since you probably don't read military contracts regularly, you have missed some of the best in doublespeak the military has to offer. In these documents can be found doublespeak that makes "interfibrous friction fastener," "multi-directional impact generator," or "manually-powered fastener-driving impact device" for hammer pale by comparison.

If the military wants to buy anything, they don't just go to the local K Mart and pick it up. Since by their definition anything the military uses is special, it has to be specially made. Nothing off the shelf for the military. You might think of it as having a custom-designed military. So someone has to draw up elaborate "military specifications" (mil-specs) for just about everything the military buys. And how those mil-specs have grown over the years. In 1951, when the air force asked Lockheed to design a new cargo plane, the specifications totaled 8 pages, while in 1980 it took 2,750 pages of specifications to request a new cargo plane from Lockheed. Of course, the increase in specifications has slowed things down a bit. In 1943 Lockheed designed and built the first American jet plane in 143 days, while the F/A-18 Hornet took nine years for development.

And the mil-specs keep growing, multiplying like wire hangers in the back of your closet, and getting just as hopelessly tangled. It takes twenty-four pages to list all the specs for T-shirts, fifteen pages for chewing gum, seventeen pages for Worcestershire sauce, twenty-two pages for a "trap, mouse," and sixteen pages for a "whistle, plastic," which include the following performance standards:

> The whistle shall be capable of emitting an audible characteristic sound when blown by the mouth with medium or high breath pressure. The center line of the air passage shall be tangent to the $13/33$-inch line radius for the solid construction whistle and to the $7/16$-inch line radius for the split construction whistle of the inner chamber so that when the whistle is overblown, the ball shall continue to rotate and the whistle shall show no reduction or cessation in sound or marked change in pitch.
>
> Note: Overblown is defined as when the breath pressure is increased to maximum, as under excitement,

so as to produce a higher pitch than the fundamental tone.

There are equally demanding specifications for the military version of the taco shell.

How to Bake a Fruitcake, Pentagon Style

When Christmas comes, can fruitcake be far behind? Now you might pick up a fruitcake or two at the supermarket while doing your Christmas shopping and let it go at that. Or, if you're real ambitious, you might even bake your own fruitcake. But if you're the military, you don't go to the grocery store, and you certainly don't bake your own fruitcake. Instead, you cook up some specifications for fruitcake—eighteen pages of specifications, complete with charts, cross-references to other publications, and four pages of amendments. Even the most elaborate recipe for fruitcake in all of my cookbooks doesn't cover one whole page, so how could those guys at the army's Research, Development and Engineering Command come up with eighteen pages of small type listing all the specifications for making a military fruitcake? Well, here's just some of Grandma Pentagon's recipe for an approved fruitcake.

Military Specification MIL-F-1499F, amended 1980, calls for candied orange peel "thoroughly deragged and processed with sugar and corn syrup to not less than 72 percent soluble solids." Grandma Pentagon's recipe also includes instructions to soak raisins "as necessary to prevent clumping," to dice the candied pineapple in quarter-inch chunks, to use candied cherries made from pitted cherries cut to yield quarter-inch to half-inch pieces, to use nuts of "the latest crop" and shortening with the "stability of not less than 100 hours. . . . Vanilla flavoring shall be pure or artificial vanilla in such quantities that its presence shall be organoleptically detected, but not to a pronounced degree." (That means you have to use enough vanilla to taste or smell it, but not so much that it overpowers the fruitcake.) "The fruitcake batter shall consist of equal parts by weight of cake batter specified in

Table I, and fruit and nut blend specified in Table II, blended in such manner as to meet requirements of 3.5."

After mixing these ingredients, you're ready to bake. "A predetermined weight of the blended fruitcake batter, sufficient to yield the specified weight, shall then be deposited into cans with liners and discs and the lids of the cans shall be clinched on loosely to allow for the escape of moisture and gases evolved during processing. Alternatively, in lieu of paper disk and liner, the can shall have an enamel interior possessing adequate product release characteristics so that not more than 5.0 percent by weight of the product adheres to the interior of the can. . . . Sealing and baking shall be so that the batter portion is heated uniformly throughout to produce a finished product having no raw, stringy or ungelatinized portions."

Now for the moment of truth. "When the cooled product is bisected vertically and horizontally with a sharp knife, it shall not crumble nor show any compression streaks, gummy centers, soggy areas, be excessively dry or overprocessed, and shall display an even grain structure throughout." The specifications conclude with the bewildering requirement that the finished product should "conform to inside contour of the can or can liner," with "no point on the top lid greater than ¾-inch from the side of the can where the cake did not touch the lid during baking."

About the only thing left out of these specifications is who gets to lick the bowl, and who gets to clean up the kitchen. If this is what it takes to bake a fruitcake for the Pentagon, how would you like to see the specifications for a new aircraft carrier?

Why have mil-specs grown so dramatically in the last few decades? Well, there is a theory that holds that all those officers have to do something, since there aren't enough enlisted men to keep the officers busy. You see, of the 12,055,884 men and women on active duty in the U.S. Armed Forces in July of 1945, 1,260,109 were officers, or 1 officer for every 9 enlisted personnel. However, on May 31, 1983, there were 2,114,341 enlisted personnel, of whom 293,026 were officers, or 1 officer for every 6 enlisted personnel. Some critics have suggested that the officer corps has become a self-perpetuating bureaucracy preoccupied with making work for itself by systematically overcomplicating every aspect of defense. What better way to keep all those officers busy than by writing all those pages of specifications? Then again, it may just be the nature of the military to make everything complicated.

How the Pentagon Simplifies Things

Still, the Pentagon is not insensitive to the mounds of paperwork and maze of doublespeak it has created as part of the procurement process, as it likes to call buying stuff. So, in 1986, with much publicity and a lot of self-congratulation, the Pentagon embarked upon the Department of Defense Contract Simplification Test Program. Before you read any further, would you like to predict the outcome of this simplification program? Have you ever been asked an easier question?

Daniel Greenberg, editor and publisher of the newsletter *Science and Government Report,* wrote in *The New York Times* of his adventures with the simplification program. Notification of the program arrived accompanied by a fifteen-page form, ten pages longer than the normal five-page form he had had to complete before the simplification program. Still, Mr. Greenberg was willing to give the program a try, in the belief that the Pentagon was really going to simplify things. I'm always touched to discover that such innocence still survives in our cynical world. After all, the previous form he had had to fill out contained such directions as, "Delete DD Form 1155r, Para Nr. 7" in favor of the "FAR/DOD Far Sup" clause on "Convict Labor APR 19(4) FAR 52.222-3." Or "If Block 10, 'Delivery to FOB Point By,' is annotated 'As Published,' this offer is only valid for 18 months from the date of order, Block 3." Anything would be better than that old form, Mr. Greenberg naively thought, so he plunged into the new form.

The new form, described as "attempting to simplify our solicitations and contracts, and relieve contractors of some of the administrative burden of contracting with the Government," did not get off to a good start: "In negotiated acquisitions, 'bid' and 'bidder' shall be construed to mean 'offer' and 'offeror.' In sealed bid acquisitions, 'offer' and 'offeror' shall be construed to mean 'bid' and 'bidder.' "

These simplified explanations were followed by fifty-eight questions and requirements. One of the requirements sought assurance that "If miniature and instrument ball bearings will be incorporated the clause of DOD FAR SUP 52.208-7000 will apply and the clause will be incorporated by reference into any resultant contract." There was a similar requirement for "high purity silicon defined as N or P type with resistivity greater than 3000 ohm-centimeter." The "Recovered Material Certification" section sought assurances that "recovered materials, as defined in section 23.402 of the Federal Acquisitions Regulations, will be used as required by the applicable specifications (IAW FAR 23.405)."

For contractors in the "$500,000 or less" category, the simplification program offered a break: exemption from "Cost Accounting Standards Notices and Certification (National Defense) (Apr 1984) FAR 52.230-1." However, this exemption was available only if "The offeror hereby claims an exemption from the CAS requirements under the provisions of 4 CFR 331.30 (b)(7) and certifies that notification of final acceptance of all deliverable items has been received on all prime contracts or subcontracts containing the Cost Accounting Standards clause or the Disclosure and Consistency of Cost Accounting Practices clause."

Mr. Greenberg doesn't say what he did with the new, simplified contract, but you can probably guess what he wanted to tell the Pentagon to do with it. For now, let your imagination go for a minute and picture what could be produced if this simplified contract were joined to the specifications for fruitcake. Then think of joining the simplified contract to the mil-specs for a new intercontinental ballistic missile. Boggles the mind, doesn't it? Is it any wonder the Pentagon builds so many things that don't work?

Even after the specifications and the contract, the Pentagon isn't finished with procurement doublespeak. In announcing the

award of a contract to the Westinghouse Electric Company, the
Pentagon issued this statement:

> [Westinghouse] is being awarded a $3,317,467 firm fixed
> price completion contract to design, develop, fabricate
> and test an advanced development model to demonstrate
> the techniques to maintain pulse-to-pulse stability in a
> tactical radar transmitter at levels necessary to support
> adequate moving target indicator performance to
> counter validated threat scenarios while operating with
> widely varying pulse widths and repetition rates to
> facilitate power management.

What all this means is that the air force is trying to develop a new
radar and needs a better transmitter to do it.

A good place to begin with military doublespeak is the *Department of Defense Dictionary of Military and Associated Terms*,
published by the Joint Chiefs of Staff. Browsing through this
book will introduce you to some fascinating terms and definitions. See if you can figure out what the definition for the term
"relateral tell" means: "relateral tell—(DOD, NATO) The relay of
information between facilities through the use of a third facility.
This type of telling is appropriate between automated facilities
in a degraded communications environment. See also track telling." I will spare you the definition of "track telling," as well as
the definitions of "back tell," "cross tell," "forward tell," "lateral
tell," and "overlap tell." The dictionary also defines "nuclear collateral damage" as the "undesired damage or casualties produced by the effects from friendly nuclear weapons."

However, the army trains its officers so that they can use nuclear weapons with a minimum of "collateral damage," as you
can see from the following course description from the catalog
of the U.S. Army's Command and General Staff College in Fort
Levenworth, Kansas:

> A154. Nuclear Weapons Employment. Scope: This course
> provides student officers an opportunity to learn how to

effectively employ nuclear weapons in a tactical context.
. . . This instruction results in a battle exercise where
students effectively plan the employment of nuclear
weapons to support a division-corps operation. . . . This
elective is designed for student officers without prior
experience or training in nuclear weapons employment.

When asked to justify the new "backpack" atomic bomb (an atomic bomb small enough to fit in a suitcase) the Defense Department wants, arms expert Richard Wagner told Congress in 1985: "Special Atomic Demolition Munitions possess an inherent capability to effect a measured qualitative change in the level of escalation of a conflict and thus retain both deterrence and defensive characteristics." Now isn't that a great reason for building a small, easily concealed, easily transported atomic bomb? And I'm sure there's not much danger of "collateral damage" from such a bomb either.

When War Isn't War

Military doublespeak starts at the top with the name of the Department of Defense. From the founding of our Republic, there has been a Department of War. Until 1947, that is, when the military pulled off the doublespeak coup of the century. On July 27, 1947, President Harry S. Truman signed the National Security Act of 1947, an act that completely reorganized the armed forces of the United States. Title II of that act carries the heading, "Establishment of the National Military Establishment," and in Section 202 establishes the post of Secretary of Defense, while Section 205(a) eliminates the Department of War: "The Department of War shall hereafter be designated the Department of the Army, and the title of the Secretary of War shall be changed to Secretary of the Army." Thus, war became "defense."

At first glance this change may not seem to be all that significant, but stop for a moment and examine the implications of this change in language. Now we can spend hundreds of billions of dollars for "defense," not war. Now members of Congress can campaign to spend more on "defense," not war. Now candidates for public office can charge their opponents with wanting to cut the $300 billion defense budget, not cut the $300 billion war budget. Now Richard Cheney, Frank Carlucci, Caspar Weinberger, and others can be the "Secretary of Defense," which is so much nicer than being the Secretary of War. And since it is the "defense" budget, Weinberger could say in 1982 that the "defense" budget was "the most important social welfare program for which the federal government must be responsible" which sounds a whole lot better than saying that the war budget is the most important social welfare program for which the federal government must be responsible.

When the State Department and NASA solicited participation by American allies in the building of a space station in 1986, they stressed the station's use for peaceful purposes only. Later, the Pentagon revealed that it wanted to use the proposed station for Star Wars research. When NASA officials expressed fears that American allies participating in the project would object, an air force official said that other countries might have misinterpreted a policy of restricting space ventures to "peaceful purposes" as meaning nonmilitary. "We will limit our use of outer space for peaceful purposes," he said. "Our philosophy is that anything the United States does, including the Department of Defense, is in the name of peace." Substitute the word "war" for "defense" in that sentence and see how much sense it makes. And since anything the Department of Defense does is for peace, Senator John Tower could say in 1982 at the commissioning of the new nuclear-powered aircraft carrier U.S.S. *Carl Vinson* that the purpose of this new warship was to "promote peace."

Changing the name of the Department of Defense back to its original name, the Department of War, would provide some real benefits. First, the change would return the historically correct name to this department of the government, a change that conservatives would surely support. Second, the original name accurately reflects the function of this department, which is to prepare for, and if necessary fight, a war. Third, a return to the original name might make Congress and the American public pay more attention to the budget appropriated for the National Military Establishment. However, if you are willing to accept "defense" instead of "war" in the title of this government agency, then perhaps you would agree to a few other changes in order to be consistent. The unpleasantness of 1914–1918 and 1939–1945 will be called "World Defense I" and "World Defense II"; Tolstoy's great novel will become *Defense and Peace*; and General William Tecumseh Sherman's comment will be changed to "Defense is Hell."

Hexiform Rotatable Surface Compression Units, and Other Pentagon Bargains

One important function of doublespeak is to hide reality, to cover up what's really going on. With doublespeak, weapons never fail, and expensive items are always very complicated and worth their high price. Sometimes military doublespeak doesn't even give you the faintest idea of what it is the Pentagon is paying all that money for. In Pentagon doublespeak, it's not a plain, ordinary steel nut; it's a "hexiform rotatable surface compression unit," which is why it cost $2,043 for just one of them. This little piece of doublespeak also allows you to say that the equipment "suffered dramatically degraded useful operational life owing to the fact that a $2,000 hexiform rotatable surface compression unit underwent catastrophic stress-related shaft detachment," which sounds a lot more impressive than saying it won't work because a 13¢ nut broke. You may call it a flashlight, but to the air force it's an "Emergency Exit Light," which is why it cost $214.

Some penny-pinchers may think that $31,672 is a lot to pay for a couch, a love seat, and twenty dining room chairs (or almost $1,500 for each piece of furniture), but not if you think of it the way the navy does. All that money was spent on "habitability improvements" for the destroyer U.S.S. *Kidd.* That ship must be really habitable after that high-priced improvement.

Then there is the "Survivable Enduring Shelter," or SES, designed by Goodyear Aerospace. Equipped with a 5,000-pound-plus payload, armor-plated shielding capable of stopping .30 caliber "projectiles" (the Pentagon's doublespeak for bullets), and an "intrusion detection system" (more doublespeak meaning a burglar alarm), the SES is designed "to meet the most stringent technical requirements for survival during a nuclear event," which is Pentagon doublespeak meaning it's supposed to be able to survive an atomic bomb attack. The SES is basically a "tactile electronics enclosure" (I have no idea what that means) placed on an existing truck chassis. Some have called the SES the Pentagon's atomic-bomb-proof camper. Just exactly what this SES is supposed to do wandering over a nuclear-ravaged landscape is never quite explained by the Pentagon, even in doublespeak.

Anomalies, and Other Reasons Missiles Don't Work

With doublespeak the Pentagon can explain that the cruise missile didn't fly out of control and crash in three pieces during a test flight in Canada. According to the air force, the missile merely "impacted with the ground prematurely." Not to be outdone by their U.S. counterparts, an official of the Canadian forces said the test flight was simply "terminated five minutes earlier than planned." When an unarmed Minuteman 3 intercontinental ballistic missile developed problems after launch and had to be destroyed by commands radioed from the ground, the air force simply announced that "An anomaly occurred during the flight which caused the early termination." Although the Bigeye aerial nerve-gas bomb has been on the drawing boards for more than twenty years, it still doesn't work. During one test drop in 1982, the bomb malfunctioned, producing what the Pentagon called "a forcible ejection of the internal bomb components." In other words, the bomb blew up.

With doublespeak, the missile can miss the target but the test can still be a success. "We did acquire the target, but we did not hit it. . . . We achieved our objectives," said Jim Kittinger, an official in the air-to-surface guided weapons office at Elgin Air Force Base. The test was the fifth consecutive failure in a series of twelve tests, according to *Defense News*.

When the House Armed Services Committee criticized the guidance system of the MX missile because, among other problems, "product integrity was marginal" (meaning the guidance systems didn't work and the missile couldn't hit its target) and some test results had been falsified, Brigadier General Charles May, who oversaw the program, said the dispute with the House committee over the test results was a matter of "dealing with the nuances in the data base" (the Committee didn't buy the false test data). In two of five tests of the new MX missile, the missile fell "outside the current accuracy requirements." In other words, the missile missed the target, which is something of a problem when you're dealing with a nuclear-armed, intercontinental ballistic missile. General May said the air force was trying to "move back in the direction" of greater accuracy. Let's hope he doesn't just move in the direction of accuracy but fixes the missile so it can hit its target. Otherwise, as a member of the House Armed Services Committee pointed out, an MX missile that's supposed to hit Moscow could land in Newark, New Jersey instead.

When the Pentagon had a missile that never worked but that it wanted to keep building, it submitted a report to Congress that defended continued funding for the failed missile this way: "Faced with the choice of maintaining a program with a history of limited or no success and the cancellation of the program with corresponding negative consequences, any consideration of the program's future should entail a full examination of plausible alternatives for mitigating the necessity of choosing between two such undesirable results." In military doublespeak, all weapons work and no weapons fail, and every weapon is worth what the Pentagon pays for it, no matter how outrageous the price.

Meals, Ready to Eat, and Other Complications

Nothing is ever simple with the Pentagon. Even a newly designed bayonet becomes a "weapons system," while the cockpit in air force fighters is now called a "Missionized Crew Station," according to *USAF Fighter Weapons Review.* When the army decided it needed a new vehicle to replace the jeep, it designed "the high mobility multi-purpose wheeled vehicle." An antisatellite weapon becomes a "kinetic kill vehicle launcher," while the smoke used in smoke bombs becomes a "universal obscurant." Even that favorite of the G.I., field rations or C-rations, has now become "MRE," or "Meal, Ready to Eat." But, just as using doublespeak to make simple things appear complex doesn't change the function of those items, so changing the name on C-rations won't make them taste any better.

When the army decided in 1982 to eliminate mixed companies of men and women in basic training, it didn't say that it made this change to improve basic training for both groups. That would have been too simple. Instead the army said that it made the change in order to "facilitate the Army's toughening goals and enhance the soldierization process." So too when testing a new boot design by having one hundred soldiers wear the new boots during obstacle course training. For the army this was "human engineering" testing. Not to be outdone, the navy proved that it could easily keep up with the army's high standard of doublespeak. In 1982, when the navy was taking the battleship U.S.S. *Iowa* out of mothballs, it had to move the ship to another pier where workers could prepare it for active duty. Seems simple enough, doesn't it? Not for the navy, which announced that the *Iowa* was moved to "facilitate the pre-activization process." And the replicas of Soviet combat vehicles that the army uses during exercises have "the same visual signatures" as the actual Soviet vehicles, officials said. That means they look like the real thing.

Doublespeak is particularly effective in explaining or at least glossing over accidents. An air force colonel in charge of safety wrote in a letter that rocket boosters weighing more than 300,000 pounds "have an explosive force upon surface impact that is sufficient to exceed the accepted overpressure threshold of physiological damage for exposed personnel." In other words, if a 300,000-pound booster rocket falls on you, you probably won't survive. In 1985 three American soldiers were killed and sixteen injured when the first stage of a Pershing II missile they were unloading suddenly ignited. There was no explosion, said

Major Michael Griffen, but rather "an unplanned rapid ignition of solid fuel."

You might think it reasonable to say that the helicopter crashed during a training exercise at Camp Lejune in 1984. After all, six Marines were killed and eleven were seriously injured. To military officials, however, it was not a crash but a "hard landing." When a seriously ill sailor was transferred to another ship for medical attention, the navy doctor noted the sailor's condition as "not salvageable." The sailor died. And the 241 marines killed in the 1983 bombing of their barracks in Lebanon were officially listed as having died of accidental causes.

The Doublespeak of War and Death

While the doublespeak of military specifications, contracts, and weapons that don't work is often humorous and frequently outrageous, the doublespeak of war and death is not. The military is acutely aware that the reason for its existence is to wage war, and war means killing people and the deaths of American soldiers as well. Because the reality of war and its consequences are so harsh, the military almost instinctively turns to doublespeak when discussing war.

In the doublespeak of war, officers do not learn how to lead their men to the rear at night. Instead they learn about "the rifle company in retrograde movement under conditions of reduced visibility." When John Lehman was secretary of the navy, he promoted a strategy that in case of war called for U.S. aircraft carriers to sail near the Soviet Union in order to strike that country's ports. Undersecretary of Defense Richard DeLauer said that such a strategy would only place the carriers in "a target rich environment." This phrase was helpfully explained in a somewhat different context by an instructor at the U.S. Army War College. Pointing to a scale model of a hypothetical Russian attack in Europe, the instructor noted that it was a classic form of Russian attack which presented a "target rich environment." He then pointed out, "That's one way of saying there's a whole lot more of them than us."

During the Vietnam War we learned that mercenaries were really "civilian irregular defense soldiers," refugees were "ambient noncombatant personnel," and enemy troops who survived bombing were "interdictional nonsuccumbers." Any sampan that was sunk was automatically called a "waterborne logistic craft." Poisoning thousands of acres of vegetation with Agent Orange was just a "resources control program" that produced "defoliation." American planes conducted "limited duration protective reactive strikes" with an "effective delivery of ordnance." When American troops attacked, it was a "pre-emptive counterattack" or an "aggressive defense." Spraying an area with machine-gun fire was "reconnaissance by fire." Sometimes American troops "engaged the enemy on all sides" (they were ambushed) and had to effect a "tactical redeployment" (they retreated). When American troops ambush the enemy it's a "proactive counterattack."

In military doublespeak, "friendly casualties," which are caused by "accidental delivery of ordnance equipment" or "friendly fire," means American troops killed by American bombs or artillery shells. In the air force, "own goal" means shooting down friendly planes. "Traumatic amputation" is what happens when arms and legs are blown off soldiers, while "aluminum transfer containers" are temporary coffins. U.S. military personnel in the Persian Gulf received "imminent danger pay" in 1987, which is not the same as combat pay since combat pay is given to troops under "hostile fire." The civilians who are killed and wounded during war are simply "collateral damage" in the doublespeak of the military. And when the marines were withdrawn from Lebanon in 1984 the Pentagon called it a "backloading of augmentation personnel."

American troops don't attack, they "assume an offensive posture," which usually occurs during a "lethal intervention" or war. "Airborne vector" means germ warfare by air, while "employment of incapacitory agents" is using nerve gas. "Locating areas for concentration of resources" means identifying targets for bombing attacks, while "eroding the will of the population" means bombing civilians. A "special weapon" is an atomic bomb.

In today's army it's not killing the enemy, it's "servicing the target."

Low-Intensity Conflict, or Violent Peace

The Pentagon even has a scale for the level of intensity of war, ranging from "low-intensity conflict" to the ultimate in "high-intensity warfare," nuclear war. The current hot topic in military planning is "low-intensity conflict," or "LIC" as those in the military like to call it. Military planners say that the army has devoted too much of its thinking and training to large-scale armored and artillery warfare in Europe and not enough to such "low-intensity conflict" as counterinsurgency in Central America, where one of the problems is to train artillery gunners to avoid "collateral damage."

Current Pentagon planning for "low-intensity conflict" proposes aiding "freedom fighters" throughout the world. A thousand-page, two-volume study entitled "Joint Low-Intensity Conflict Project" prepared by the CIA, State Department, and Pentagon states that "low-intensity conflict is neither war nor peace. It is an improbable compilation of dissimilar phenomena that, like the Cheshire cat which seems to fade in and out as you look at it, leaving only its mocking smile, bedevils efforts at comprehension." The study discusses terrorism as one type of "low-intensity conflict" that will be used and states that "low-intensity conflict" also includes virtually all acts of violence in the Third World, ranging from domestic turmoil, drug trafficking, and political assassinations to hostage taking, guerrilla insurgencies, revolution, and civil war.

At a Pentagon-sponsored conference on "low-intensity warfare," retired army General Paul F. Gorman said that this type of conflict "is inherently repugnant to Americans, a conflict which involves innocents, in which noncombatant casualties may be an explicit object." Writing in the March 1985 issue of *Military Review,* a U.S. Army journal, Lt. Col. Richard Brawn stated that "Low-intensity conflict is a pseudonym for a war without full political support—a war without the needed political will." The U.S. Navy, in its own inimitable doublespeak, calls the concept of low-intensity conflict "violent peace."

The Language of Military Recruitment

The following help-wanted ad appeared in newspapers around the United States in 1986:

> Deck Hands. Immediate opening with international maritime organization seeking to man rapidly expanding fleet. Relocation necessary at our expense. On the job training, good salary, excellent benefits, world travel. Ages 17–34. High School Diploma required. Must be in good physical condition.

This was a recruiting ad for the U.S. Navy, otherwise known as an "international maritime organization."

This ad is in keeping with the campaign by the military services to use the language of business to portray themselves as a corporation whose product is defense. Such language avoids the reality that this corporation is really an organization whose function is to wage war in which employees of the corporation kill other people and are killed and maimed themselves.

Using the language of the business world—jobs, pay, training, benefits, advancement, experience, and career development— the military portrays the unpleasant aspects of military life as not just palatable but desirable. In the world of the military corporation, combat is just one of the functions of the corporation, almost like marketing or sales.

In the modern military corporation combat does not involve killing and death, but is a "challenge" that will "test your strength, stamina and spirit" and slake "your thirst for adventure," as the army's "Combat Arms" pamphlet presents it. To meet this challenge, you will "charge out of a Bradley fighting vehicle or jump from a helicopter in full daylight . . . ready to meet the opposition, head-on." You won't "kill the enemy" or even "service the target," but "meet the opposition," as if you were negotiating a business deal or trying to beat a competing company in a sales pitch to a customer. While the brochure stresses skill, courage, stamina, spirit, teamwork, intelligence, and confidence, it never mentions pain, suffering, killing, or death. War as it's fought in this pamphlet is fought by soldiers who are corporate employees working to advance the goals of their employer.

A marine brochure portrays combat as good preparation for civilian life by promoting the corporate view of military life. A marine in the "field" (military brochures never say "battlefield") does not face an enemy who wants to kill him but faces instead "challenges." The infantry is "the cutting edge," while serving in the field artillery, driving a tank, or transporting marines from ship to beachhead in an assault vehicle will train you to be a "combat engineer." All of these jobs will give you "the right qualifications for top-notch occupations," as well as qualify you to return to civilian life trained in "engineering and construction."

The military has relentlessly advertised military service as being just like any other career, and even better than many. "Be all that you can be," advertises the army. But it never mentions that sometimes all you can be is dead. The military corporation is the one corporation whose business is killing and whose product is death and destruction. Only doublespeak allows the military to avoid talking about the reality of its function in our society.

The Pentagon's Propaganda Document

Around March of every year, during congressional budget hearings, the Pentagon issues a warning that America's prestige and power are on a dangerous decline; or that the military has been neglected for too long; or that our defenses have seriously eroded, leaving our national security at grave risk; or that our lead in one or more major areas of the arms race is rapidly diminishing; or that a window of vulnerability has opened or is about to open; or a gap of one kind or another is looming; or that the military balance is shifting inexorably against the United States. And every year the Pentagon proposes the same remedy to the decline, gap, or window it has discovered: a massive increase in military spending.

As part of this yearly campaign to increase its budget, the Pentagon began publishing in 1981 a series of booklets titled *Soviet Military Power,* which purport to be assessments of Soviet military strength. Several hundred thousand copies of the 1987 edition of this 180-page booklet were distributed free to members of the press and others throughout the world, at a cost of approximately $1 million to taxpayers. While this booklet has become an official source of information, it is filled with misstatements of fact, exaggerations of the numbers and capabilities of Soviet weapons, and hidden assumptions used to create incomplete and misleading comparisons of military power.

In his 1987 book, *Soviet Military Power: The Pentagon's Propaganda Document, Annotated and Corrected,* Tom Gervasi points out that "By every significant measure of comparison, the United States has always held, and continues to hold, a commanding lead in strategic power." But what can the Pentagon do about the facts? "It can only avoid mentioning them, misrepresenting them, or, as it does frequently" in *Soviet Military Power,* "simply lie." For example, many publications follow the Pentagon's false report of the three-thousand-kilometer range of the Soviet AS-15 air-to-ground missile, when in fact its range has never exceeded twelve hundred kilometers.

Gervasi has marshaled an enormous amount of evidence to enable him to assess the facts of the Pentagon's claims. The Pentagon's booklet, of course, presents only its point of view and ignores everything that might counter its arguments. Soviet bombers are described as approaching within "80 kilometers of the Alaskan coast," but the booklet fails to mention that U.S. bombers "cross right over that coast, into Soviet territory." The Pentagon booklet says the Soviet Union sends a "flow of arms and hostile activities into our own hemisphere," yet the booklet doesn't mention that the United States "sustains a 'flow of arms' to more than 100 nations in every hemisphere." The booklet is also filled with false and deceptive maps, illustrations, and statistical tables.

As Sissela Bok warned in her book, *Lying: Moral Choice in Public and Private Life,* a society "whose members were unable to distinguish truthful messages from deceptive ones, would collapse," because individual choice and survival depend upon the trust provided by "some degree of truthfulness in speech and action. . . . Even the devils themselves, as Samuel Johnson said, do not lie to one another, since the society of Hell could not subsist without the truth, any more than others."

General Westmoreland Rewrites History

As Orwell pointed out, history can be and often is rewritten to suit the needs of the present. General William Westmoreland, who had been a commander of U.S. forces in Vietnam, tried a little rewriting of history himself, especially since a famous photograph from the war in Vietnam did not present the picture of the war the general likes to believe.

On June 8, 1973, South Vietnamese planes accidentally dropped napalm bombs on a village. Huynh Cong (Nick) Ut of the Associated Press happened to be just outside the village at the time of the bombing and took photographs of the injured civilians who were running from the flaming village. One of the photographs he took showed Phan Thi Kim Phuc, a seven-year-old South Vietnamese girl, naked, badly burned, and screaming, running from a wall of fire and smoke. The photograph won the Pulitzer Prize in 1973.

On January 15, 1986, General Westmoreland said in a speech to a group of businesspeople in Florida that he did not believe the girl was burned by napalm. He said an investigation determined that she had been burned in an accident involving a hibachi, an open grill.

When reporters asked the army for copies of the results of the investigation General Westmoreland referred to in his speech, the army responded that it could find no record of any such investigation. In an interview with *The Miami Herald* after his speech, General Westmoreland said he did not remember the extent of the investigation, nor did he recall who had told him that the girl had not been burned by napalm. "If this girl was burned by napalm that hit a thatched hut, that didn't happen every day. That didn't happen very often at all," the general said. But then generals don't experience war the way soldiers do, and the way civilians caught between two armies experience it.

If any wars are fought in the future, we won't have to worry about rewriting history after the war is over in order to satisfy the faulty memories of the generals who directed the war. At least we won't have to if General Westmoreland has his way. The good general said in 1982 that in any future war involving the United States, the news media will have to be censored. According to General Westmoreland, censorship will be necessary to insure the support of the public. "Without censorship things can get terribly confused in the public mind," said the general.

Secretary of Defense Caspar Weinberger demonstrated in 1985 just how deftly words can go down the memory hole. During an interview on Canadian television, Secretary Weinberger was asked if in the future a defense against Cruise missiles is developed, launchers might be placed in Canada, beneath the route that low-flying Soviet Cruise missiles would have to take to reach the United States. "I don't have any idea as to where the defenses would be placed," Weinberger replied. "They would first be placed in the most effective way. But I think what we would try to do would be to locate the best places for defenses. Some might be here, some might be in the United States, some might be at sea. It just depends on where the most effective technical place for them to be put."

The phrase "some might be here" touched a nerve in Canada, so the Pentagon tried to rectify the problem, saying that Weinberger's remark was "severely misinterpreted." Chief Pentagon spokesperson Michael Bruch told reporters, "I'm going to make you read the whole thing, so you can see what the secretary did say." But in the transcript sent to the Pentagon from the American embassy in Ottawa, the offending phrase "some might be here" was missing. "It was completely inadvertent," said Carol

Della Penta, information assistant at the embassy in Ottawa. She said the phrase was dropped in retyping the manuscript.

The Missile Didn't Crash, It Just Ceased to Fly

Secretary Weinberger seemed to have a lot of trouble with Cruise missiles. His statements about Cruise missiles had to be rewritten frequently. In testimony before the Senate Foreign Relations Committee in 1985, Secretary Weinberger said that "the Soviets demonstrated their defense against Cruise missiles a couple of days ago when they shot down one of their errant missiles that was on its way into Finland." Later that day, Weinberger repeated his contention that the "Soviets have already demonstrated one method by shooting down their Cruise missile that somehow got away from them." Still later that day, Pentagon spokesman Michael Bruch had to rewrite Weinberger's statements. Bruch said that Weinberger "did not mean to imply that the missile was shot down. The Soviets didn't shoot the missile down. It ceased to fly." If General Westmoreland had his way, these are the people who would censor the news during a future war so things wouldn't get terribly confused in your mind.

When he needed to, Secretary Weinberger could use doublespeak to mislead. The most critical element in the Star Wars defense, which Weinberger championed so strenuously, is the x-ray laser, which is powered by a nuclear detonation, or an atomic bomb. But detonating an atomic bomb aboveground would violate the U.S.–Soviet test ban treaty. So Weinberger simply referred to a "nuclear event" when he testified about Star Wars during a congressional hearing.

1984—Grenada Style

The 1983 invasion of Grenada produced more than enough doublespeak. What started as an invasion became a "rescue mission" and ended up being, in those immortal words of the Pentagon, a "pre-dawn vertical insertion." What is even more fascinating is that the insertion was not conducted by the United States Army,

Navy, Marines, and Air Force. No, Grenada was inserted by the "Caribbean Peace Keeping Forces," as they were officially called.

It was a tough insertion. So tough that the army awarded 8,612 medals to individual Americans involved in the insertion, although there were no more than 7,000 officers and soldiers on the island. Asked for an explanation, the army said that medals were a "valuable and effective leadership tool to build unit morale and esprit."

After the insertion, American military commanders were asked why there had been such a lack of intelligence information about Grenada. General John Wickham said military intelligence about the island was so deficient because the timing of the operation prevented the military from "developing a greater architecture of human intelligence."

But it was Admiral Wesley L. McDonald, who put it much more forcefully: Why was military intelligence so lacking? Said Admiral McDonald, "We were not micromanaging Grenada intelligencewise until about that time frame." Here is a phrase to stir the hearts of brave fighting men everywhere, equal to John Paul Jones, "I have not yet begun to fight"; Oliver Hazard Perry, "We have met the enemy, and they are ours"; and General Anthony McAuliffe at Bastogne when he said "Nuts" to the German demand that he surrender. But then maybe Admiral McDonald's comment is the best summary of the state of the U.S. military today.

After the insertion of Grenada was completed, Brigadier General Jack Farris, commander of the 82d Airborne Division's forces on the island, said that the future role of the United States Army on Grenada was to build a police force that would prevent leftist revolutionaries from ever again seizing power on the island. General Farris said the United States had brought in sophisticated computers to register and keep track of the island's remaining leftists, with the help of an extensive police intelligence system built by Americans. "You develop a human-intelligence network, whereby you have your police and your agents throughout the country and find out who the bad guys are. . . ." Then, he continued, "You build a data base on those people, on thousands of them, and bring them all in and pick up all these people and question them. You put them all in a data base, and that's how you stamp out something like that."

General Farris noted that Prime Minister Maurice Bishop, who had been killed in a coup, had had widespread support. "Bishop was a very popular guy. . . . And there was grass roots support for the Bishop regime." However, General Farris noted that even though the Bishop government was popular, he recognized the need to prevent another revolutionary leader from coming to power in Grenada. "The grass roots support is not there. And we have to prevent it from developing again," General Farris said.

Perhaps General Farris could name the "human intelligence network" of police and agents he was developing the Thought Police. Then he could name all the citizens of Grenada Winston Smith, right after he established the Ministry of Love.

Doublespeak and Iran Air Flight 655

On July 3, 1988, the U.S.S. *Vincennes*, a U.S. cruiser on patrol in the Persian Gulf, shot down Iran Air flight 655, a commercial airliner carrying 290 people. The official investigation into that incident by the United States Navy produced a report that found that, although the personnel on the *Vincennes* committed a multitude of errors, no American military personnel were responsible for shooting down the airliner. Using doublespeak, Secretary of Defense Frank Carlucci, Admiral William Crowe, and Rear Admiral William Fogarty, author of the investigation report, placed the blame on the Iranians for forcing the *Vincennes* to shoot the airliner down.

The United States Navy's investigation report on the shooting down of the airliner was titled *Investigation Report: Formal Investigation into the Circumstances Surrounding the Downing of Iran Air Flight 655 on 3 July 1988.* The official press conference releasing and discussing the report was held on August 19, 1988. Both the report and the press conference were filled with the doublespeak of omission, distortion, contradiction, and misdirection.

One reporter called the "heavily censored report" an "enormous jigsaw puzzle with key pieces missing" because it presented an incomplete and frustrating picture. In addition to censoring a great deal of information, such as the names of almost all the participants, including the former commander of the U.S.S. *Vincennes,* the report also lacked any original source information, such as statements by participants and any of the data recorded by the ship's computers. While the report pretended to be detailed and complete—by giving such information as the air and sea temperatures, the wind speed and direction, the relative humidity, the evaporation duct height, the surface pressure, the visibility estimate, and the ceiling at the time of the shooting—it did not contain something as basic and as important as a map showing the course, over time, of the *Vincennes,* its sister ships, the Iranian airliner, and the Iranian gunboats. As one reporter noted, such a map would show important details such as "whether or not the plane was headed directly toward the *Vincennes,* or if it made any last-minute turn toward the ship that could have been interpreted as a fighter rolling in to attack." Yet Secretary of Defense Frank Carlucci said that "I believe the facts to the extent they can be known are clearly presented in the report. . . . We chose not to withhold anything."

At the news briefing held to release and discuss the report, Admiral William Crowe said that "a number of mistakes were made": First, Captain Will Rogers of the *Vincennes* concentrated on the fact that the airliner was three to four miles off the median line of its assigned air corridor (he did so despite navy procedure for taking such a deviation into account; moreover, the report reveals that the ship's radar mistakenly placed the center line of the commercial air corridor to the west of its actual point, so the airliner was actually where it was supposed to be). Second, the airliner was reported as descending, when the radar on the *Vincennes* in fact showed it was climbing. Third, the airliner was reported to be emitting a signal identifying it as an F-14 fighter plane, when in fact the ship's equipment showed it never emitted such a signal and indeed emitted a constant signal identifying itself as a commercial airliner. Fourth, the report by the Combat Information Center officer standing directly behind Captain Rogers that the airplane was possibly a commercial airliner was not acted upon. Finally, the *Vincennes* failed to monitor the constant communications between the airliner and the control tower at Bandar Abbas airport, failed to follow up on the commercial flight schedules that showed that flight 655 would be in the air about that time, and failed to note that the airliner was not emitting any of the radar signals (such as fire control or missile guidance) necessary for an attack.

Despite what *Time* magazine called this "catalog of errors committed by the crew," and despite Admiral Crowe's admission that "some of the information given to Captain Rogers during the engagement proved not to be accurate," Secretary Carlucci said "these errors or mistakes were not crucial" to the decision to shoot the airliner down. Carlucci went on to say that "the question is not whether mistakes were made. . . . The question is whether the mistakes were critical and whether they were due to culpability or negligence, and the finding is that they were not." Admiral Crowe claimed that "to say there were errors made . . . is not necessarily to suggest culpability."

A reported asked: "Are you saying that these mistakes are in no way responsible for the downing of this airliner? You use the word crucial, but there is some responsibility here, and these mistakes are in no way responsible for that." Secretary Carlucci replied, "If your question is had these mistakes not been made would the events have unfolded in a different direction, obviously no one can say for sure. It is the judgment of those who have investigated this, and it is Admiral Crowe's judgment which I accept, that the errors were not crucial to the decision."

When a reporter observed: "You say these mistakes weren't crucial, but it seems to be the accumulation of mistakes that was crucial," Carlucci replied: "I don't know how you can say that."

A reporter noted that a report issued earlier by the General Accounting Office on the training of the crews operating the Aegis radar system concluded that "The absence of stress biased results in favor of Aegis and left the actual performance in a more realistic environment unknown." Yet when it was noted that the official report stated that "stress . . . may have played a major role in this incident" Secretary Carlucci insisted that "the training had been adequate."

Admiral Crowe also said that "there are a series of recommendations looking at what can be done to improve both the system and the people operating it." But when a reporter said, "So the equipment itself and the procedures did contribute to the errors made," Admiral Crowe replied, "No, the equipment functioned as designed. We cannot find any errors in the equipment." "Then it wasn't designed correctly?" asked a reporter. Admiral Crowe replied, "I'm not indicating it wasn't designed correctly. I am indicating that as you go through experience with any weapon system you improve the design."

Neither Secretary Carlucci nor Admiral Crowe, nor the report itself, addressed the fact that, based upon virtually the same evidence available to Captain Rogers, the commander of the frigate *Sides,* eighteen miles away, had immediately identified the airplane as a civilian airliner.

It was not all the mistakes by the crew of the *Vincennes* which led to shooting down the airliner, according to the official report as endorsed by Admiral Crowe and Secretary Carlucci. Indeed, the report never stated that anyone on the *Vincennes* was responsible. Instead, in the best tradition of blaming the victim, the report and Admiral Crowe blamed the Iranians for making the *Vincennes* shoot down the airliner.

In the section entitled "Opinions," the report stated that "Iran must share the responsibility for the tragedy by hazarding one of their civilian airliners by allowing it to fly a relaatively [*sic*] low altitude air route in close proximity to hostilities. . . ." This statement contradicts an earlier section of the report which noted that the airliner was taking off and climbing steadily to its assigned altitude at the time it was shot down.

In his memorandum endorsing the report, Admiral Crowe stated: "I believe that the actions of Iran were the proximate cause of this accident and would argue that Iran must bear the principal responsibility for the tragedy."

When a reporter asked Admiral Crowe: "You said the Iranians are partially responsible. Do you have indications that the Bandar Abbas airport was aware that there was fighting going on between the *Vincennes* and Boghammers?" Admiral Crowe replied, "When we say Iranians we don't distinguish between the people at Bandar Abbas Airport and the people controlling the ships that are engaged in the fire fight."

Another reporter asked Admiral Crowe: "You're making the assumption that they work together on joint operations. Is that really the case?" He replied that "whether it's the case or not, the point is they were all Iranians."

A subsequent report prepared by an international panel of aviation experts for the International Civil Aviation Organization laid the blame for the disaster squarely on the navy. The report found that the crew of the Iran airliner had performed properly, while the crew of the U.S.S. *Vincennes* failed in a number of areas. It was only through doublespeak that the Pentagon could avoid responsibility for shooting down the civilian airliner. But then the Pentagon is well practiced in doublespeak.

It's Just a Radiation Enhancement Weapon

Military doublespeak that calls a rear-view mirror a "retro reflector," that refers to the layoff of civilian mechanics as placing them on "non-duty, non-pay status," that calls cowardice being "philosophically disillusioned," and chewing out someone "verbal counseling" isn't all that misleading, nor all that consequential. But you'd better be able to figure out a lot of the other doublespeak the military uses, because it can have very serious consequences. You need to know that the "Mark 12A re-entry system" is really the nuclear warhead on an ICBM missile; that the "physics package" Secretary of Defense Frank Carlucci is talking about is the nuclear warhead on an Intermediate Range Ballistic Missile located in Europe; and that when Secretary Weinberger called for a "major expansion of force structure" he was calling for an increase in the number of combat divisions in the army.

For fifteen years the Pentagon got funding for the neutron

bomb from Congress by calling it a "radiation enhancement weapon." In 1977 the Pentagon wanted to begin production of the bomb, so it again sought money from Congress to build its "radiation enhancement weapon." Congress was all set to approve funding for this new weapon when Walter Pincus, a reporter for *The Washington Post*, revealed the reality of the weapon, and how the Pentagon planned to use it. A staff member for the Senate Appropriations Committee said that because of the "radiation enhancement" doublespeak, some legislators "didn't understand the full implication of it." But because of the articles by Walter Pincus explaining what a "radiation enhancement weapon" is, what it does, and what it was to be used for, Congress at that time changed its mind and decided not to build the neutron bomb.

What is a "radiation enhancement weapon," and how does the Pentagon plan to use it? The Pentagon described it as "an efficient nuclear weapon that eliminates an enemy with a minimum of damage to friendly territory" by killing people while leaving buildings intact. Now we know what the Pentagon considers really important. "Save the real estate!" might be the battle cry for the next war. The neutron bomb works by attacking the central nervous system: the body convulses, limbs shake, the nervous system fails so that all of the automatic body functions, even breathing, are affected. Death comes within forty-eight hours from respiratory failure or swelling of tissues in the brain.

The Pentagon developed the neutron bomb for use against an enemy occupying army. A Pentagon official said that "We were going to use it over our own territory, if necessary"—territory including San Francisco, Los Angeles, New York, Chicago, Boston, Detroit, Seattle, Honolulu. The Pentagon, which also called the bomb "the cookie cutter," claimed that it would kill people inside less than a three-quarter-mile radius without harming allied soldiers and civilians nearby. The Pentagon assumed that an occupying enemy would be considerate enough to place civilians outside any such radius. In 1981, after Congress changed its mind and approved funding to build the bomb, the Pentagon called it an "enhanced radiation device." In 1984, the Pentagon changed the name again and started calling it an "enlarged radiation" weapon.

In 1982 a meeting was called in the White House to find a new and appealing name for the MX missile. When someone suggested calling the missile the "Peacemaker," the name that was finally selected, Robert McFarlane, national security adviser to President Reagan, said, "I suppose widowmaker wouldn't do?" Later, President Reagan mistakenly called the missile the "Peacekeeper," a name that it still has today. With military doublespeak, what you don't know or understand might just kill you.

CHAPTER VII

Nothing in Life Is Certain Except Negative Patient Care Outcome and Revenue Enhancement: Your Government at Work

When Governor Nelson Rockefeller of New York was campaigning for president and was asked to explain his position on the Vietnam War, he said:

> My position on Vietnam is very simple. And I feel this way. I haven't spoken on it because I haven't felt there was any major contribution that I had to make at the time. I think that our concepts as a nation and that our actions have not kept pace with the changing conditions. And therefore our actions are not completely relevant today to the realities of the magnitude and the complexity of the problems that we face in this conflict.

"What does that mean, Governor?" asked a reporter. "Just what I said," replied Governor Rockefeller.

Political doublespeak is often language that sounds impressive but really says nothing. As George Orwell wrote, it is language that obscures meaning "like a cuttlefish squirting out ink." Gobbledygook, or bureaucratese, is such a common form of political and government doublespeak because it allows the speaker to appear intelligent and able to handle a difficult, complicated subject while suggesting that the audience is too stupid to understand what the speaker is saying. As Governor Rockefeller implied, he had been perfectly clear, and he couldn't help it if the reporter was too dumb to understand his comments. In other words, if we're confused, the fault lies with us, not with the politicians who use doublespeak.

In addition to saying nothing, political doublespeak also allows the speaker to sound sincere, concerned, and thoughtful. When a constituent wrote to Senator David Durenberger, urging him to vote against aid to the Nicaraguan Contras, the Senator replied with a letter that contained such sentences as:

> I think you will agree with me that the United States and its democratic allies have a responsibility to encourage democracy, peace, economic development and reform in Central America. This policy should apply to regimes of the right—like Panama—as much as it should apply to regimes of the left—like Nicaragua. As you know, I have stated many times that this important goal can be carried out only through a comprehensive policy in the region—a policy with definitive objectives, rather than piecemeal reactions to political and military events.

If this statement really represents Senator Durenberger's thinking on aid to the Nicaraguan Contras, then the honorable senator from Minnesota must have a thinking process somewhat similar to overcooked mush. More insultingly, he expects people to accept his doublespeak as legitimate language.

Unfortunately, such doublespeak is so common in what passes for political discourse in this country that we have come to expect it, even from presidents. In 1981, when President-elect Ronald Reagan was asked if he could go along with the terms of agreement to release the American hostages in Iran, he said, "If what I understand, if it is true, that I was told what I understood, yes, I thought that made sense." And no one was bothered that a man who used such language was about to be sworn in as president.

President Reagan got better at doublespeak during his years in office, especially when he had to face the Iran-contra scandal. At a press conference on March 19, 1987, the president was asked: "Mr. President, is it possible that two military officers who are trained to obey orders grabbed power, made major foreign policy moves, didn't tell you when you were briefed every day on intelligence? Or did they think they were doing your bidding?" To which President Reagan answered: "I don't know. I only know that that's why I've said repeatedly that I want to find out. I want to get to the bottom of this and find out all that has happened and so far I've told you all that I know. And you know the truth of the matter is, for quite some long time, all that you knew was what I'd told you." If Senator Durenberger's statement reflected a mind of mush, what can be said about the mind of the man who uttered this statement?

Although just vice-president at the time, George Bush demonstrated more than once that he can use the doublespeak of gobbledygook to avoid taking a position and accepting responsibility for his actions—or nonactions. In 1987 Mr. Bush explained his views on the policy of selling arms to Iran by saying,

> I think it's debatable, and I think on the surface you can make a case that it's wrong. Having said that, when you look at the whole policy and look at Iran's geographic standing and look at the problems facing them, if a small shipment establishes contact with moderate elements, and if it results down the line in a solution to the Iran-Iraq war, I think we can argue that it was right. On the surface, selling arms to a country that state-sponsors terrorism, of course, clearly, you'd have to argue it's wrong, but it's the exception sometimes that proves the rule.

With doublespeak, Vice-President Bush can take a firm nonposition, favoring the arms sale and opposing it, leaving his audience as bewildered as Governor Rockefeller's. But unlike Governor Rockefeller, Vice-President Bush was elected president.

Politicians who use doublespeak see nothing wrong with using such language to mislead the voting public. According to former President Richard Nixon, a president is not always "lying in an immoral sense" when he says something he doesn't believe. Mr. Nixon is quoted in a 1982 article in *The New York Times* as saying that as a candidate "you have to dissemble. . . . There's a lot of hypocrisy and so forth in political life. It's necessary in order to get into office and in order to return to office." So much for expecting our political leaders to be truthful and speak clearly to us.

Once upon a time (actually, it was 1912), in a faraway land (actually it was New York, which isn't as far away as you think), a voter became upset when the candidate for whom he voted promptly proceeded, once he was in office, to ignore all the promises he had made during the campaign. The voter became so upset he sued the politician for breach of oral contract. After all, reasoned the disillusioned voter, weren't the promises made by a politician during a campaign a promise to the voters? And didn't those same oral promises constitute an oral contract between the candidate and the voter, a contract in which in exchange for the voter's vote the candidate promised to do certain things if elected?

Unfortunately, this tale takes place in New York, which is in the real world and not in a fairytale kingdom where people and life are far more truthful and honest. In New York, the judge ruled that "a contract cannot be based on an ante-election promise to voters generally by a candidate for public office, so as to give a voter a right to restrain the promisor from violating same." In other words, there's no legal way voters can make politicians keep their promises, once they have been elected, so politicians are free to say whatever they want during an election campaign and then do whatever they want once they're in office. (*O'Reilly* v. *Mitchell*, 85 Misc. 176, 148 N.Y.S. 88 [Sup.Ct. 1914].)

Probably few if any candidates for office know about the New York court decision. In fact, they display their talent for using doublespeak so frequently it's almost as if they think the ability to use doublespeak is an important qualification for office. Alexander Haig was famous for his use of doublespeak as secretary of state, especially the doublespeak he used to justify the murder of four American women in El Salvador. Running for president didn't change Haig's use of doublespeak. During the Republican presidential primaries in 1988 he said that "America as a nation, in relative terms, no longer has the demographic assets that enable us to survive incompetence, malfeasance, less than perfection in the conduct of our affairs." Mr. Haig's campaign didn't go very far because so few "demographic assets" voted for him in the primary elections.

During his campaign for president, Reverend Pat Robertson insisted that he was not a "television evangelist" but a "Christian broadcaster," a "religious broadcaster," or a "Christian businessman." The Reverend Robertson even went so far as to charge Tom Brokaw of NBC News with "religious bigotry" when Brokaw called him a "former television evangelist." But the Reverend Robertson proved he could use doublespeak with the best of those seeking the presidency. When asked to explain his idea for dealing with the deficit by declaring a year of jubilee and canceling the debt, the Reverend Robertson said, "Certainly the trouble that we run into economically, if you use the term Kondratieff long-wave cycle, is a cycle of debt accumulation of which we have in our country now, $10 trillion, we have it about every 54, 56, 58 years on an exponential basis. . . ." You have to wonder if politicians go to school to learn to speak this way, or whether it's just natural for them to use doublespeak, like Orwell's cuttlefish uses its ink.

How Political Ads on TV Lie

Even the ads politicians run on television can't be trusted. It's not just the doublespeak in these ads you have to watch out for, but the pictures themselves. If you think the camera doesn't lie, then you might want to buy shares in a cheese-mining company on the moon.

According to Ron Harris, chief editor at the National Video Center in New York, "Political commercials are now filled with special effects." Mr. Harris ought to know because he was the postproduction editor responsible for the special effects in the famous George Bush commercial during the 1988 New Hampshire primary accusing Robert Dole of "straddling" the issues. Even Senator Dole's media advisers credit this commercial with igniting Bush's campaign. What special effects, you ask?

While a political commercial may not show the candidate doing battle with invaders from Mars, the effects in some commercials are just as special as any found in science fiction movies. The Bush commercial contrasted a photograph of Bush and his supposedly clear position on the issues with a photograph of Dole who, the commercial said, "straddled" the issues. On the surface, it appeared to be a fairly clear-cut political commercial. But let's look at the commercial a little more closely for the magic performed by Ron Harris.

For the Bush commercial, Harris used a variety of subtle, almost subliminal, techniques. The picture of Dole was flipped so that his hair was parted on the wrong side and his face appeared awkward. Then, too, "these are not great pictures of Dole," said Harris. They look "almost as if he was in mid-attack." On the other hand, the pictures of Bush not only caught him in a good mood, but every time the photograph of Bush appeared a thin halo of light outlined the back of his head. Dole was given no such halo.

Another Bush commercial called "Presidential Temperament" offered alternating snippets of Bush's best comments contrasted to Dole's worst. Even with the volume turned off Bush came across as the stronger candidate because his words were always framed by a blue background while Dole's words were framed in black. Even the people surrounding Bush were colorfully dressed, while the people in Dole's background looked washed out.

In another commercial Bush was seen delivering a speech to what appeared to be an enthusiastic crowd. It seemed as if every word Bush uttered was greeted with wild cheers, whistles, and applause. But even as the viewer heard the cheering the camera panned across a room of listeners who were sitting quietly with their mouths shut. All the cheering was on the sound track. Ron Harris claims that without a well-edited sound track the commercial would have been "a good 30% weaker."

Throughout all of Bush's commercials, certain techniques were always used. Every time Dole's words appeared on the television screen Ron Harris made sure they were underlined in hot-tempered red while Bush's words were always underlined in a cool, calm blue. Bush was also either wearing blue, had blue curtains in the background, or was framed by a blue background.

There is other magic Ron Harris can perform if called upon to do so. He can make sure a hair is never out of place or eliminate a shiny bald spot. He can even make a candidate's nose smaller if necessary. All of these "special effects" are used without the slightest sense that there is any dishonesty involved in such political commercials. So the next time you see a television commercial for a candidate, watch carefully for these "special effects" because what you see is not necessarily what you will get, because now the camera always lies.

Tried Any Initiatives Lately?

For quite awhile, when politicians had nothing to say because they had no ideas or simply didn't know what was going on, they would fall back on that handy little piece of doublespeak, "process," as in the "Camp David process," the "Contadora process," or the "peace process." But "process" lost its luster, so another meaningless yet impressive word had to be found. Some genius at doublespeak came up with "initiative." In case you haven't noticed, this is the era (age? decade? year? month? moment?) of the initiative. For politicians, "initiative" has become THE word to use when discussing any program that is more goal than fact, more hope than reality, more hype than substance.

Throughout the Iran-contra hearings, everyone spoke of the "Iran initiative," the "Nicaragua initiative," the "arms initiative," the "peace initiative," and any number of initiatives. While this wonderfully vague word was never really explained, it allowed a seemingly precise discussion of incomplete, insincere, failed, duplicitous, or disastrous actions. But those using the word so freely and so imprecisely were right in step with using what has become the most popular word in Washington, if we ignore the frequent use of the word "recall" as in the sentence "I don't recall."

How do politicians initiate? Let us count the ways. There is, of course, the "Strategic Defense Initiative," but the Defense Department also announced the "Strategic Computer Initiative," and the "Air Defense Initiative." And President Reagan announced the "Superconductivity Initiative," while continuing the "Caribbean Basin Initiative," the "International Youth Exchange Initiative," and the "U.S.–Soviet Exchange Initiative."

If all those initiatives aren't enough to keep everyone busy, there's a special assistant for "park initiatives" in the National Park Service, an "Office of Quality Control Initiatives" in the Labor Department, and a "Defense Spares Initiatives Office" in the Defense Logistics Agency. Not to be outdone, Senator Sam Nunn proposed a "Conventional Defense Initiative."

When politicians run out of ideas or solutions, or when they want to sound like they're doing something when they haven't the faintest idea what to do, they come up with initiatives. Initiatives only start, they don't finish, which explains why there have been so many Middle East peace initiatives, but no real peace in the Middle East. Initiatives, initiatives everywhere, but not a success in sight.

Doublespeak, the Language of Government

While politicians often use doublespeak to avoid taking a position or accepting responsibility, or to lie and mislead, government workers often use doublespeak simply because it's the only language they know. They really think they are communicating a message with their doublespeak. Their audience, however, is just as bewildered and baffled as any politician's.

Maybe it's not reasonable to expect people who work in government agencies with names like the "Federal Insurance Administration, Office of Risk Assessment, Technical Operations Division, Production Control Branch of the Federal Emergency Management Agency" (or to those in the know, "FIA/ORA/TOD/PCB/FEMA," an agency that employs exactly four people) to use clear language. Still, there are those in Washington who do try every once in awhile to clarify complicated names. Take, for example, William H. Manley of the Veterans Administration who in 1988 sent out a memorandum announcing that the title "Supply Service" had been changed to "Office of Acquisition & Materiel Management Service." See how hard the people in Washington are working to make things simpler? Sort of reminds you of the crew at the Pentagon simplifying the language of their contracts.

People in government write things like this notice which appeared in the federal government's publication *Commerce Business Daily* (June 27, 1988), calling for bids for the job of "Deinstallation of Institutional Conduct of Fire Trainer from present location and reinstatement of its permanent location. . . ." Another notice called for bids for the "outsulation" of a building. But sometimes government bureaucrats get caught by their own doublespeak. The Energy Department proposed the following new regulation in 1983: "Nothing in these regulations precludes the secretary or his delegate from designating information not specifically described in this regulation as unclassified controlled nuclear information." When asked if the proposed regulation meant that the Secretary of Energy or any low-level bureaucrat to whom he hands the power of censorship can suppress any information, including unclassified information long in the public domain, officials were unable to answer since they weren't sure what the regulation meant. Now this is language without thought, language produced without bothering to engage the higher thinking faculties. The problem, however, is that such language affects your life.

When communicating with ordinary mortals, meaning people who don't understand their doublespeak, government agencies can create some confusion. One poor taxpayer didn't have the slightest notion what this letter from the U.S. Civil Service Commission meant:

> This notice assures you that the second (corrected) tax statement we sent to you is accurate. . . . The original statement we sent to you understated your beginning balance of retirement contributions. The second statement corrects this error. . . . We are sending this notice to all annuitants who received accurate corrected copies because some annuitants were sent corrected copies by mistake.

Another taxpayer received a letter from the Office of Management and Budget with this concluding paragraph: "Since data is central to the issue of refined implementation guidance and legislation defers implementation, we believe it is advisable to examine the data that your organization is assembling to preclude any such unintended effects." Try not to think of it as doublespeak but as another example of your tax dollars at work.

It's Not a Tax Increase, It's Revenue Enhancement

Somehow taxes always seem to bring out the doublespeak in politicians and the Internal Revenue Service. In fact, look at the name of the tax collector—"Internal Revenue Service." Now that's a nice piece of doublespeak. It reminds you how the IRS services you every April.

Once taxes were what you expected to pay for government services. After all, someone has to pay for police, fire fighters, roads, schools, garbage collection and disposal, sewage treatment plants, and all those other services provided by government. But now taxes have become the dreaded "T" word, feared and shunned by politicians at all levels of government. Yet we all know that taxes are necessary. So politicians use doublespeak to talk about taxes and tax increases because with doublespeak there are no taxes and certainly no such thing as a tax increase.

If you live in California, you might have mistakenly thought that there was going to be an increase in state taxes in 1988. Faced with a $1 billion "hole" in the state budget, Governor George Deukmejian of California and his director of finance Jesse Huff both insisted that any changes in the tax laws should not be construed as a tax increase, even though some people would pay more taxes than they were under current laws. "It is not a tax increase," Huff said. "It is an adjustment of a windfall this year." Now don't you feel better? You're not going to pay any more in taxes; you're just going to have your windfall adjusted.

President Reagan campaigned saying there would be a tax increase only over his dead body, so doublespeak was used to increase taxes without stepping over the president's dead body. But it took a little work to come up with the doublespeak needed to say tax increase without saying it. When Congress refused to freeze Social Security cost-of-living increases, President Reagan said he would consider taxing the Social Security benefits of the wealthy. Senator Robert Dole called the president's proposal a "recapture of benefits," while White House spokesperson Larry Speakes called the plan a "replacement of revenues."

The favorite doublespeak for tax increase used by the Reagan Administration was "revenue enhancement," which replaced "tax enhancement." According to The New York Times, Lawrence A. Kudlow, chief economist of the Office of Management and Budget, admitted he had invented the phrase in 1981 so the dreaded "T" word could be avoided, especially in a proposal for a $3 billion tax increase. He also proudly admitted that he had invented "receipts strengthening," but that doublespeak was rejected and "revenue enhancement" was chosen as the preferred term. When asked why he would use such a phrase as "revenue enhancement," Mr. Kudlow is quoted as saying, "There's no better way to sell economic theory than by the euphemistic route." Even Mr. Kudlow's seemingly honest admission uses doublespeak when he calls a proposed tax increase "economic theory."

With the doublespeak of "revenue enhancement," President Reagan could approve House Bill 4961, known by its doublespeak title as the "Tax Equality and Fiscal Responsibility Act of

1982," a bill which raised $99 billion in tax revenues, and still maintain that there would be a tax increase only over his dead body. Senator Robert Dole called the bill a "reform bill, not a tax increase bill." See how easy it is? You're not paying more in taxes; you're just reforming the tax law and enhancing government revenue.

It's Not Revenue Enhancement, It's User Fees

It didn't take too long for everyone to catch on to the real meaning behind the doublespeak of "revenue enhancement," so other phrases such as "tax base broadening," "tax base erosion control," and "update the revenue mechanism" started to appear. When the Reagan Administration proposed a plan in 1982 to increase the federal gasoline tax by five cents a gallon with the funds to be spent repairing highways, bridges, streets, and mass transit, White House deputy press secretary Larry Speakes denied that it was a gasoline tax but said instead that it was a "user's fee" imposed "on those who use cars and gasoline." Moreover, it wasn't a public-works program but a "construction program on work that needs doing." Thus, there was no reversal of President Reagan's opposition to increasing taxes and spending money to provide jobs.

The discovery of the term "user fee" for "tax increase" really opened up all kinds of opportunities for raising taxes without raising them. In January 1987, Treasury Secretary James Baker acknowledged that the Reagan Administration's new budget called for some selected tax increases. In remarks made before the Senate Budget Committee, Mr. Baker said that in the 1988 budget "there are $6.1 billion of receipts, revenues—call it what you will—that, I think it's fair to say, probably represent [higher] taxes." But Mr. Baker insisted that these selected tax increases did not violate President Reagan's firm objection to a tax increase since President Reagan opposed a general tax increase. Senator Warren Rudman asked Mr. Baker to explain how excise taxes on items such as cigarettes differ from administration proposals such as the administration's proposed $1 "fee" on airline tickets for flights into and out of the United States. "Excise taxes are excise taxes. And they're taxes," Mr. Baker replied. He said that "user fees" for government services shouldn't be considered taxes. Senator Lawton Chiles suggested the government impose a "user fee" on corporate mergers. When Mr. Baker objected that user fees apply to government services not private transactions, Senator Chiles answered, "I'm talking about a user fee to fund the Antitrust Division" of the Justice Department.

In February 1987, however, Budget Director James Miller insisted that the proposed budget did not contain tax increases, but rather "increased receipts" and "offsetting collections." Are these tax increases? "The answer is a definite *no*," declared Mr. Miller. The $1 per ticket fee for airline and cruise tickets into and out of the United States is a "user charge" that will be applied toward the cost of running the U.S. Travel and Tourism Administration. When it was pointed out that the proposed fee would raise more than double the amount necessary to fund the agency, with the surplus going to the Treasury, Mr. Miller suggested that the surplus be considered an "investment."

Single-Purpose Agricultural Structures, and Other Tax Reforms

So nobody likes to pay taxes, even when they're called "user fees." So everybody knows, and complains, that the tax law is hopelessly confused and confusing. The original income tax law was sixteen pages long but has over the years grown to over sixteen thousand pages, containing such passages as "The term 'taxable distribution' means any distribution which is not out of the income of the trust, within the meaning of section 643(b), from a generation-skipping trust to any younger generation beneficiary who is assigned to a generation younger than the generation assignment of any other person who is a younger generation beneficiary." With the tax law filled with such doublespeak, taxpayers increasingly demanded that Congress do something to clarify and simplify the law and the language of the law. But like the Pentagon and any other agency of government, Congress only complicates things whenever it tries to simplify them.

The doublespeak of taxes only got worse with the Tax Reform Act of 1986, a title that was itself a wonderful piece of doublespeak. Running some 1,489 pages, this simplified tax law contains such simplified language as "For purposes of paragraph (3), an organization described in paragraph (2) shall be deemed to include an organization described in section 501 (c)(4), (5) or (6) which would be described in paragraph (2) if it were an organization described in section 501 (c)(3)." There were so many errors in the bill that Congress had to pass a bill 446 pages long explaining and correcting all of them. If Congress keeps simplifying the tax law, it will take a major portion of the federal budget just to print copies of it.

The Tax Reform Act of 1986 calls chicken coops and pigpens "single-purpose agricultural structures," thereby giving farmers a special depreciation deduction denied other businesses. The act also declares that Don Tyson and his sister-in-law Barbara Tyson run a "family farm." Their "farm" has twenty-five thousand employees and grosses $1.7 billion a year, but because the bill calls them a "family farm" they get tax breaks that save them $135 million. Nor were the Tysons alone in receiving special largess from Congress. In a series of articles in *The Philadelphia Inquirer*, investigative reporters Donald Barlett and James Steele revealed hundreds of such deceptive passages in the act and how such passages granted billions of dollars in tax exemptions to corporations and influential, wealthy individuals, all done through the use of doublespeak.

Among the dozens of sections of the act that Barlett and Steele cite is one that states,

In the case of a partnership with a taxable year
beginning May 1, 1986, if such partnership realized net
capital gain during the period beginning on the first day
of such taxable year and ending on May 29, 1986,
pursuant to an indemnity agreement dated May 6, 1986,
then such partnership may elect to treat each asset to
which such net capital gain relates as having been

distributed to the partners of such partnership in proportion to their distributive share of the capital gain or loss realized by the partnership with respect to each asset.

This doublespeak applies only to the partners of the Bear Stearns and Companies, Inc., a Wall Street investment banking and brokerage company, and saves them $8 million in taxes. The chairman of the company, who received $5.7 million in cash compensation in 1986, was already the highest-paid executive of any publicly-held Wall Street brokerage firm.

Barlett and Steele also pointed out that while the tax bill was touted as socking it to corporations, the increase in taxes for corporations was insignificant. In 1940, corporations paid 57 percent of all income taxes collected by the government, while individuals paid 43 percent. In 1985, individuals paid 85 percent, while corporations paid only 15 percent. Even after the 1986 Tax Reform Act went into effect, corporations paid only 17 percent of all income taxes collected, which is below the 1980 level of 21 percent. The doublespeak in this act is some of the most powerful and expensive you will ever come across. So the next time you hear politicians talk about "tax reform" or "tax simplification," hang onto your wallet because they're going to complicate the law with even more doublespeak, and they're going to raise your taxes.

Unlawful or Arbitrary Deprivation of Life, and Other State Department Doublespeak

Want a good job? Well, if you were hanging around Washington, D.C. in 1976, you could have applied for the job of Consumer Affairs Coordinator at the State Department. According to the announcement for this position, "The purpose of the Department's plan is two-fold, to confirm and reinforce the Department's sensitivity to consumer rights and interests as they impact upon the Department and to take those steps necessary and feasible to promote and channel these rights and interests with respect to the maintenance and expansion of an international dialogue and awareness." The announcement goes on to state that the job of coordinator would be to "review existing mechanisms of consumer input, thruput and output, and seek ways of improving these linkages via the consumer communication channel." Of course, as clear and specific as this description is, it leaves out the most important qualification for the job: you had to know Henry Kissinger, since the job was specifically created for one of his friends. This is the same Henry Kissinger who in his memoirs called bombs and bullets "consumables."

Secretary of State Alexander Haig gained fame for his doublespeak, if not his creative use of words. In testimony before a Senate committee, Haig told Senator John Glenn that his question could not be answered "in the way you contexted it." Haig went on to say, "I'll have to caveat my response, Senator." Haig also expressed his hope that the Soviets would do nothing "to exacerbate the kind of mutual restraint that both sides should pursue," and often spoke of "nuanced and fundamentally sharp departures" and "nuance-al differences." He was also careful not to "saddle myself with a statistical fence" and pointed out that "the very act of definitizing an answer" could cause problems. But all of this language was only warming up for statements such as, "This is not an experience I haven't been through before." However, he reached even greater heights when he told the Senate Foreign Relations Committee in 1982 that a continued weapons buildup by the United States is "absolutely essential to our hopes for meaningful arms reduction."

Secretary Haig's language fit right in at the State Department, where they have "non-papers," which are discussion papers that are not attributed to an individual. They also have "non-meetings," during which they discuss the "non-papers." In 1981, when El Salvador treasury police dragged twenty-three men from their homes and killed them, and killed seven more men inside their homes, a State Department spokesperson said that "the police had probably overreacted." In 1988 the State Department warned embassy employees in Budapest that "it must be assumed that available casual indigenous female companions work for or cooperate with the Hungarian government security establishment." In other words, local prostitutes are probably spies for the Hungarian government. Those people at the State Department sure have a way with words.

With doublespeak, the State Department can reject the World Court and still accept it. Even though the United States had already announced that it would not accept the World Court's jurisdiction in the charges brought against the United States by Nicaragua, representatives of the United States were present at the court. When asked why they were present, Davis Robinson, legal adviser to the State Department, said, "That we are here shows our continuing commitment to the International Court of Justice and the rule of law."

Doublespeak also allows the State Department to explain a policy of being neutral while choosing sides in a war. Although the United States was publicly neutral in the Iran-Iraq war, the United States provided "battlefield-related intelligence" to Iraq. Asked to explain how this intelligence assistance squared with the administration's professed neutrality, Phyllis Oakley, spokesperson for the State Department, said, "We're neutral on the outcome." That's something like giving one guy a gun when all the other guy has is a stick, and then insisting that you're neutral about the outcome of the fight.

In 1982, when four members of Congress called for a ceasefire and a negotiated settlement to the civil war in El Salvador, which had started after a military junta seized power in 1979, State Department spokesperson Dean Fischer said, "We believe that a negotiation on power sharing as proposed by the guerrillas would constitute a usurpation of the right of the Salvadoran people to determine the nature of their own government." However, the State Department later saw no usurpation of the right of the Nicaraguan people to determine the nature of their own government when the department supported the claims of the Nicaraguan guerrillas to share in the government.

Cleaning Up the Contras with Doublespeak

First the State Department had to legitimize the Nicaraguan guerrillas by giving them the right kind of name, and the right kind of definition to that name. So instead of calling them guerrillas, the State Department called them Contras, and then "Freedom Fighters," after President Reagan used that term. But sometimes the doublespeak gets ahead of events. According to Jim Anderson of United Press International, the 1987 edition of the State Department's *Dictionary of International Relations and Terms* had to be recalled because it contained a fallacious definition. The State Department said that there was an error in the definition of the term "Contras," who were defined as a group of "counterrevolutionaries" that "comprise former members of the Somozist National Guard, dissident right-wing former Sandinistas and the Miskito Indian minority." Since these groups weren't exactly the kind of people you'd normally think of as "Freedom Fighters," the State Department simply wrote another definition more in keeping with the image of the guerrillas it wanted to present to Congress and the American public. In a particularly nice touch of doublespeak, the supervision of the "covert" war waged by the U.S.-funded guerrillas against Nicaragua was directed by the State Department's "Agency for Humanitarian Assistance."

Changing the definitions of words to suit its purposes is not new with the State Department. In the weeks after the invasion of Grenada, U.S. military forces arrested over eleven hundred Grenadians and others suspected or accused of opposing the invasion. Since the U.S. forces had no legal authority to arrest anyone on the island, the State Department simply denied that anyone was arrested. "We are detaining people," said a State Department official. "They should be described as detainees." Let's hope that the police in the United States don't use the State Department's doublespeak.

The State Department is required by Congress to prepare each year a full report on the status of human rights in 163 countries around the world. Now the State Department had a problem because some of the governments that the United States supports engage in the systematic abuse of the human rights of their citizens. It's hard to come up with a positive report on the status of human rights in countries like South Africa, Guatemala, El Salvador, Iran, and Chile, especially when some governments kill a lot of their citizens. To smooth over the problem a little, the State Department announced in its 1,485-page 1984 report that it would no longer use the word "killing" in its reports. Instead it will use the phrase "unlawful or arbitrary deprivation of life." "We found the term 'killing' too broad and have substituted the more precise, if more verbose, 'unlawful or arbitrary deprivation of life,' " said Elliott Abrams, then assistant secretary of state for human rights. The State Department finds the world—and Congress and the American public—a lot easier to deal with as long as it uses doublespeak.

Sometimes State Department doublespeak isn't just carefully crafted language designed to mislead. Sometimes it's just plain lying. Assistant Secretary of State for Inter-American Affairs Elliott Abrams admitted in his testimony during the Iran-contra hearings that he "deliberately misled Congress on three occasions about his knowledge of foreign aid to Nicaraguan rebels." His excuse for lying to Congress was that "he wasn't authorized to tell the truth." Later, Senator Claiborne Pell, chairman of the Senate Foreign Relations Committee, refused to allow Abrams to testify before the committee, because it had been revealed that "information [Abrams] had supplied the committee in October 1986 was at odds with the facts." In a letter to the committee, Abrams wrote that "I regret that my October statements to the Congress on this subject—which I believed to be absolutely true—proved to be inaccurate." If you ever talk to Mr. Abrams, be sure to ask him if he's "authorized to tell the truth," otherwise everything he tells you may prove to be "inaccurate."

Grain-Consuming Animal Units, and Other
Concerns of the Government

The federal government produces doublespeak like Japan produces cars—in an endless, unbroken stream in all shapes and sizes for all kinds of functions. In addition to being a prime government product, doublespeak is also the essential fuel of government. It is the gas and oil that makes the government engine run because without doublespeak the federal government wouldn't operate. Sometimes it seems that without doublespeak there would be no government.

You may remember that the Department of Agriculture gave us "deep-chilled chickens" and "mechanically separated meat." This is also the government agency that in 1981 came up with the brilliant regulation saying that ketchup could be used as one of the two vegetables required for a balanced meal in the school lunch program. Not only does the department refer to cows, pigs, chickens, and other farm animals as "grain-consuming animal units" in its monthly feed outlook report, but it also classifies white farmers as "non-minorities."

The Department of Agriculture issues "marketing orders" to farmers, orders which strictly control the amounts of produce that farmers can sell to processors. Thus the department can control how much produce goes from the farmer to the market, no matter how much the farmer grows thus controlling the price consumers will pay. In 1981, the department admitted that this practice caused "price enhancement" for consumers, but it defended the practice and didn't change it.

Also in 1981 the department proposed a change in the standards that allow a maximum permissible percentage of "checks" or cracked shells in eggs at retail stores. "This change would merely align the tolerance for 'checks' to more accurately reflect what is already happening under today's egg production and marketing practices," said Donald L. Houston, administrator of the department's Food Safety and Quality Service. In other words, the present standard isn't being followed so the department will just change the standard. Remember that the next time you try to find a carton of eggs with none of them broken.

When he was Secretary of the Interior, James Watt said, "I never use the words Republican and Democrats. It's liberals and Americans." In keeping with this use of language, Secretary Watt also said that "Virtually every action I have taken has been part of a strategy to protect the environment." As part of his strategy to protect the environment, Secretary Watt championed the Wilderness Protection Bill, which he claimed would ban oil and gas leasing in most wilderness areas until the year 2000. However, the bill would also open closed wilderness areas to mining after the year 2000, and would allow the president to open any wilderness area before 2000 because of a "national emergency," a term not defined in the bill.

Among Secretary Watt's other actions to protect the environment were reducing the staff of the Office of Surface Mining (which enforces the strip-mining reclamation law) from one thousand to six hundred; increasing offshore oil drilling; offering the first onshore Alaskan oil and gas leases since the 1960s; adding four Pacific Ocean basins to a California offshore lease sale (these tracts lie in valuable fishing areas not far from some of California's most treasured beaches, yet the tracts contain only twelve days' worth of oil); advocating oil and mineral exploration in the Bob Marshall Wilderness Area in Montana; and proposing that environmental quality as a major policy objective of the Interior Department be dropped. These were just a few of the ways in which Secretary Watt protected the environment.

Secretary Watt was in good company with his doublespeak. In 1983, Frederic Andre, a member of the Interstate Commerce Commission, said that the commission should not worry about bribes in the trucking business, because bribes are "one of the clearest instances of the free market at work." When other members of the ICC insisted that bribes were wrong, Andre replied, "Well, they are just discounts. . . . A bribe is a rebate, is it not?" With this kind of doublespeak, the Mafia could quickly become a respected corporation, calling extortion insurance payments, for example.

Government agencies never kill animals or cut down trees. In

1981, G. Ray Arnett, Assistant Secretary of the Interior, explained the difference between hunting and killing as "You kill rats, but you harvest game." In 1983, when the federal government launched a program to gas over 7 million chickens in an effort to contain an influenza virus in Pennsylvania, it said it had "depopulated" the birds. The Park Service calls killing dangerous grizzly bears in Yellowstone Park "renaturalization." Under a program of "vegetation manipulation," the Department of the Interior proposed clear cutting hundreds of acres of aspen trees in scenic areas around the famous resort town of Aspen, Colorado, in 1983. Al Wright of the Bureau of Land Management said, "There are several valid forest-management purposes in managing the aspen." "Managing" is doublespeak for "cutting down."

With doublespeak, selling public lands is called "asset management" for the Bureau of Land Management and death becomes a "serious adverse effect" from the use of E-Feral Aqueous Solution, as the Food and Drug Administration noted in 1984. Doublespeak allows Secretary of Energy Donald Hodel to propose a new security classification called "Unclassified Controlled Nuclear Information," which covers information not subject to classification because it poses no threat to national security. Violators of the new classification would be subject to a fine of up to $100,000. Not to be outdone in the quest for security, a National Security Planning Group chaired by Robert McFarlane in 1985 issued National Security Directive 196 recommending "that the U.S. Government adopt, in principle, the use of aperiodic, non-lifestyle counterintelligence-type polygraph examinations." President Reagan signed the directive, thus requiring over 100,000 Americans who work for the government to submit to lie-detector tests at any time.

When is a flight delay not a flight delay? When the Federal Aviation Administration is doing the counting. The FAA counts as delays only those flights that are held up by air traffic controllers because of bad weather or too many planes in the sky. "We don't pay attention to schedules," said FAA spokesperson Fred Farrar. Thus, the FAA's most often cited statistic that about one in seventeen flights is delayed is doublespeak.

When it comes to airplane accidents, the official doublespeak really flows. The National Transportation Safety Board, in FAA Accident Investigation Records, uses the phrase "controlled flight into terrain" for airplane crashes. When a passenger airliner barely missed colliding with another airliner during takeoff, the NTSB called it a "runway incursion," while the FAA called it a "pilot deviation." When a helicopter crashed, killing three people, the NTSB cited as the probable causes of the crash: "flying into bad weather and failure to maintain clearance from the ground." And according to the FAA, the propeller blade didn't break off, it was just a case of "uncontained blade liberation."

Let's Go for a Primary Recreational Contact

In 1987, the Environmental Protection Agency announced that pollution control efforts had been so effective that parts of the Delaware River in Philadelphia were suitable for "primary recreational contact," meaning you could go swimming in the river. Such doublespeak isn't too surprising, because in 1981 EPA Administrator Anne Gorsuch banned the term "acid rain" and required that only the phrase "poorly buffered precipitation" could be used. But in 1981 the EPA also decided to make doublespeak the official language of the agency.

John Hernandez, deputy EPA administrator, explained that words like "hazard" were on their way out at the EPA. "Hazard" had through overuse become "a trigger-word that excites the American public needlessly," according to Mr. Hernandez. Instead of "degree of hazard," Hernandez said he wanted "to talk about 'degree of mitigation of risk,'" and he changed the name of the Office of Hazardous Emergency Response to the "Office of Emergency and Remedial Response." The EPA would also avoid the word "cancer-causing." Thus, the EPA decided not to publicize new findings that certain wood preservatives might cause cancer, nor would it identify toxic chemicals that have been found to cause genetic abnormalities or birth defects. "It might scare too many people," said one EPA press aide. Also, EPA "enforcement personnel" were to be called "compliance assistance officers."

An example of the new language policy in action occurred when in a draft press release it was said that a Los Angeles chemical dump had "exploded and burned." (The fire at the dump caused explosions that sent seven-hundred-pound drums hundreds of feet in the air.) When the draft press release came back from EPA Administrator Anne Gorsuch's office the word "exploded" had been deleted, along with the names, descriptions, and possible adverse health effects of the chemicals involved. Thus does doublespeak function as the official language of the EPA.

The doublespeak flows in the government, whether people in government are talking to the public or to each other. The Bureau of Land Management issued a press release in 1986 which began, "In a move to add administrative procedures regarding compliance with statutory requirements, the Department of the Interior's Bureau of Land Management (BLM) today published a rulemaking concerning federal coal leasee qualifications." This doublespeak simply means that the BLM intends to crack down on coal leases. An official in the Department of Commerce who had requested a pay raise was told that "Because of the fluctuational predisposition of your position's productive capacity as juxtaposed to government standards, it would be monetarily injudicious to advocate an increment." In other words, no pay raise.

The 1984–1985 report of the Offices of Research Development and Technology of the Federal Highway Administration stated that "A study is attempting to validate non-accident measures as safety measures of horizontal curves and unsignalized intersections on two-lane rural highways where low traffic volumes make accidents a questionable safety measure." This doublespeak seems to mean that the FHA is attempting to solve safety problems at locations where no safety problems exist by developing a nonaccident measure of what the problem might be if one did exist. But then again, it might mean something entirely different. Who knows what meaning lurks in such doublespeak?

William O'Connor, special counsel to the U.S. Merit Systems Protection Board, was asked in a hearing before a Senate Judiciary subcommittee if he would advise a private client to disclose wasteful government spending. Mr. O'Connor responded like a true bureaucrat: "I would say that cost analysiswise it was counterindicated."

When a Final Report Isn't Final

Until 1988, the Commerce Department issued a series of three estimates of the gross national product for each quarter. The first report, based upon preliminary data, was called the "preliminary" GNP estimate. The two subsequent reports were called, respectively, the "first revision" and "second revision."

But Robert Ortner, undersecretary for economic affairs in the Commerce Department, decided that such clear language had to go. Ortner decided to call the "preliminary" GNP estimate the "advance" GNP estimate, while the "first revision" was renamed the "preliminary" report and the "second revision" was renamed the "final" report. However, the "final" report won't really be final because each July the Commerce Department revises all the quarterly estimates for the preceding three years, and every three years the department revises GNP figures even further back. Thus, the "final" report means "subject to change." "It's 'final' up until the annual July revision," Ortner said. "It finally becomes 'final' after three years." Couldn't this guy find something better to do with his time?

Sometimes the very name of an agency is doublespeak, like the Department of Defense. The name of the Energy Department is another example of doublespeak. What do you think the Energy Department does? Well, you're wrong. When the Energy Department was formed in 1977, it was assigned the task of freeing America from dependence on imported oil and achieving "energy independence" for America through the development of renewable energy resources such as wind, water, sunlight, and thermal energy. However, things have changed at the Energy Department.

The 1987 budget for the Energy Department was $12.8 billion of which $2.3 billion was for production of nuclear-warhead components and final warhead assembly; $1.8 billion for production of plutonium, uranium, tritium, and other warhead ingredients; $1.6 billion for designing and testing warheads; and $600 million for "Star Wars" research. Oh yes, the budget also provided $76 million for energy conservation and $92 million for renewable energy resources. Fully 65 percent of the 1987 budget went for nuclear weapons research and production. So much for freeing America from dependence on imported oil and developing renewable energy resources. I'll bet you never thought of building nuclear weapons as the main function of the Energy Department.

The Doublespeak of Redefinition

Doublespeak can also mean redefining widely used words, giving them a new meaning that is the opposite of their generally accepted meaning. The Federal Communications Commission has a thirty-nine-year-old policy called the "fairness doctrine," which requires broadcasters to present all sides of controversial public issues. In 1982, Mark S. Fowler, chairman of the FCC, said in a speech to a meeting of the National Association of Broadcasters that "it's one thing for stations to follow principles like fairness or equal time. I call that not only sensible but good business. It's another when the government enforces those rules. That, I call censorship."

Because the "fairness doctrine" was only a FCC rule and lacked the standing of law, Congress passed a bill in 1987 that would have made the "fairness doctrine" law. President Reagan vetoed the bill, saying that it was "antagonistic to the freedom of expression guaranteed by the First Amendment." Thus does the requirement that all sides be heard on controversial public issues become "censorship."

You may have called it a means test for Medicare benefits, but that's not the way Edwin L. Dale, Jr., of the Office of Management and Budget saw it. Mr. Dale said he wouldn't call it a means test but preferred to call it a "layering of benefits according to your income." See what redefining a word can do?

The redefinition of words is a particularly powerful form of government doublespeak. In 1982, Treasury Secretary Donald Regan told reporters, "I hope and believe that over the next three to five years we'll be trying for full employment. The definition is now 6.5 percent unemployment." In 1964, a 6.5-percent unemployment rate was considered so excessive that it was cause for President Lyndon Johnson's Great Society and War on Poverty programs. Now, through the power of redefinition by the government, a 6.5-percent unemployment rate is transformed into "full employment."

Guilty Until Proven Innocent: The Doublespeak of the Supreme Court

Doublespeak can and does occur in Supreme Court decisions. In 1974, in *Gedulding* v. *Aiello,* the court ruled that California's continued exclusion of pregnant women from benefits under its health insurance program did not discriminate against women. The court reached this conclusion by pointing out that "The program divides potential recipients into two groups—pregnant women and nonpregnant persons." Thus, the program does not violate the Equal Protection clause of the U.S. Constitution and therefore does not discriminate against women.

In 1987, in *United States* v. *Salerno,* No. 86-87, the U.S. Supreme Court upheld the constitutionality of the Bail Reform Act, which allows jailing persons who have been accused but not convicted of crimes. Writing for the majority opinion, Chief Justice William Rehnquist engaged in doublespeak to justify what one legal scholar called "the great tool of totalitarian governments," detention without trial.

Rehnquist dismissed the argument that the Bail Reform Act violates the Excessive Bail Clause of the Eighth Amendment by saying that "this Clause, of course, says nothing about whether bail shall be available at all." (The full text of the Eighth Amendment is: "Excessive bail shall not be required, nor excessive fines imposed, nor cruel and unusual punishments inflicted.") Rehnquist also maintained that preventive detention is not punishment but "regulatory" because "the mere fact that a person is detained does not inexorably lead to the conclusion that the government has imposed punishment.... To determine whether a restriction on liberty constitutes impermissible punishment or permissible regulation, we first look to legislative intent." Rehnquist then found that "The legislative history of the Bail Reform Act clearly indicates that Congress did not formulate the pretrial detention provisions as punishment. . . ." Thus, imprisonment without trial becomes "regulatory" and not "punishment" simply because Congress intended it that way.

Rehnquist also called a person accused of a crime and denied bail on the grounds of "dangerousness" a "putative offender." Thus, someone who is accused of a crime but not yet tried is presumed guilty until proven innocent and can be held in jail because of "the likelihood of future dangerousness." Doublespeak served the Supreme Court well in arriving at this decision.

The CIA and Its Unilaterally Controlled Latino Assets

The Central Intelligence Agency is pretty secretive. So secretive, in fact, that not much of its doublespeak leaks out to the public, but when it does, it's some of the best around. After all, this is the agency that called killing a suspected double agent "elimination with extreme prejudice" and referred to the Latin American mercenaries it hired to carry out raids in Nicaragua as "unilaterally controlled Latino assets." The CIA also does things like classify a report as "Secret Noforn Nocontract Orcon," meaning that no one is to see the document without the permission of the writer of the report. In a nice touch of doublespeak, the CIA calls the department responsible for designing and executing covert actions, such as illegally overthrowing a foreign government, the "Department of International Affairs." Since it's in the spying business, or "intelligence gathering" as it likes to say, the CIA must be careful that none of its employees does anything bad, like talk out of school. So the agency has a "quality control" program, which includes subjecting its employees to lie detectors, wiretapping, audits of their finances, surveillance, and investigations of their acquaintances and travels.

Help Wanted

Getting a job with the CIA is no easy task. In its help-wanted ads, the CIA never uses words like "spying," "wiretapping," "breaking and entering," or "killing," nor do its ads mention illegally overthrowing governments, recruiting mercenaries, bribing foreign officials, lying to Congress, or all those other exciting things the CIA does. What the ads do stress is "intercultural sophistication," "communication skills," and "solid ethical standards," plus "a gift for dealing with people" and "integrity of performance." Best of all is the doublespeak used to describe the major function of the CIA, which is spying. The ads say that "Prudent foreign policy decisions depend on solid knowledge. The most important decisions depend on information our adversaries seek to conceal. A truly extraordinary group of men and women serve abroad as the key players in our national effort to fill these critical information gaps." You won't be spying; you'll just be "filling critical information gaps."

If you want to see the kind of people the CIA is interested in hiring, just look at who they have working for them. Alan Fiers was the CIA's top Central American operative. During the Iran-contra scandal, he contradicted his earlier sworn testimony to Congress that he had no knowledge of individuals providing military aid to the Contras. But Fiers defended his testimony that Lt. Col. Oliver North was not providing arms to the Contras, by claiming that North was merely "causing that to happen." He defended as "an honest answer, not a complete answer" his testimony that he had "no idea" who owned the cargo plane downed inside Nicaragua. He called his testimony "technically correct but specifically evasive." Mr. Fiers was obviously demonstrating those "solid ethical standards" that the CIA requires of all its employees.

Another successful employee of the CIA is Dewey Claridge,

former head of the CIA's clandestine operations in Latin America, who also demonstrated the qualities that the CIA looks for in its employees. In secret briefings for senior staff members of the House Intelligence Committee in 1985, Claridge told how CIA-supported Contras killed "civilians and Sandinista officials in the provinces, as well as heads of cooperatives, nurses, doctors and judges." Claridge insisted that such killings did not violate a 1981 executive order signed by President Reagan forbidding political assassinations. "After all, this is a war—a paramilitary operation," Claridge said. He went on to say that the term "assassination," by the CIA's definition, did not apply to killings in Nicaragua. "These events don't constitute assassinations because as far as we are concerned assassinations are only those of heads of state. I leave definitions to the politicians," Claridge said. (President Reagan's order, signed December 4, 1981, said, "No person employed by or acting on behalf of the U.S. government shall engage in or conspire to engage in assassinations. No agency of the intelligence community shall participate in or request any person to undertake activities forbidden by this order.") Mr. Claridge certainly demonstrates the qualities so valued by the CIA: "solid ethical standards," "a gift for dealing with people," "intercultural sophistication," and "first-rate communication skills."

Helping People to Be Persuasive in Face-to-Face Communication the CIA Way

If you do have "first-rate communication skills" and "intercultural sophistication," you might be called upon to write something like the *Psychological Warfare Manual* prepared by the CIA for the Nicaraguan guerrillas fighting the government of Nicaragua. Using your "first-rate communication skills," you would give advice on the "selective use of violence" to "neutralize" Nicaraguan officials, such as court judges, police, and state security officials; suggest hiring professional criminals to carry out "selective jobs"; propose arranging the death of a rebel supporter to create a "martyr" for the cause; and give directions on "the agitation of the masses in a demonstration," with men equipped with "knives, razors, chains, clubs, bludgeons" joining a peaceful demonstration and marching "slightly behind the innocent and gullible participants." And as you wrote such a manual, you would remember that its purpose was, in the words of William Casey, director of the CIA, "to make every guerilla persuasive in face-to-face communication" and to develop "political awareness," because its "emphasis is on education. . . ."

You wouldn't have to worry that writing such a manual was illegal. After all, White House spokesperson Larry Speakes said that investigations conducted into the manual concluded that "there had been no violation by CIA personnel or contract employees of the Constitution or laws of the United States, executive orders or presidential directives." Mr. Speakes simply ignored the fact that U.S. law forbids supporting actions aimed at overthrowing another country's government, unless there is a declaration of war. He also ignored the presidential directive regarding assassinations that had been approved by President Ford and reissued by President Reagan.

NASA and the Challenger Anomaly

You may have called it an accident, but to NASA (National Aeronautics and Space Administration) it was an "anomaly" when the space shuttle Challenger blew up. And NASA didn't conduct an investigation into the accident. As Kay Parker of NASA said, flight simulators were being used by experts "working in the anomaly investigation."

When NASA reported that it was having difficulty determining how or exactly when the Challenger astronauts died, Rear Admiral Richard Truly reported that "Whether or not a cabin rupture occurred prior to water impact has not yet been determined by a superficial examination of the recovered components." The phrase "recovered components" refers to the bodies of the astronauts. Admiral Truly also said that "Extremely large forces were imposed on the vehicle as evidenced by the immediate breakup into many pieces." He went on to say that "Once these forces have been accurately determined, if in fact they can be, the structural analysts will attempt to estimate the effect on the structural and pressure integrity of the crew module." NASA also referred to the coffins of the astronauts as "crew transfer containers."

During the investigation into the causes of the accident, the doublespeak flowed. Arnold Aldrich, manager of the National Space Transportation Systems Program at Johnson Space Center, said that

> The normal process during the countdown is that the countdown proceeds, assuming we are in a go posture, and at various points during the countdown we tag up on the operational loops and face to face in the firing room to ascertain the facts that project elements that are monitoring the data and that are understanding the situation as we proceed are still in the go condition.

In testimony before the commission investigating the Challenger accident, Allen McDonald, an engineer for Morton Thiokol, the maker of the rocket, said he had expressed concern about the possible effect of cold weather on the booster rocket's O-ring seals the night before the launch:

> I made the comment that lower temperatures are in the direction of badness for both O-rings, because it slows down the timing function.
>
> McDonald also commented on his concern on the eve of the launch about the effect of cold weather on the O-rings: I told them I may be naïve about what generates launch commit criteria, but I was under the impression that that was generated based on the qualification of all elements or sub-systems of the space shuttle; that anything that was outside that qualification was a launch-commit criteria, and we never went outside that envelope. And I don't know why NASA would ever

launch below 40 degrees Fahrenheit if that's what the
SRM was qualified to.

Larry Mulloy, manager of the Space Shuttle Solid Rocket
Booster Program at Marshall Space Flight Center, responded to
a question assessing whether problems with the O-rings or with
the insulation of the liner of the nozzle posed a greater threat to
the shuttle by saying, "The criticality in answering your question, sir, it would be a real foot race as to which one would be
considered more critical, depending on the particular time that
you looked at your experience with that."

After several executives of Rockwell International, the main
contractor to build the shuttle, had testified that Rockwell had
been opposed to launching the shuttle because of the danger
posed by ice formation on the launch platform, Martin Ciof-
foletti, vice-president for space transportation at Rockwell, testified, "I felt that by telling them we did not have a sufficient data
base and could not analyze the trajectory of the ice, I felt he
understood that Rockwell was not giving a positive indication
that we were for the launch."

Officials at Morton Thiokol, when asked why they reversed
earlier decisions not to launch the shuttle, said the reversal was
"based on the re-evaluation of those discussions." The presidential commission investigating the accident suggested that this
statement could be translated to mean there was pressure from
NASA. If this is the way the people who build and operate the
space shuttle program talk, you have to wonder how the thing
ever gets off the ground. But then maybe that's just the way they
talk when they make a mistake and don't want to talk about it.

Splash and Spray Suppression Devices,
and Other Acts of Congress

Congress is one of the greatest sources of doublespeak, if for no
other reason than the tax laws that it produces. Still, there is
plenty of other doublespeak flowing from those hallowed halls.
Unlike other legislative bodies, Congress doesn't have a recess

but a "district work period," as in the "Independence Day District Work Period." When Congress does work, it considers bills like the "Uranium Revitalization, Tailings Reclamation and Enrichment Act," a bill which would forgive payment of the $8.8 billion the nuclear utility industry owes to the government. Or the "Sugar Export Enhancement Program," a bill that provides a $100-million-a-year subsidy for a few sugar producers. Or a bill that laid the groundwork for President Reagan's "Star Wars" program which was called the "People Protection Act."

The language in the bills Congress passes is just as confusing as any found in the tax law. Here's a section of the bill amending the Higher Education Act of 1985: "Title III of the Act is amended (1) in section 311(b), by striking out 'section 358(a)(1)' and inserting 'section 360(a)(1)'; (2) in section 312(b)(1)—by inserting 'which' before 'is' each place it appears in subparagraph (C) and (D)—by inserting 'which' before 'has' in subparagraph (E)." When you do figure out congressional doublespeak, you usually discover another outrage.

In 1981, Congress passed a bill for a natural-gas pipeline from Alaska, a bill that allowed the corporation that owned the pipeline to collect from utility customers for the natural gas that the customers were not receiving while the pipeline was being built. This procedure was called "prebilling." Although the bill graciously allowed customers to share in the expense of building the pipeline, there was no provision for them to share in the profits of the pipeline, once it was built with their money.

The 1982 tax bill contained a provision that makes tax-deductible the bribes, or "grease," that American companies pay illegally to foreign government officials to get things done faster, or get them done at all. Michael Samuels, director of the International Division of the U.S. Chamber of Commerce, explained that "Grease is unfortunately a word that makes it sound greasy or dirty, which it isn't. It's more like paying a headwaiter $5 for a better table, very much like a tip." The Senate Finance Committee report on the provision put it this way: "These are payments made to government officials to facilitate administrative actions that are non-discretionary on their part. Thus, payments to a customs official to expedite goods through customs are allowed as a deductible under this bill." Isn't doublespeak wonderful? Now bribes are just "tips," or "payments to facilitate non-discretionary administrative actions."

Congress does wonderful things with doublespeak in the bills it passes. Mud flaps on trucks become "splash and spray suppression devices," and an intentional state of mind is defined as "one's state of mind is intentional as to one's conduct or the result of one's conduct if such conduct or result is one's conscious objective." Section 503 of the Rehabilitation Act of 1973 states that a person cannot be discriminated against because of a handicap, and mental illness, drug addiction, and alcoholism are considered "handicaps." As Representative John B. Breaux said in 1981, when asked if his vote could be sold, "No. It can be rented." So the congressional doublespeak machine chugs right along, making a better if somewhat more expensive life for you and me through doublespeak.

Government doublespeak goes from the ridiculous to the serious. Highways are called "urban penetrators," and dust becomes "airborne particulates." The government doesn't clear slums, it "rehabilitates blighted areas." It doesn't condemn homes and neighborhoods, it "exercises its right of eminent domain." The government doesn't tap your telephone, it just engages in "electronic surveillance."

Local Government Gets in on the Act

Doublespeak isn't confined to just the federal government in Washington. It can be found at all levels. Local bureaucrats—municipal, county, and state—get in on the act just as much as those pros in Washington. One bewildered resident of Illinois received the following notice from the Office of the Secretary of State, Springfield, Illinois:

> Persons who are employed by any unit of local
> government, or by a school district, defined to include
> community college district, and are compensated for

services as employees and not as independent
contractors at the rate of $35,000 per year or more and
other persons so employed who are compensated at a
rate of less than $35,000 per year for such employment,
if they receive fees for professional services rendered for
the State or any unit of local government or school
district, defined to include community college district, in
such an amount that their total income from public
employment, including such fees, is $35,000 per year or
more.

Not only is this hopelessly confused and confusing doublespeak,
it's not even a sentence. What exactly is the recipient of this letter
supposed to do?

In 1984, the city of Allentown, Pennsylvania, submitted a "proposal for the creation and evolution of a 'Safe House' structure
designed for female children involved in prostitution." The proposal contained jargon and run-together sentences such as:

It is an extremely doubtful and naive assumption that
children independently execute physical and
psychological resolutions which present themselves as
commodity allotments within a business doctrine,
therefore motivation of the individual is included to
provide a workable justification development as related
to the operation and pre-requisites of the "safe house"
concept.

You have to hope that they got the money for the "safe house
structure," despite this prose. It seems like a good idea.

Government doublespeak is bad enough, but when government bureaucrats join with lawyers to produce doublespeak,
we're in big trouble. Just look at those ballot propositions and
ordinances, which are written by government specialists in doublespeak and by lawyers, who seem to know only doublespeak.
In 1982, voters in the town of Wildwood Crest, New Jersey, were
asked to vote on the following question:

Shall the ordinance proposed by petition and providing
for amending Ordinance No. 564 of the Borough of
Wildwood Crest, so as to establish free beaches in the
Borough of Wildwood Crest, in the County of Cape May,
State of New Jersey; to provide for the repeal of any
portion of Ordinance 564 which establishes rules and
regulations for the beaches in the Borough of Wildwood
Crest, in the County of Cape May, State of New Jersey;
to provide for the repeal of any portion of Ordinance
564 which establishes rules and regulations for the
collecting of fees for the use of beaches and distributing
of badges; to repeal rules and regulations establishing
penalties for failing to pay beach fees be adopted?

In other words, if you are *against* charging a fee to use the public
beaches you should vote "yes," but, if you are *for* charging a fee
to use the public beaches, you should vote "no." Now that's great
doublespeak. But you have to wonder what kind of minds produced this language.

Now take a deep breath, hold it, and read this ordinance from
a town in Wisconsin:

132.06 Use of receptacle by other than owner; as to junk
dealers. The using by any person or persons or
corporation other than the owner or owners thereof, or
his, her, its or their agent, of any such can, tub, firkin,
box, bottle, cask, barrel, keg, carton, tank, fountain,
vessel or container, for the sale therein of any substance,
commodity or product, other than that originally therein
contained, or the buying, selling, or trafficking in any
such can, tub, firkin, box, bottle, cask, barrel, keg,
carton, tank, fountain, vessel or container, or the fact
that any junk dealer or dealers in cans, tubs, firkins,
boxes, bottles, casks, barrels, kegs, cartons, tanks,
fountains, vessels or containers, shall have in his or her
possession any such can, tub, firkin, box, bottle, cask,
barrel, keg, carton, tank, fountain, vessel, or container,

so marked or stamped and a description of which shall
have been filed and published as provided in s.132.04,
shall be, and it hereby is, declared to be, prima facie
evidence that such using, buying, selling or trafficking in
or possession of is unlawful within the meaning of
ss.132.04 to 132.08.

In other words, if junk dealers reuse containers they will be
fined. Now, the question I know you want to ask after reading
this perfectly clear statute is, just what is a firkin?

Some local governments don't talk about trucks driving on a
highway, they talk about the "dynamic behavior of articulated
vehicles traversing random flexible pavements." But then they
also call a highway a "soft wheel infrastructure system." Other
states may have road signs, but according to Scott L. Pickard of
the Massachusetts Department of Public Works, they're really
"ground-mounted confirmatory route markers." Other cities
may need more parking spaces downtown, but in Minneapolis–
St. Paul they have a "parking deficit." Other states may have
emergency vehicles, but according to the California State Department of Transportation they're really "major incident response units." And drivers in New Jersey don't pay a surcharge
on their already-highest-in-the-nation car insurance; they pay a
"Residual Market Equalization Charge."

The report of the panel investigating the collapse of the Teton
Dam in Idaho in 1977, which killed 14 people, concluded that the
tragedy was due to "an unfortunate choice of design measures
together with less than conventional precautions." After two sky-
walks at the Hyatt Regency Hotel in Kansas City collapsed in
1981, killing 114 people and injuring another 200, a study of how
Kansas City administered its construction guidelines disclosed
"a number of deficiencies which tend to weigh heavily on the
negative side of a competency scale."

In Easton, Connecticut, the garbage committee is called the
"Solid Waste Task Force," while New Canaan, Connecticut, does
not have a dump but a "volume reduction plant." In Philadelphia, Pennsylvania, a lot of dumps are called "recycling facili-

ties." Hanover, New Hampshire, no longer has a Sewer Commissioner but a "Waste Water Manager." Paradise Valley, Arizona, didn't build a community recreational center; it built a "multigenerational facility."

The Trenton State Prison in New Jersey no longer has a death house; now it's called the "capital sentences unit," where, by the way, "execution technicians" administer lethal injections. At the Greenhaven Correctional Facility in Stormville, New York, death row is now called the "Unit for Condemned Prisoners." And in 1984, the District of Columbia Court, in a ruling later rejected by the U.S. Supreme Court, ruled that the lethal injection drugs used to carry out the death penalty in Texas must be certified "safe and effective."

Steve Schwalb, director of adult detention for King County, Washington, insisted that it's not a jail but the "King County Correctional Facility," and the people who work there aren't guards but "corrections officers." In a blow for clear language, Jared Karsetter, business agent for Public Employees Union Local 519, which represents these prison guards, said, "That's a jail. It's not a correctional facility. We don't correct anybody."

In Pennsylvania, there is the "Youth Development Center," which is much nicer than saying reform school or prison for juveniles. But then the state prison is called the state "correctional facility" and the warden is called the "superintendent" and solitary confinement cells are called "individual behavior adjustment units." Can't you see the movie? James Cagney is the tough convict and Pat O'Brien is the warden. Snarls Cagney to O'Brien: "Go ahead, superintendent. Throw me in the individual behavior adjustment unit. I can take it." Somehow it's not the same.

The Pennsylvania State Office of Mental Health and Mental Retardation has adopted the term "eloped" instead of escaped for patients, now called "residents," who have run away from state institutions, now called "centers." Pennsylvania also changed the name of the Department of Public Welfare to the "Department of Human Services." Once upon a time this department was known as the "Department of Public Charity."

Two members of New Jersey Governor Tom Kean's staff did not have chauffeurs; that would violate state law. However, according to Thomas Thurston, chief of the governor's staff, "Both have aides who drive." Jim Thomas, Oklahoma state personnel director, was asked why eleven department heads had received substantial raises when Governor George Nigh had imposed a thirty-day state spending freeze. "These were not raises per se," said Thomas; it was just that the jobs were upgraded.

Maybe those jobs were real tough ones like this one. Here's the advertisement for the job of "Senior Staff Analyst" in the lawyer's office of the South Florida Water Management District in West Palm Beach,

> This is a professional administrative support system job
> functioning at the Office/Department Staff level to assist
> in the execution of the organization's policies,
> procedures and programs. The job is assigned the
> responsibility to improve administrative performance
> through the development, institution and maintenance of
> diverse procedures, methods, and systems designed to
> assure adherence to prescribed policies and directives
> and promote operational efficiencies within the
> Office/Department and ultimately within the district.

It's a tough job, but somebody's got to do it. But then, this description is as clear as the definition of "exit access" in a government fire-prevention pamphlet for homes for the elderly: "Exit access is that part of a means of egress that leads to an entrance to an exit."

Mayor Marion Barry of Washington, D.C. refused to identify the programs he was going to cut in 1983 to try to avert a projected $110-million budget deficit because the public would be confused by all the budget numbers. "I made the decision that really we ought to communicate better with people by not getting them confused with all these numbers." Some people still say the Philadelphia police dropped a bomb that started a fire, killing eleven people and destroying sixty-one houses in 1985, but, according to the official report, it wasn't a bomb but an "entry device."

Colorado State Representative A. J. Spano was tired of Denver being classified the city with the second dirtiest air in the country in 1979. But Mr. Spano didn't start a campaign to clean up Denver's dirty air. Instead, he introduced, and the Colorado House Transportation Committee passed, a bill to change the nomenclature of the state's air quality scale. According to Mr. Spano's new scale, the level of pollutants called "hazardous" by the federal government scale was called "poor," while "dangerous" was called "acceptable," "very unhealthful" was called "fair," "unhealthful" was called "good," and "moderate" was called "very good." With doublespeak there is no problem with air pollution in Denver.

Anthony B. Gliedman, commissioner of housing preservation and development in New York, knows how to confront the problem of urban decay. Faced with thousands of crumbling, abandoned tenements in the South Bronx, one of the worst sections of urban decay in America, in 1983 Mr. Gliedman announced a $300,000 federal grant to expand a program to improve the images of rundown neighborhoods. The money wasn't used to renovate or rehabilitate run-down housing. It was used to put vinyl decals over the windows of the abandoned buildings to give them a cheery, lived-in look. The decals look like curtains, or venetian blinds, or flower pots with geraniums blossoming. Said Mr. Gliedman, "We want people to feel good about their neighborhood. Morale is very real. Perception is reality." As Thomas Jefferson should have written, "We hold these perceptions to be self-evident. . . ." Or was it something about the pursuit of life, liberty, and perceptions?

Ronald Reagan and Doublespeak

During his time in office, President Ronald Reagan demonstrated that he is a master of doublespeak. At times, his doublespeak left you breathless, not just because it was so outrageous, but because it was said with such sincerity and conviction. President Reagan is an expert at language that simply has no connection to reality, words that simply do not align with any known fact, words that avoid all responsibility.

Some of Reagan's doublespeak is fairly common. He changed the SALT talks to the START talks and referred to the September 1 Plan instead of the Camp David Accords. He stopped talking about a balanced budget and instead stressed the need for a "down payment" on the budget deficit. The budget deficits that candidate Reagan called "evil" President Reagan said were a "necessary evil in the real world today." In his defense budgets U.S. troops were called "men" and "personnel," while they were "American boys" when they were under fire or killed. President Reagan emphasized the need for "redeployment," "reconcentration," and a "move to a little more defensive position," where once he had accused President Carter of vacillation and retreat.

It was fairly routine political doublespeak when President Reagan said in his 1987 State of the Union address that the Soviet Union "found the resources to transfer $75 billion in weapons to client states in the past five years" and then two sentences later criticized Congress for cutting his "request for critical U.S. security assistance to free nations by 21 percent this year." The Russians send "weapons" to "client states," while the United States sends "security assistance" to "free nations."

President Reagan also used language that denied reality. After contending that he did not want a summit meeting during the 1986 congressional election campaign, especially a meeting held outside the United States, President Reagan met with Premier Gorbachev in Iceland. "This in no way discounts what we've said about a summit," said President Reagan. "This is not a summit." And that was not doublespeak.

After Congress passed and he had signed the 1982 tax increase bill, President Reagan insisted that the tax increase was not the "greatest single tax increase in history." Instead, he said the tax bill was the "greatest tax reform in history." Moreover, he insisted that the tax bill "absolutely does not represent any reversal of policy or philosophy on the part of this Administration or this President." The tax bill was estimated to cost taxpayers $217 billion over five years. Doublespeak sure helped President Reagan keep his pledge of no tax increase.

A summit wasn't a summit, and a tax increase wasn't a tax

increase. Such a denial of reality was a common form of double-speak for President Reagan. After the National Commission on Excellence in Education reported in 1983 that the federal government shares the responsibility for meeting the needs of gifted, handicapped, disadvantaged, and bilingual students, and that it has "the primary responsibility to identify the national interests in education," President Reagan described the report as a "call for an end to federal intrusion."

Even numbers were doublespeak for President Reagan. In 1982, when he vetoed a supplementary appropriations bill, he said in a nationwide radio address that he had done so because the bill meant that "required funding in virtually every major defense program" had been slashed by Congress. He claimed that the bill cut funding for military personnel by 52 percent, for operation and maintenance by 92 percent, for procurement by 83 percent, and for military construction by 77 percent. However, President Reagan deliberately didn't mention that the reductions applied only to the supplemental funding passed each summer to cover unforeseen expenses. In fact, he had asked for $218.9 billion for the Defense Department, and Congress had granted $215.8 billion, or 98.6 percent of what he requested, or a reduction of only 1.4 percent of what he had requested.

Then there was good old gobbledygook. When asked what "Star Wars" is, President Reagan replied, "Well, I will present the same thing that I told those others. My concept of the strategic defense system has been one that, if and when we finally achieve what our goal is, and that is a weapon that is effective against incoming missiles, not a weapon system that is effective against incoming weapons, missiles."

In the doublespeak of President Reagan the way to arms reduction was build more weapons. As he said in his speech presenting his budget for fiscal year 1986, "ultimately our security and our hopes for success at the arms reduction talks hinge on our determination that we show here to continue our program to rebuild and refortify our defenses." Or as he said in 1982, "A vote against MX production today is a vote against arms control tomorrow."

While he was publicly criticizing the Democrats in Congress as "ready to surrender" in Lebanon because of their congressional resolution calling for withdrawal of the marines, President Reagan had already privately decided to pull the marines out of Lebanon. Larry Speakes, White House spokesperson, said that the president had criticized the resolution because it was interpreted as urging "a complete withdrawal of the U.S. forces" from Lebanon. "That is not what we've done," said Speakes. But then Secretary of Defense Weinberger also denied that the marines had been withdrawn from Lebanon. "The marines are being deployed two or three miles to the west," he said. Of course, that meant the marines had been taken out of Lebanon and placed back on ships.

In a speech to deputies of the Costa Rican National Assembly in 1982, President Reagan said, "Any nation destabilizing its neighbors by protecting guerrillas and exporting violence should forfeit close and fruitful relations with the people of the United States—and with any people who truly love peace and freedom." If you believe President Reagan's words, then the United States should forfeit close and fruitful relations with people who truly love peace and freedom, because shortly after this speech, news reports revealed that the United States, through the CIA, was recruiting, arming, equipping, and directing "clandestine military operations against Nicaragua." And in 1987 President Reagan called his requested $270 million for arms and equipment for the Contras so they could carry on their war against Nicaragua "peace insurance."

On September 15, 1982, President Reagan told a gathering of black Republicans that he felt compelled to respond to "the suggestion that we Republicans are taking a less active approach to protecting the civil rights of all Americans. No matter how you slice it, that's plain baloney. Look at the record." He also said, "The level of activity of the administration in investigating and prosecuting those who would attempt to deny blacks their civil liberties by violence and intimidation has exceeded the level of every past administration."

On the same day as the president's speech, the Washington

Council of Lawyers, a bipartisan association of attorneys from private firms, government, and public interest groups, published a report that concluded that "the administration has retreated from well-established bipartisan civil rights policies" in several areas. President Reagan cited statistics that showed that during his term "the number of suits filed by the [Equal Employment Opportunity] Commission increased by 13 percent." But the figures he used were not from "the first full year of this administration" as he claimed, but were based instead on the last four months of the Carter Administration and the eight months before Reagan appointees took over the commission. In the last year of the Carter Administration, 400 cases of discrimination were recommended to be taken to court, while during the six-month period ending March 31 only 31 cases (out of 108 recommended) were approved to be taken to court. So much for taking an active approach to protect the civil rights of all Americans.

It Wasn't an Exchange of Arms for Hostages, or Was It?

The Iran-contra affair was perhaps the biggest scandal and biggest controversy of the Reagan Administration. It was also the occasion for a great deal of doublespeak, as everyone involved in the affair tried to deny knowing about it, participating in it, or approving it. For President Reagan, it just didn't happen; or, if it did happen, he didn't know about it; or, if he did know about it, he didn't approve it; or, if he did approve it, the arms weren't traded for hostages. Wading through President Reagan's doublespeak on Iran-contra can leave you thoroughly confused, which is probably the purpose of his doublespeak. Here, in chronological order, are just some of the statements he made on the sale of arms to Iran and illegal aid to the Contras.

On November 11, 1986, President Reagan said,

> Our government has a firm policy not to capitulate to
> terrorist demands. That no-concessions policy remains in
> force, in spite of wildly speculative and false stories
> about arms-for-hostages and alleged ransom payments.

> We did not—repeat—did not—trade weapons or
> anything else for hostages nor will we . . . The charge
> has been made that the United States has shipped
> weapons to Iran as ransom payment for the release of
> American hostages in Lebanon, that the United States
> undercut its allies and secretly violated American policy
> against trafficking with terrorists. Those charges are
> utterly false. The United States has not made concessions
> to those who hold our people captive in Lebanon. And
> we will not. The United States has not swapped
> boatloads or planeloads of American weapons for the
> return of American hostages. And we will not.

Later, on November 25, President Reagan claimed ignorance, saying, "I was not fully informed on the nature of one of the activities undertaken in connection with this initiative." But on December 6, the president seemed to have changed his position when he said, "While we are still seeking all the facts, it's obvious that the execution of these policies was flawed and mistakes were made. Let me just say it was not my intent to do business with Khomeini, to trade weapons for hostages, nor to undercut our policy on antiterrorism."

But on February 20, 1987, President Reagan claimed he didn't remember: "Try as I might, I cannot recall anything whatsoever about whether I approved an Israeli sale in advance or whether I approved replenishment of Israeli stocks around August of 1985. My answer, therefore, and the simple truth is, I don't remember—period."

On March 4, 1987, the president used doublespeak to both admit and deny that there had been an arms-for-hostages deal:

> A few months ago I told the American people I did not
> trade arms for hostages. My heart and my best
> intentions still tell me that's true, but the facts and the
> evidence tell me it is not. As the Tower board reported,
> what began as a strategic opening to Iran deteriorated,
> in its implementation, into trading arms for hostages.

. . . As I told the Tower board, I didn't know about any
diversion of funds to the Contras. But as President, I
cannot escape responsibility.

But in a press conference on March 19, President Reagan
again contradicted himself:

It could be that the policy was flawed in that it did
deteriorate into . . . arms for hostages. . . . I did not see
that as trading anything with the kidnappers. They didn't
get any advantage out of this. . . . So, I still believe that
if someone in my family was kidnapped and I went out
and hired someone that I thought could get that person
safely home, that would not be engaging in ransom of
the victim.

When asked about whether he could have forgotten about
being told of the diversion of funds from the Iran arms sales to
the Contras, President Reagan replied, "Oh, no. You would have
heard me without opening the door to the office if I had been told
that at any time."

But on March 26, we're back to the arms-for-hostages admission again: "It sort of settled down to just trading arms for hostages, and that's a little like paying ransom to a kidnapper. If you
do it, then the kidnappers are just encouraged to go kidnap someone else."

Then on May 3 President Reagan denied any knowledge of
people in his administration soliciting money from private citizens and foreign governments to support the Contras, a denial
that was at variance with the facts. "With regard to whether
private individuals were giving money to support the Contras,
yes, I was aware that there were people doing that. But there was
nothing in the nature of a solicitation by my Administration, to
my knowledge, of anyone to do that." Then on May 13 the president admitted that he did and didn't know about the solicitation
of money from a foreign government: "There was no solicitation
that I know of or anything of the kind. I did know, and had been

informed, that he [King Fahd of Saudi Arabia] was helping, but I never brought it up."

Finally, on May 15 the president claimed he knew everything that had been going on and had been kept informed:

And here there's no question about my being informed. I've known what's going on there. As a matter of fact, for quite a long time now, a matter of years, I have been publically speaking of the necessity of the American people to support our program of aid to those freedom fighters down there in order to prevent there being established a Soviet beachhead here in the Western hemisphere, in addition to the one we already have in Cuba. And to suggest that I am just finding out or that things are being exposed that I didn't know about—no. Yes, I was kept briefed on that. As a matter of fact, I was very definitely involved in the decisions about support to the freedom fighters. It was my idea to begin with.

But then on June 11 the president claimed he hadn't been kept informed: "Well, I wasn't giving those orders because no one had asked or had told me what was truly happening there."

Finally, on July 15, President Reagan again claimed that he had not been told about the diversion of funds to the Contras. When asked whether he was surprised by Rear Admiral John Poindexter's denials that the president was aware of the diversion of funds to the Contras in Nicaragua, President Reagan replied: "What's new about that? I've been saying it for seven months." All this from the "Great Communicator." And still the question remains: did he or didn't he? Does anyone know?

One very powerful doublespeak word revealed during the Iran-contra hearings was the word "finding." It's a small word with a lot of power, and President Reagan and the State Department knew how to use this powerful piece of doublespeak. An amendment to the 1974 Foreign Assistance Act states that no money can be spent for CIA operations abroad "unless and until the President finds that such operation is important to the national security." On January 18, 1986, President Reagan signed a "Finding" authorizing the sale of arms to Iran outside of the provisions of the law and outside the reporting requirements for foreign military sales. A year later, on January 9, 1987, another "Finding" signed by the president directed the CIA to provide the Contras with intelligence information and equipment despite the congressional ban on military aid to the Contras because the president deemed it "important to the national security." The "Finding" on Iran has never been rescinded. When the House Foreign Affairs Committee asked whether the arms embargo still applied to Iran under the terms of the Anti-Terrorism Act of 1986, the State Department replied in writing that this "determination remains in effect," but added this parenthetical reservation: "(The foregoing is, of course, without prejudice to the authority of the Executive Branch to carry out transfers of defense articles under other legal authorities, such as pursuant to special intelligence Findings.)" It seems that under the heading of "Finding" the president does not have to obey the law.

Surreptitious Entries and Stonewalling: The Legacy of Watergate

During the congressional hearings into the Watergate scandal, television viewers were introduced to the doublespeak of Watergate, a language designed to hide reality with words, to separate words from truth, to avoid responsibility. In the doublespeak of Watergate, burglary became a "surreptitious entry" or an "intelligence-gathering operation," burglars became "plumbers," illegal acts were "inappropriate actions," flattery was "stroking" or "puffing," subornation of perjury was "coaching," government-sponsored crimes were "White House horrors" or "dirty tricks," blackmail payments were "laundered money" or "increments . . . in the form of money," covering up a crime was "containing" or "confining a situation," and conspiracy to obstruct justice was "biting the bullet" or "stonewalling."

Sports metaphors were popular in the doublespeak of Watergate. There was a "game plan" with the "team players" doing the "downfield blocking" so the chief could "shoot the gap" or "throw the long bomb." And, as John Mitchell reminded us, "when the going gets tough, the tough get going." Come on team, let's get out there and commit a burglary for the coach.

At all times the language of Watergate functioned to remove the speaker from the event and from any responsibility for the event. People would only "recollect to the best of their ability," and they would never lie, only "misspeak." President Nixon could "initiate" "security operations" designed to "strengthen internal security procedures." This language does not reveal but conceals, does not communicate but misdirects, does not clarify but obscures.

During the congressional hearings into the Iran-contra affair, there were echoes of the doublespeak of Watergate. But the doublespeak of the participants in the Iran-contra affair was far more sophisticated and complex than the doublespeak of Watergate. By comparison, the doublespeak of Watergate seems almost simple, yet the doublespeak of Iran-contra had the same function as the doublespeak of Watergate: to hide reality with words, to separate words from truth, to avoid responsibility.

Cleaning Up the Historical Record: The Doublespeak of Lt. Col. Oliver North

On June 25, Assistant Attorney General Charles J. Cooper testified before the Joint Select Committee on Secret Military Assistance to Iran and the Nicaraguan Opposition that he would not believe the testimony of Lt. Col. Oliver North, whether or not under oath. Subsequently, during North's second day of testimony, after he had admitted that he had on different occasions lied to the Iranians, his colleague Maj. Gen. Richard Secord, congressional investigators, and the Congress, and that he had destroyed evidence and created false documents which he had purported were accurate, North then asserted to the joint congressional committee that everything he was about to say would be the truth. You should keep these comments in mind when evaluating the language of Oliver North.

North used the words "residuals" and "diversions" to refer to the millions of dollars of profits that were intentionally created by overcharging Iran for arms so that the money could be used to finance the Contras. North also said that he "cleaned things up," he was "cleaning up the historical record," he "fixed" things up, and that he "took steps to ensure" that things never "came out," meaning he lied, destroyed official government documents, and created false documents. Some documents weren't destroyed, but were "non-log," or kept "out of the system so that outside knowledge would not necessarily be derived from having the documents themselves."

North was also careful not to "infect other people with unnecessary knowledge." He explained how the Nicaraguan Humanitarian Assistance Office provided humanitarian aid in "mixed loads." According to North, "mixed loads meant you took beans and Band-Aids and boots and bullets." For North, people in other countries who helped him were "assets" and "Project Democracy" was a "euphemism I used at the time" as the name of the organization that was building an airfield for the Contras.

North was particularly good at lying without calling his actions lying. In speaking of a false chronology of events that he helped construct, North said that he "was provided with additional input that was radically different from the truth. I assisted in furthering that version." He mentioned "a different version from the facts" and called the chronology "inaccurate." North also claimed that he and William Casey, then head of the CIA, together falsified the testimony that Casey was to give to Congress. "Director Casey and I fixed that testimony and removed the offensive portions. We fixed it by omission. We left out—it wasn't made accurate, it wasn't made fulsome, it was fixed by omission." Official lies were "plausible deniability."

While North was often eager during his testimony to give long speeches in support of the Contras, to attack Congress, and to explain his curious handling of money, he could at times be very evasive. For example, when asked, "When you say acknowledged, you mean they acquiesced?" North replied, "No one ever came back and asked for it again." After admitting that "it was wrong to misrepresent facts to the Congress," North was then asked if "it wasn't wrong to misrepresent facts to the attorney general of the United States?" To which North replied (after conferring with his lawyer), "I have testified as to what I believed to be right and wrong before, and you have that, and it's on the record."

North also claimed that he had not reported a $1-million bribe offered to him by Ghorbanifar because "everyone involved in it knew what baksheesh is. And it was expected." When pressed why he hadn't reported the attempted bribe, North replied, "Actually it wasn't expected; it was un — it was not unexpected." When asked again if he had reported the incident to his superiors, North replied, "I may have. I don't recall, sir."

North, a man noted for having a steel-trap memory, a man who once was told by William Casey to "put away the notebook" because if "I couldn't remember it, I didn't belong in the business," suffered frequent memory lapses and often could not "recall" information. On the final day of his testimony he replied that he could not recall over thirty times in the space of less than three hours.

While North admitted that he had shredded documents after being informed that officials from the attorney general's office wanted to inspect some of the documents in his office, he denied that he had shredded the documents so the officials could not see them. "I would prefer to say that I shredded documents that day like I did on all other days, but perhaps with increased intensity. . . ." he said.

North could also use the passive voice to avoid responsibility. When asked, "Where are the non-logged documents?" he replied, "I think they were shredded." Again, when asked on what authority he agreed to allow Secord to make a personal profit off the arms sale to Iran, North replied with a long, wordy response filled with such passive constructions as "it was clearly indicated," "it was already known," and "it was recognized," but he never answered the question.

North implied that those who opposed aid to the Contras were assisting the cause of communism: "And thank God somebody put money into that account and the Nicaraguan resistance didn't die, as perhaps others intended; certainly the Sandinistas, and Moscow and Cuba intended that. . . ." The use of the word "others" coupled with the independent clause beginning "certainly" lumps together all who oppose aid to the Contras and aligns Congress with promoting the aims of the communists.

Indeed, North later charged that

> it is the Congress which must accept at least some of the blame in the Nicaraguan freedom fighters' matter. Plain and simple, the Congress is to blame because of the fickle, vacillating, unpredictable, on-again, off-again policy toward the Nicaraguan Democratic Resistance—the so-called Contras. . . . When the executive branch did everything possible within the law to prevent them from being wiped out by Moscow's surrogates in Havana and Managua, you then had this investigation to blame the problem on the executive branch.

North does not explain what "blame" he is speaking of, nor does he explain what the "blame" is for. He speaks vaguely of the Freedom Fighters "matter." And according to North, while the "executive branch" (meaning North, McFarlane, Poindexter, Casey, Secord, and others) worked to save the "Freedom Fighters," Congress was more concerned with an investigation "to blame the problem" on just the very people who were fighting so hard to keep the forces of Moscow at bay. North does not explain what "problem" the Congress is investigating.

For North, the whole investigation by Congress was just an attempt "to criminalize policy differences between co-equal branches of government and the Executive's conduct of foreign affairs." Lying to Congress, shredding official documents, violating laws, and conducting unauthorized activities were all just "policy differences." But North was generous with the committee; he conceded that "I think there's fault to go on both sides.

I've said that repeatedly throughout my testimony. And I have accepted the responsibility for my role in it." While North accepted responsibility, he did not accept accountability.

This final statement bears close reading for it reveals the subtlety of North's language. North states as fact that Congress was at fault, but at fault for what he doesn't specify. But note also that he accepts responsibility only for his "role" in "it." He does not accept responsibility for any specific action, only for his "role," whatever that may have been. In short, while he may be "responsible" (not guilty) for violating the law, Congress shares in that responsibility for having passed the law.

One of North's most interesting uses of language occurred when he declared that

> the American people ought not to be led to believe . . .
> that we intentionally deceived [them] or had that intent
> to begin with. The effort to conduct these covert
> operations was made in such a way that our adversaries
> would not have knowledge of them, or that we could
> deny American association with it, or the association of
> this government with those activities. And that is not
> wrong.

Indeed, North complained that "one of the things that disturbs me about the way this [the hearing] is proceeding is that we constantly are coming back to the fact that the American people haven't been told everything." North never did explain how the American people were to be informed of these covert operations, especially since he testified that "I didn't want to show Congress a single word on this whole thing."

But North also testified that knowledge of his covert operations on behalf of the contras was not secret to our "adversaries." "*Izvestia* knew it. The name had been in the papers in Moscow. It's been all over Danny Ortega's newscast, Radio Havana was broadcasting it. It was in every newspaper in the land." But when asked, "All our enemies knew it and you wanted to conceal it from the United States Congress?" North replied, "We wanted to be able to deny a covert operation. . . ."

North also insisted that "the president could authorize and conduct covert actions with unappropriated funds." When asked, "And in such event, to whom would the president be accountable?" North answered, "To the American people . . . that elected him . . . they can vote him out of office." But, North was reminded, "covert action is secret and he [the president] doesn't tell them about it, there's no way the American people can know about it to be able to vote him out of office on that basis, is there?" To this North replied, ". . . I believe the president has the authority to do what he wants with his own staff. . . ."

Welcome to the world of doublethink, where, as George Orwell observed, one can hold two contradictory beliefs in one's mind simultaneously and accept both of them; a world where war is peace, slavery is freedom, and defying a law is complying with it; a world where North could participate in drafting a letter to Congress saying that "we are complying with the letter and spirit of Boland" while admitting what the letter really meant was that "Boland doesn't apply to us and so we're complying with its letter and spirit." A world where noncompliance is compliance.

North also testified that, after two members of Congress had been briefed by President Reagan about the imminent bombing of Libya, they "proceeded immediately to waiting microphones and noted that the President was going to make a heretofore unannounced address to the nation on Libya. I will tell you the volume of fire over the Libyan capital was immense that evening. Two American airmen died as a consequence of that antiaircraft fire. As best we can determine, they alerted our enemies."

But as was later pointed out, for over a week before the raid, top administration officials were telling reporters that such a raid was possible, and over fourteen accounts leaked from administration sources appeared in the press or on television. When Senator William Cohen asked North, "So the notion that somehow when lives are at stake Congress cannot [be] and has not been trusted is not the correct perception?" North replied, "I did not try to leave that impression, Senator."

North also charged that after U.S. fighters had intercepted an Egyptian airliner carrying terrorists believed responsible for the hijacking of the cruise ship *Achille Lauro*, "a number of members of Congress" made revelations "that very seriously compromised our intelligence activities." According to *Newsweek* magazine, it was North himself who leaked details of the interception to one of its reporters. It was North who told *Time* magazine correspondent David Halevy that the Israelis were the major source of intelligence during the *Achille Lauro* affair, information that Halevy reported in the July 1987 issue of *The Washingtonian*. As the *Wall Street Journal* noted: "Reagan Administration foreign-policy strategists were incredulous when Oliver North assailed Congress for leaks. They say he was renowned for selective leaking of information that might help his causes. 'Ollie,' says one top national security official, 'was the biggest leaker in this administration.' "

Finally, after North completed his testimony, it was revealed that he had been part of a National Security Council operation designed to leak top-secret intelligence to the media through the U.S. State Department's "Office of Public Diplomacy," as part of a vast, expensive, and sophisticated worldwide campaign to turn international opinion against the Sandinista government of Nicaragua and to persuade Congress to renew aid to the Contras.

Daniel Schorr, the commentator for Public Television and National Public Radio who won three Emmy awards for his coverage of the Watergate hearings, observed how North never really answered many questions but instead "would slide away from the most probing questions, how he would fall back on generalizations about patriotic motives, obedience to authority, reverence for his commander-in-chief, devotion to family, the crushing pressure under which he had worked, the threat of assassination, and his dedication to saving Contras in Nicaragua and hostages in Lebanon."

North disclaimed all responsibility for his actions, claiming "I was authorized to do everything that I did." Yet when he was asked who gave him authorization, North replied, "My superiors." When asked which superior, he replied: "Well who—look who sign—I didn't sign those letters to the—to this body." And North's renowned steel-trap memory went vague or forgetful again.

The Doublespeak of John Poindexter

In the world of Admiral John Poindexter, one does not lie but "misleads" or "withholds information." Likewise, one engages in "secret activities," which are not the same as covert actions. In Poindexter's world, one can "acquiesce" in a shipment of weapons while at the same time not authorize the shipment. One can transfer millions of dollars of government money as a "technical implementation" without making a "substantive decision." One can also send subordinates to lie to congressional committees if one does not "micromanage" them. In Poindexter's world, "outside interference" occurs when Congress attempts to fulfill its constitutional function of passing legislation. Poindexter's world is a world of doublespeak and doublethink.

For Poindexter, withholding information is not lying. When asked about North's testimony that he had lied to a congressional committee and that Poindexter had known that North intended to lie, Poindexter replied:

> there was a general understanding that he [North] was
> to withhold information. . . . I . . . did not expect him to
> lie to the committee. I expected him to be evasive. . . .
> I'm sure they [North's answers] were very carefully
> crafted, nuanced. The total impact, I am sure, was one
> of withholding information from the Congress, but I'm
> still not convinced . . . that he lied. . . .

Yet Poindexter protested that it is not "fair to say that I have misinformed Congress or other Cabinet officers. I haven't testified to that. I've testified that I withheld information from Congress. And with regard to the Cabinet officers, I didn't withhold anything from them that they didn't want withheld from them."

Poindexter did not explain how it is possible to withhold information that a person already knows.

Poindexter insisted that when the American people vote for a president, they vote knowing what his foreign policy is, and they vote for that policy. Therefore, the president should be free to carry out that policy without any interference. Yet, when asked if he was suggesting that when people voted for President Reagan they were voting to send arms to Iran, Poindexter responded, "I think that [selling arms to Iran] is a tactical decision . . . that most Americans would think that they didn't have enough information to make a decision one way or the other."

When reminded that President Reagan had said that "As president, I have always operated on the belief that given the facts, the American people will make the right decision," Poindexter replied, "I think the President is absolutely correct. . . . I don't think the American people necessarily . . . want to know those details of how the President goes about implementing his foreign policy."

Poindexter was reminded that evaluations of his performance as aide to the chief of naval operations noted that he "reads and understands every paper and report that comes into the office. Furthermore, he retains fully, recalls accurately and evaluates with a keen sense of what is important—and what isn't." More than one evaluation referred to his "photographic memory." To which Poindexter responded, "It's important to note that the description he was giving there was a description of the way I functioned as an aide to him in a position of much less responsibility than I had as national security adviser." During one day of testimony, Poindexter responded some 184 times that he could not remember.

During his last day of testimony, Poindexter was reminded by Senator Sam Nunn that he had testified that "the President would have approved the decision [to use money from arms sales to Iran to support the Contras] at that time if I had asked him." Nunn then asked if "after reading the denials by the White House issued since your testimony, do you still believe the President would have approved that decision if you had asked him?"

The following exchange then took place between Poindexter and Nunn:

"I do . . ."

"So the denials from the White House have had no effect on your testimony?"

"No, they have not."

"That means, Admiral, you must believe the White House is now misleading the American people."

"No, I, I . . . I don't think so."

"How can that be?"

"At this point I can't speak for the White House. I don't know what they've got in mind over there."

"Well, I would just observe, Admiral, and you can refute this if you like, the White House statements directly contradict your testimony, and you're standing by your testimony, so your testimony directly contradicts the White House statements."

"That is correct. That appears to be obvious."

Poindexter concluded his five days of testimony by insisting that "what I have testified, as I swore at the beginning of these hearings, is the absolute truth and the whole truth."

The doublespeak of Oliver North and John Poindexter certainly rivals that of President Reagan. All three men used doublespeak to mislead their audiences, avoid answering questions, and construct a reality at variance with the facts. All three men used language that pretended to communicate but didn't, language designed to make the bad seem good, the negative appear positive. Their language did not extend thought but sought to limit it.

The Doublespeak of Responsibility

We normally think of someone who claims responsibility for an act as being the person on whom praise or blame, reward or punishment, should fall. However, we now witness people such as President Nixon, President Reagan, Oliver North, and John Poindexter, among many others, saying, "I'm responsible" but not really accepting responsibility. The assumption seems to be that, with the admission of responsibility nothing else needs to be said or done. The problem is settled and everyone can go home. There is no sense of blame or punishment connected with gross negligence, lying, deception, and illegal acts. Yet simply saying "I'm responsible" isn't really accepting responsibility but avoiding it; it is denying responsibility while laying claim to it. Maybe the next time the police catch some bank robbers, the robbers should simply claim responsibility and then walk away with the money, secure in the knowledge that the police won't hold them accountable.

CHAPTER VIII

Winnable Nuclear Wars and Energetic Disassemblies: Nuclear Doublespeak

I n March 1975, a worker was testing for air leaks in some of the pipes at the Brown's Ferry nuclear plant in Decatur, Alabama. And what sophisticated, high-tech equipment did this worker use to locate those leaks? Why a lighted candle, what else? When you go crawling around all the pipes in a nuclear power plant with a lighted candle, you can expect exactly what happened at Brown's Ferry. Sealing foam on the pipes caught fire, spreading quickly to the insulation on electrical cables serving the reactor control room. In no time the electrical controls for the valves, pumps, and blowers were gone, as well as the instruments on which the engineers in the control room depended for information on the status of the reactors. The control room filled with smoke as the operators tried to shut down the reactors. About seven hours after it had begun, the fire was finally extinguished.

The Nuclear Regulatory Commission appointed a review group to study the accident, which the review group insisted on calling an "event" or an "incident." Their official report found that the specific cause of the fire was an "undesirable combination of a highly combustible material . . . and an unnecessary ignition source. . . ." Thus did the NRC use nukespeak to deal

252

with one of the most serious reactor accidents in U.S. history, an accident that cost over $240 million for repairs and replacement power.

The function of nuclear doublespeak is to avoid reality, to control and direct any discussion of nuclear power and weapons, and ultimately to make any real public discussion of nuclear power, weapons, and war impossible. Nuclear doublespeak is language that pretends to communicate but doesn't, that makes the negative aspects of nuclear power appear positive and the unpleasant side-effects and possible disasters appear tolerable. It is language designed to conceal the realities and dangers of nuclear power.

When the atom bomb was first revealed to the public, it was presented as part of the development of the new "atomic age," an age that would see "energy so cheap it isn't worth making a charge for it," as physicist R. M. Langer put it. Atomic power, which had the slight disadvantage of including the atomic bomb, would lead us to a new world with "unparalleled richness and opportunities for all." Thus were born the "Atoms for Peace" and "Project Plowshare" programs for the peaceful use of atomic power.

At first the word "atom" was very popular. The Atomic Energy Commission was established by the Atomic Energy Act of 1946 and given control over the production of fissionable material. More important, it was also given control over all information concerning atomic energy. With this control began the doublespeak of nuclear power, the official language designed to make "our friend the atom" seem like just another technological advance. Now we could look forward to "Project Plowshare," which would use atomic bombs to dig harbors and canals, remove mountains, and even dig mines.

Glenn Seaborg, chairman of the AEC in the 1960s, suggested that a small atomic bomb could be used to close the Straits of Gibraltar, thus causing the Mediterranean Sea to rise so that it could be used to irrigate the Sahara desert. The fact that Venice and other sea-level cities would be flooded out of existence was just an issue of advantage versus disadvantage to Seaborg: "Of course, the advantages of a verdant Sahara would have to be weighed against the loss of Venice and other sealevel cities."

By the 1970s, the word "atomic" had lost its magic glow, so it was replaced by the more acceptable and less frightening "nuclear." Nothing is atomic anymore, now everything is nuclear, from "nuclear devices" (instead of atomic bombs) to "nuclear" (not atomic) power plants. Sometimes the preferred doublespeak is "energy," as in the Energy Research and Development Administration.

In 1974 the Atomic Energy Commission was dissolved and its functions were split between two agencies. The "Energy Research and Development Administration (ERDA)," which is responsible for developing nuclear weapons, was placed in the newly created Department of Energy, while the Nuclear Regulatory Commission (NRC) was created for the purpose of promoting and regulating commercial nuclear power. Thus it was that the Department of Energy became responsible for designing, developing, and manufacturing atomic or nuclear weapons, devoting over 65 percent of its annual budget to producing weapons.

Maximum Credible Accidents

When it comes to talking about problems with nuclear power plants, the NRC uses nothing but doublespeak. In a 1988 series of articles on the problem-plagued Oyster Creek nuclear power plant in New Jersey, reporter David Vis of *The Press* in Atlantic City discussed how the members of the Nuclear Regulatory Commission "are masters of saying something without saying it." Vis discovered that, in the language of the NRC, alarms don't go off; "system monitoring indicators are affected." NRC inspectors never say they've discovered machinery prone to breaking down; they say that "a failure mode has been identified." Equipment doesn't fail, fall apart, crack, explode, or disintegrate; it "fails to meet functioning criteria as per design requirements and specifications." NRC personnel would never say that a particular plan, action, or procedure was a bad idea, unsuccessful, wrong,

or just a plain waste of time; they say that "management attention and initiatives to meet and address these concerns have not
been entirely successful."

In the doublespeak of the NRC, nothing ever "is" or "isn't."
Instead it "may be," "could be," and "might be," or "perhaps
could be." Conversely, it "may not be," "could not be," "might not
be," or "could perhaps not be." With everything in the conditional, the NRC can never be pinned down to any exact meaning
in any of its documents or statements. And you thought the
Cheshire Cat gave Alice problems.

The Oyster Creek nuclear power plant is located in the middle
of a densely populated area. In case of a severe accident, the
design of the plant is such that, in the words of the NRC, it would
allow "immediate high consequences" (meaning radioactive
contamination) to people living downwind. This is the NRC's
doublespeak for a whole lot of people will die from radiation
sickness.

In the doublespeak of the NRC, equipment is never badly designed or poorly made. In 1987 the NRC reported that it had
identified "a potential failure mode for the containment torus-to-
drywell vacuum breakers" in the Oyster Creek plant. In other
words, these valves may not work the way they should when they
are needed in an emergency.

The containment system at the Oyster Creek plant was designed to "absorb the energy release of a maximum credible
accident involving the rupture of the reactor coolant system,"
according to a description of plant systems prepared by the
plant's operator. Yet the list of "maximum credible" accidents
did not include a complete loss of coolant and emergency coolant, a failure of safety systems, operator error, core damage, or
meltdowns, because the NRC believed the chance of any of these
accidents occurring was "incredible." Thus can the NRC make a
nuclear power plant safe by simply using doublespeak.

Seismic and Other Events

NRC documents and reports are filled with nuclear doublespeak designed to say something without saying it. On April 22, 1987, the NRC issued a "Memorandum and Order" relating to the emergency zone around the Seabrook nuclear power plant in New Hampshire. The memorandum noted that "seismic events involving large ground accelerations (initial event, perhaps followed by strong aftershocks) can degrade the efficacy of emergency plan implementation, increase the likelihood of earlier than expected containment failure, and degrade operator performance." In other words, the emergency plan can't handle an earthquake.

The memorandum also notes that "Numerous incidents recently reported in NRC Information Notices regarding licensed nuclear power plants attest to the thesis that there are instances of hardware components having safety significance that have not on random demand performed in accordance with the design intent for those components. . . ." In other words, there are important and crucial parts of nuclear power plants that when actually used do not live up to the performance claims made by the manufacturers.

In a 1983 report on a series of "events" at the Salem, New Jersey, nuclear power plant, the NRC concluded that the malfunctions were the "results of insufficient management involvement in establishing a safety perspective, in requiring attention to detail and in insuring procedural adherences." Victor Gilinsky, a member of the NRC, said improper maintenance of the safety system was related to "multiple management breakdowns." In other words, these people don't know how to run a nuclear power plant.

No matter what the issue or the problem, the NRC can come up with the doublespeak needed to smooth it over and cover it up. It was reported in 1985 that the number of equipment failures causing shutdowns at the Davis-Besse nuclear power plant in Oak Harbor, Ohio, had been above average for the industry. The plant had also had a large number of failures that required reporting to the NRC. When asked by the House Subcommittee on Energy Conservation and Power if the risk at the Ohio plant was higher than elsewhere, the NRC responded: "There are preliminary indications that its core damage or melt frequency may well be above average. There are no indications that the frequency of severe releases, and thus offsite radiological risk, is above average." James K. Asselstine, a member of the NRC, added that he believed that Davis-Besse was "one of those plants that dominate the probability of a severe accident." Now that's dealing with the problem and the question in a clear, straightforward way. You have to wonder if the people in the nuclear power industry think the way they talk, because if they do, we're all in a lot of trouble.

There are times, however, when you have to believe that the NRC uses doublespeak as a deliberate way to mislead the public and cover up what's really going in nuclear power plants. The 1975 Sunshine Act requires that all meetings of government bodies be open to the public and that written records of the meetings be kept. In 1985 the NRC amended its Sunshine Act regulations so that it could meet in private "nonmeeting gatherings" without written records of what took place in such "nonmeetings." Members of the NRC argued that the closed meetings fostered "congeniality" and that open meetings tended to have a "chilling effect" when it came to testing ideas among the members of the NRC. So the NRC decided that its general discussions, technical briefings, and "brainstorming" sessions about safety were not "meetings" as defined by the Sunshine Act. So maybe the NRC really does know how to use clear language when it wants to. Maybe it also knows how to use doublespeak when it wants to keep the public confused and in the dark about issues and problems related to nuclear power and the safety of nuclear power plants.

Sometimes it seems as if everyone associated with nuclear power plants uses doublespeak to cover up their mistakes. In 1986 disaster-preparedness officials in St. Petersburg, Florida, distributed a booklet showing evacuation routes to be used in case of a disaster at the St. Lucie nuclear power plant on Hutchinson Island on Florida's east coast. The map in the booklet showed a nonexistent bridge along one route and suggested that some evacuees could drive down a road to a Florida turnpike interchange that did not exist. When these problems were pointed out to officials, they said they were "working" on them. Did that mean they were going to build a bridge and a turnpike so their map would be accurate? Or did it mean they would draw a new map? Or did it mean they were going to come up with a new emergency plan?

Nuclear doublespeak must be learned. In 1982 the Energy Department and the Nuclear Regulatory Commission spent $10,000 for a "Witness and Media Skills Clinic" designed to teach some of their employees how to answer questions from reporters and members of Congress, especially during an emergency situation similar to the one at Three Mile Island in 1979. Participants were told to give the "impression that things are going well" and to "avoid embarrassment." They were asked, "what position do you want the public to hear?" They were also told how to "handle questions for which I don't want to give the answer," while still managing "to look good." One participant was a TMI contractor executive who acknowledged that TMI radiation detectors had malfunctioned and were potentially dangerous. If talking to the manufacturer he would say the devices had been "very misleading." But "if the critic is an anti-nuke" he would say that "these are radiation monitors, not safety-related equipment, and therefore not required to operate correctly under accident conditions."

Normally Expected Abnormal Occurrences

The NRC and the nuclear power industry have developed a whole lexicon of doublespeak which they use to downplay the dangers of nuclear power plants and nuclear accidents. An explosion in a nuclear power plant is called an "energetic disassembly," an "energy release," or a "rapid release of energy," while a fire in a nuclear power plant is called "rapid oxidation" or an "incendiary event." A reactor accident is an "event," an "unusual event," an "unscheduled event," an "incident," an "abnormal evolution," a "normal aberration," or a "plant transient." In one report on accidents at nuclear power plants, one "abnormal occurrence" occurred so frequently that it was called a "normally expected abnormal occurrence." Nuclear power plants need never be concerned about earthquakes, just "seismic events." Plutonium contamination at a nuclear power plant is referred to as "infiltration," "migration," a "breach of containment," or "plutonium has taken up residence." A meltdown at a nuclear power plant is a "core disruptive accident."

The NRC even uses doublespeak when counting accidents at nuclear power plants and reporting them to Congress. In one report, the NRC counted as one "abnormal occurrence" accidents at nineteen different reactors. How do nineteen accidents become one accident? Since the nineteen different reactors all had the same design flaw, and since the NRC counts "generic" problems such as design flaws built into many different reactors as one problem, the "abnormal occurrence" caused by this design flaw was really only one accident, not nineteen, even though it occurred at nineteen nuclear power plants in different locations across the country. See how easy it is to make nineteen equal one with the NRC's nuclear doublespeak?

In nuclear doublespeak, heating the water around a nuclear power plant so that vegetation and animal life dependent on the water are killed is called "thermal enrichment." Radioactive waste is simply "spent fuel," while "health effects" are the deaths and injuries caused by nuclear accidents. The clouds of radioactive gas released accidentally by nuclear power plants are called "off-gas." The amount of radioactivity that a human body can absorb and still live is called the "body burden." When the nuclear power industry talks about the "benefits versus risks" of nuclear power, what it really means is "we'll do what we want to make a profit and you'll take all the risks." And when the nuclear power industry or the NRC says, "Let us put this in perspective," what they really mean is, "Let us divert attention from the real issue to something else so we can avoid the problem and talk about what we want to talk about."

When a nuclear power plant loses plutonium through theft or

incompetence, plant operators just note the loss as an "inventory discrepancy" in the "Materials Unaccounted File" or "MUF." The systematic theft of plutonium from a nuclear power plant is called a "diversion." And when the operators of a nuclear power plant say there is "no evidence of diversion," they really mean that they can't prove the missing plutonium has been stolen and they have no idea who is doing it.

But sometimes you just have to laugh at this language, especially when it's supposed to be taken seriously. After all, what other reaction can you have when you read the following help-wanted ad in a newspaper: "Person to work on nuclear fissionable isotope molecular reactive counters and phase cyclotronic uranium photosynthesizers. No experience necessary." Maybe this is how the nuclear power industry finds workers who look for leaks in the pipes by using a lighted candle.

The doublespeak of the NRC and the nuclear power industry is designed to make nuclear power acceptable. It is language designed to prevent a serious, thoughtful, informed debate on an important subject. Moreover, the doublespeak used by the NRC covers up and avoids the serious safety and operating problems that exist in too many nuclear power plants. The doublespeak of the NRC and nuclear power industry must be eliminated if we really want to discuss the role of nuclear power in our society. But the doublespeak of nuclear power pales in comparison to the doublespeak of nuclear weapons and nuclear war.

It's Just a Nuclear Exchange

The doublespeak of nuclear weapons and nuclear war provides language with which to think the unthinkable. If you think about just one atomic bomb going off in your city, the picture you get is almost incomprehensible. And it becomes almost impossible to picture the effects of ten nuclear warheads landing on your city, or the over fifty thousand nuclear warheads the United States and the Soviet Union have landing on cities across the United States and the Soviet Union. Yet there are those whose profession it is to think the unthinkable, to plan for bringing about the end of the world. In order to think the unthinkable, it is necessary to use doublespeak.

On the ABC-TV program "Nightline" for April 22, 1982, the following exchange took place between moderator Ted Koppel and his guest, Herman Kahn.

> KOPPEL: And a final quote. "Since we wish to be able to limit Soviet behavior, to deter them from acts which cannot be met by limited means, we must have a credible first-strike capability." The writer, Herman Kahn; the book, *On Thermonuclear War.* Mr. Kahn is with us now here at Harvard. Dr. Kahn, would you still hold to that view?
>
> KAHN: I think the exact term was "not incredible," and there's a distinct difference. You really can't achieve a capability which looks like it would be used, but you can achieve a capability which the other side cannot feel will not be used if he's too provocative. And the term "not incredible" really carries an extraordinary amount of weight.
>
> KOPPEL: There is a potential on this program tonight for us to drown in double negatives. I wonder if you could put that into a straightforward sentence, Professor Kahn.
>
> KAHN: Absolutely not. And let me spend a minute on that. The attempt to put these in straightforward sentences simply confuses. Take the concept of "not probable." Not probable is, say, less than .5; improbable is less than .1. Therefore, not improbable is quite different from probable. It's called a *litote* [*sic*], and it's a perfectly legitimate grammatical construction.

George Orwell suggested that those who use the "not un-" formation could cure themselves by memorizing this sentence: "A not unblack dog was chasing a not unsmall rabbit across a not ungreen field." But Kahn's doublespeak is deliberately and carefully created, so he isn't interested in clear language when discussing nuclear weapons and nuclear war.

General Daniel Graham, former director of the Defense Intelligence Agency, demonstrated the kind of clear thinking involved in planning for nuclear war. General Graham wasn't impressed by the argument that there is no need to build more nuclear weapons because there are already enough nuclear weapons to kill every human being on earth two and one-half times, a situation known as "overkill." The good general dismissed this argument by saying that "There are also enough rocks on earth to kill the world's population several times over. Organizing them into a system for the purpose is quite another matter."

Winnable Nuclear Wars

With nuclear doublespeak it's possible to talk about "war" and "win" without even using these words. A nuclear war is called the "ultimate in high-intensity warfare," or, better yet, a "nuclear exchange," something like exchanging Christmas gifts. No one wins in such an "exchange," they "prevail," a word that avoids discussing the implications of what it means to "win" a nuclear war.

When Geroge Bush was campaigning for the presidency in 1980, he didn't yet know that you use the word "prevail" and not "win" in talking about nuclear war. Reporter Robert Scheer asked Bush, "How do you win in a nuclear exchange?" Bush replied, "You have survivability of command and control, survivability of industrial potential, protection of a percentage of your citizens, and you have a capability that inflicts more damage on the opposition than it can inflict on you. That's the way you have a winner. . . ." When Scheer then asked, "Do you mean like 5 percent would survive? Two percent?" Bush answered, "More than that—if everybody fired everything he had, you'd have more than that survive." Mr. Bush's doublespeak allows him to redefine "survivability" and "win" so that the unthinkable becomes thinkable.

In 1972 Secretary of Defense Melvin Laird proposed building an antiballistic missile base to protect Washington, D.C., thus insuring the "survivability of command and control" that George Bush thinks essential to winning a nuclear war. At the time of Laird's proposal, Admiral Thomas Moorer, chairman of the Joint Chiefs of Staff, defended the proposed base, saying: "We look on the [Federal] decision-making process as a very important component of the over-all deterrence package." What Adm. Moorer was saying was, while everyone else from New York to Los Angeles may be wiped out, the Soviet Union would tremble to know that all those bureaucrats and politicians in Washington would survive and would go on making the decisions that got us in that predicament in the first place. That's what is meant by winning a nuclear war, and that's what is meant by deterrence.

Many nuclear war strategists talk about a "winnable nuclear war." Colin Gray, a Defense Department consultant, said in 1982 that "The United States must possess the ability to wage nuclear war rationally." Mr. Gray didn't explain how a nuclear war could be "rational." The "winnable nuclear war" strategy includes planning for a "broken-backed war," in which any survivors would continue fighting after first, second, and retaliatory strikes had failed to settle the conflict. And Alice thought the logic of Wonderland was bizarre and irrational.

Nuclear doublespeak allows India to call its atomic bomb a "peaceful nuclear device," while allowing those who plan for nuclear war to talk about a "nuclear umbrella," as if you can be protected from falling nuclear bombs as you can be protected from rain. The "Strategic Defense Initiative" is called "Star Wars" or the "Peace Shield." The evacuation of millions of people from cities during a nuclear attack is called a "fallout sojourn in the countryside" or "crisis relocation." At all times nuclear doublespeak not only avoids talking about the reality of nuclear weapons and nuclear war, but it also attempts to make nuclear weapons appear nonthreatening, even benign. The room that houses the twenty-four nuclear-armed missiles on a Trident submarine is called the "Christmas tree farm," while a particular kind of nuclear attack on a military target is a "cookie cutter."

Naming the Unspeakable

When conducting tests of nuclear weapons, the Pentagon is very careful to make sure that the code name for the test is nonthreatening. The bomb that destroyed Hiroshima was named "Little Boy," while the bomb that wiped out Nagasaki three days later was named "Fat Boy." Since the beginning of the nuclear age, the United States has tested over seven hundred "nuclear devices," each of which has had its own nonthreatening, nonnuclear name.

After using such names as "Nancy" and "Harry," scientists went on to use the names of trees, mountains, and planets. Names associated with golf ("Backswing"), mixed drinks ("Daiquiri"), and parts of sailboats ("Rudder") have been used. Even names of cheeses have been used ("Edam," "Stilton," "Camembert," "Muenster," and "Dana Bleu"). Roger Ide, director of the test program at Livermore Laboratory in Berkeley, California, took a seven-pound wheel of Dana Bleu cheese with him to a test named after that cheese. "I like to bring some of the cheese for the people in the control room to try before the shot goes off," he said.

At the Department of Energy in Washington, D.C., Terry Egan is the "weapons information specialist" responsible for approving all the names for nuclear tests. She points out that the names must be easy to pronounce, they must not have been used before, and they cannot be controversial. Egan issued a memorandum in 1981 after she had had to turn down a number of names. The memorandum pointed out that "words should not be submitted for approval that connote or imply by their meaning aggressiveness, a relation to war, weapons, explosives, the military, potentially sensitive situations or other categories that in some way reflect on weapons programs." So it looks like we will never see a nuclear weapon or nuclear test with a name such as "Grim Reaper," "People Eliminator," "Earth Destroyer," or "Shatterer of Worlds."

Even those who design and test nuclear weapons use doublespeak to justify their work. Scientists at Livermore defend their work by pointing out that "we are making antiweapons." Says Lawrence West, one of the scientists, "My primary interest is not trying to find better ways to kill people, but better ways to kill arms. . . . I don't think I fall in that category, of working on weapons of death. We're working on weapons of life, ones that will save people from the weapons of death."

Megatons and Megadeaths

In the world of nuclear doublespeak, peace is achieved by living under the constant threat of nuclear war, a policy known as "MAD," or "mutually assured destruction" which constitutes "deterrence." The doublespeak of nuclear planners is composed of cool, crisp, nonthreatening language that speaks not of millions of dead but "megadeaths." The killing power of nuclear bombs is measured in "megatons" or "MT," while the efficiency of nuclear missiles is calculated by their "yield to weight ratio." The pattern in which the multiple warheads from one missile land is called a "footprint." Cities are "bargaining chips," "soft targets," or "countervalue targets," which during a nuclear war would be "taken out" by "clean, surgical strikes."

Nuclear weapons are called "sophisticated weapons systems" and are categorized as "strategic," "tactical," or "theater" weapons. Nuclear warheads, which are called "reentry vehicles," "the product," or "the physics package," are "delivered" by a "bus" after getting the "go code." "Fratricide" means one of your own warheads destroying another of your warheads, while a "nucflash" is an accident that has the potential to start an actual war.

The electronic system designed to prevent the unauthorized firing of nuclear weapons is called "PAL," or "permissive action links." Nuclear weapons accidents are called "bent spears" or "broken arrows." According to the official definition of the term "broken arrow," such accidents can include the unauthorized or accidental detonation of nuclear weapons; the nonnuclear detonation of a nuclear device; radioactive contamination from a nuclear weapon; the seizure, theft, or loss of a nuclear weapon; or any public hazard from an accident involving a nuclear weapon. The doublespeak of "broken arrow" neatly avoids the frightening reality of a nuclear accident and allows us to talk about such accidents without confronting the disaster they would bring.

The cornerstone of nuclear war policy is "deterrence," yet no one bothers to define this term. What is deterrence? Basically, nuclear deterrence is a mutual suicide pact between the United States and the Soviet Union. Deterrence means that if you attack me, you may kill me, but I will kill you before I die. This situation is also known as the "balance of terror." Everything that is done to plan and prepare for a nuclear war is done in the name of "deterrence."

Yet as some nuclear strategists have pointed out, "one person's deterrent is another person's threat." When the United States hardened its missile silos and launch control facilities, and dispersed and hardened its command and control facilities, the measures were called "improving survivability" and "stabilizing" because they reduced "vulnerability" to a Soviet first strike. However, when the Soviet Union undertook the very same measures, U.S. officials denounced them as "destabilizing" and evidence of Soviet intent to "absorb" U.S. "retaliation" and "undercut our deterrent." "Deterrence" has become so vague and so widely used that it is a word without meaning. No matter what new nuclear weapon is proposed, it is always justified as "enhancing deterrence," and no one bothers to question what exactly "deterrence" is—whether it's a good idea, how it works, what it leads to, and how any new weapon can ever "enhance" something as vague as "deterrence."

Building Up While Building Down

In 1983 the United States proposed to the Soviet Union a "build down" of nuclear missiles, an example of doublespeak that is right up there with "negative economic growth" and an "increasing decreasing rate of inflation." Basically, a "build down" would require that the United States and the Soviet Union scrap two nuclear missiles for each new one they produce. Sounds good, doesn't it? But this is doublespeak, remember, so you have to look for the real meaning. Although it sounds like progress in reducing the threat of nuclear war by reducing the number of missiles each side has, "build down" really increases the threat because each of those new missiles that would replace the two old ones would be bigger, more accurate, and carry more warheads that are more powerful. That's how nuclear doublespeak works to say one thing but mean another.

Doublespeak is useful when the government wants to get around a treaty that it no longer wants to honor. Article V of the 1972 Antiballistic Missile Treaty bans the testing of ABM systems or components of such systems in space: "Each side undertakes not to develop, test, or deploy ABM systems or components which are sea-based, air-based, space-based, or mobile land-based." The treaty does allow some limited development and testing and deployment of fixed land-based systems such as interceptor missiles and radars. In 1986, the Reagan administration suddenly claimed that Article V did not apply to new types of ABM systems. Thus, there are no restraints on the development and testing of new space-based lasers and other new systems crucial to the development of the "Star Wars" program. Critics of this new interpretation of the treaty called it the "revisionist" view as opposed to the "traditional" view. The Reagan administration called its new view the "broad" view and called the opposing view the "restrictive" view. Abraham Sofer, the State Department legal adviser who developed the new view, denied that the administration's reinterpretation represents a sudden change of perspective. Some officials in the Reagan administration called the new view of the treaty the "legally correct interpretation (LCI)." These officials maintained that "LCI" allows the testing and deployment of defensive systems based on "OPP," meaning exotic systems such as lasers that are based on "other physical principles," in contrast to such older defensive systems as interceptor missiles. Secretary of Defense Caspar Weinberger said that "broad" and "restrictive" were not the correct terms. Rather the correct terms are "right" for the new interpretation and "wrong" for the old.

Secretary Weinberger had used doublespeak before to "re-interpret" a treaty to get the result he wanted. In 1982 he used doublespeak to get around a problem posed by the language of the SALT II treaty. Although the treaty was never ratified by the Senate, President Reagan said that the United States would observe it. Part of the treaty specifies that "each party undertakes not to start construction of additional fixed ICBM launchers." When asked whether his proposal to build new bases for the MX missile was a violation of SALT II, Weinberger said that a "silo is not a launcher," which certainly must be news to the people who build those silos and the air force personnel who sit in the underground rooms ready to launch the missiles.

Peacekeepers and SS-20s

Patriotic, nonthreatening names are given to U.S. missiles, while the Soviet Union's missiles are given cold, stark numbers. The United States has the "Peacekeeper," "Midgetman," "Minuteman," "Pershing," "Sergeant York," "Poseidon," "Atlas" and "Titan," while Soviet missiles are designated "SS-20," "SS-21," "SS-22," "SS-24," and so on to higher numbers. The increasing numbers give the impression that the Russians are developing new generations of missiles faster than the United States. However, the numbers on the Soviet missiles include missiles tested but never deployed, or missiles that were only slightly modified. Meanwhile, U.S. missiles are constantly improved without changing their names.

Nuclear doublespeak is filled with acronyms which are cool, precise, rational, and authoritative. Those who use these acronyms appear to possess such qualities themselves, and they appear knowledgeable and objective when discussing nuclear weapons and war. Acronyms also allow those discussing nuclear war to distance themselves from the horrible reality of such a war. The acronyms abound: "ICBM, SLBM, IRBM, INF, RDF, SDI, SRBM, GLCM, SLCM, FOBS, BAMBI, MARV, MIRV, MAD, BMD" are just a few. One of the best is "CBM," which means "Confidence Building Measure." A "CBM" is anything that improves communication between the United States and the Soviet Union and thereby reduces tension and lowers the risk of starting a nuclear war through miscalculation.

Words such as "escalation dominance," "preemptive strikes," "sub-holocaust engagements," and a "surgically clean counter-force strike" permeate nuclear doublespeak, a language that defines "peace" as "strategic stability," meaning a balance in the numbers and types of nuclear weapons possessed by the United States and the Soviet Union. It is language which uses such words as "zero option," "window of vulnerability," "flexible response," and "triad" when discussing the most important issue in the world today: nuclear war and nuclear weapons. It is the doublespeak that can have the most important effect on our lives, and failure to eliminate or at least understand such doublespeak may well mean the end of our world. We ignore such doublespeak at the risk of our lives.

APPENDIX A

Quarterly Review of Doublespeak

Published in January, April, July, and October, the *Quarterly Review of Doublespeak* brings together in one publication examples of current doublespeak as well as articles, book reviews, cartoons, and other materials illustrating, criticizing, and analyzing doublespeak. The January issue carries the announcements of the winner of the annual Doublespeak Award, and the winner of the George Orwell Award for the work that has made an outstanding contribution to the critical analysis of public discourse. Each twelve-page issue includes a bibliography of resources such as books, articles, and other materials that aid in the study and analysis of public language in general and doublespeak in particular.

Subscription: $8.00 (U.S.) per year.
Address: Quarterly Review of Doublespeak
        National Council of Teachers of English
        1111 Kenyon Road
        Urbana, IL 61801

APPENDIX B

Recipients of the Doublespeak Award

The Doublespeak Award is an ironic "tribute" to American public figures who have perpetrated language that is deceptive, evasive, euphemistic, confusing, or self-contradictory. Following George Orwell's intention of exposing inhumane, propagandistic uses of language, the Committee on Public Doublespeak restricts the Award to misuses of language with pernicious social or political consequences that are more worthy of censure than the kind of garden-variety jargon, gobbledygook, or solecisms emphasized by many current critics of language.

1988 Secretary of Defense Frank Carlucci, Admiral William Crowe, and Rear Admiral William Fogarty. For the language they used in the report, *Formal Investigation into the Circumstances Surrounding the Downing of Iran Air Flight 655 on 3 July 1988,* and the language they used during the press conference held on August 19, 1988, to release and discuss that report. See pages 185–189 of this book, for their doublespeak.

1987 Lt. Col. Oliver North and Rear Adm. John Poindexter. For the language they used when testifying before the Select Committee on Secret Military Assistance to Iran and the Nicaraguan Opposition. See pages 241–250 of this book, for their doublespeak.

1986   NASA, Morton Thiokol, and Rockwell International.
For the language they used throughout the Challenger tragedy
and the subsequent investigation of the accident by a
presidential commission. See pages 5–6 and 222–224 of this
book, for their doublespeak.

1985   The Central Intelligence Agency. For the doublespeak
used in the CIA publication, *Psychological Warfare Manual,*
prepared for rebels fighting the government of Nicaragua. See
pages 221–222 of this book, for this doublespeak.

1984   The U.S. Department of State. For the doublespeak it
used in the weeks after the invasion of Grenada, and for the
doublespeak used in its official reports on the status of
human rights in countries around the world. See pages 3, 6–7,
and 209–210 of this book, for this doublespeak.

1983   President Ronald Reagan. For the doublespeak he
used in a speech to deputies of the Costa Rican National
Assembly, and for naming the new MX intercontinental
ballistic missile the "Peacekeeper." See pages 235 and 191 of
this book, for his doublespeak.

1982   The Republican National Committee. For a
television commercial on Social Security produced during the
congressional campaign. See pages 16–17 of this book, for
this doublespeak.

1981   Secretary of State Alexander Haig. For testimony
before congressional committees on the murder of three
American nuns and a layworker in El Salvador. See pages
17–18 of this book, for his doublespeak.

1980   President-elect Ronald Reagan. For the doublespeak
he used during the 1980 presidential campaign, which was
filled with inaccurate assertions and statistics, and
misrepresentations of his past record. He claimed that as
governor of California he had refunded $5.7 billion in
property taxes but failed to mention he had raised taxes by
$21 billion. Even after it was disproved, he continued to

claim Alaska had more oil than Saudi Arabia. He claimed General Motors had to employ 23,300 full-time employees to comply with government-required paperwork. However, General Motors pointed out it had 4,900 persons to do all its paperwork. Reagan continued his misstatements, omissions, misrepresentations, and exaggerations throughout his campaign, even though his misuse of language was constantly pointed out by others.

1979   The Nuclear Power Industry. For the whole lexicon of doublespeak used before, during, and after the Three Mile Island accident, which has served to downplay the dangers of nuclear accidents. See pages 258–260 of this book, for this doublespeak.

1978   Earl Clinton Bolton, Executive Vice-President, University of California. For a memorandum he wrote for the CIA in 1968, titled "Agency-Academic Relations," which advises academics to defend themselves by explaining their CIA involvement "as a contribution to . . . proper academic goals. . . . It should be stressed that when an apology is necessary it can best be made: (1) by some distant academic who is not under attack, (2) in a 'respectable' publication of general circulation (e.g., *Harper's, Saturday Review, Vital Speeches,* etc.) and (3) with full use of the jargon of the academy. . . . Two doctrines fiercely protected by the academy are 'academic freedom' and 'privilege and tenure.' . . . When attacked for aiding the Agency the academic (or institution) should base a rejoinder on these sacred doctrines."

1977   The Pentagon and the Energy Research and Development Administration. For calling the neutron bomb an "enhanced radiation device" and a "radiation enhancement weapon," which is "an efficient nuclear weapon that eliminates an enemy with a minimum degree of damage to friendly territory." See pages 3, 15, and 189–191 of this book, for their doublespeak.

1976 The U.S. Department of State. For an announcement of the position of consumer affairs coordinator who would "review existing mechanisms of consumer input, thruput, and output, and seek ways of improving these linkages via the 'consumer communication channel.'" See pages 206–207 of this book, for this doublespeak.

1975 Yasir Arafat, Leader, PLO. For his answer to a charge that the PLO wanted to destroy Israel, "They are wrong. We do not want to destroy any people. It is precisely because we have been advocating co-existence that we have shed so much blood." See page 161 for his doublespeak.

1974 Colonel David Opfer, U.S. Air Attaché in Cambodia. After a U.S. bombing raid in Cambodia, he told reporters: "You always write it's bombing, bombing, bombing. It's *not* bombing! It's air support!"

APPENDIX C

Recipients of the George Orwell Award for Distinguished Contribution to Honesty and Clarity in Public Language

The Orwell Award was established in 1974 by the Committee on Public Doublespeak of the National Council of Teachers of English to recognize each year a work that has made an outstanding contribution to the critical analysis of public discourse.

1988 Donald Barlett and James Steele. Reporters for **The Philadelphia Inquirer.** In a series of articles (April 10–16, 1988), Barlett and Steele revealed how hundreds of deceptive passages in the Tax Reform Act of 1986 granted billions of dollars in tax exemptions to corporations and influential, wealthy individuals, all done through the use of deceptive language.

1987 Noam Chomsky. On Power and Ideology: The Managua Lectures. Boston: South End Press, 1987.

1986 Neil Postman. Amusing Ourselves to Death: Public Discourse in the Age of Show Business. New York: Elizabeth Sifton/Viking, 1985.

1985 Torben Vertergaard and Kim Schroder. The Language of Advertising. New York: Basil Blackwell, 1985.

1984 Ted Koppel. Moderator of ABC–TV program, "Nightline." For his long-sustained role as moderator of an important news program which has contributed to the common good by its extensive analysis of topical news. Ted Koppel has been a model of intelligence, informed interest, social awareness, verbal fluency, and fair and rigorous questioning of controversial figures. The national audience, the citizens in this democracy, have benefited from his attempts to seek honesty and openness, clarity and coherence, to raise the level of public discourse.

1983 Haig A. Bosmajian. The Language of Oppression. Lanham, MD: University Press of America, 1983.

1982 Stephen Hilgartner, Richard Bell, and Rory O'Connor. Nukespeak: Nuclear Language, Visions, and Mindset. San Francisco: Sierra Club Books, 1982.

1981 Dwight Bolinger. Language: The Loaded Weapon. New York: Longman, 1980.

1980 Sheila Harty. Hucksters in the Classroom. Washington, DC: Center for Study of Responsive Law, 1979.

1979 Erving Goffman. Gender Advertisements. Cambridge: Harvard University Press, 1979.

1978 Sissela Bok. Lying: Moral Choice in Public and Private Life. New York: Pantheon, 1978.

1977 Walter Pincus. Reporter for the Washington Post. One of those reporters for whom the term "gadfly" truly applies. The government's attempt to slip the neutron bomb through, unnoticed, in an ERDA appropriations bill was deceptive, and it was caught because a methodical, patient journalist knew his job, knew the jargon.

1976   Hugh Rank. Intensify/Downplay Approach. Rank
has developed a schema that offers a much-needed, concise,
fresh, and practical approach to the analysis of the language
of persuasion and propaganda.

1975   David Wise. The Politics of Lying. New York:
Random House, 1973.

INDEX OF DOUBLESPEAK

GENERAL INDEX